Saints In Rome
And Beyond

A Guide For Finding
The First Class Relics Of The Saints

Rev. Mr. Daniel L. Thelen

Printed By:
Lulu Press, Inc.

Copyright © 2015 by Daniel L. Thelen

All Rights Reserved.

ISBN: 978-0-9861547-0-6

Pictures taken by author.

For the online website and interactive maps please visit:
www.saintsinrome.com

It is my hope that this book may help pilgrims to fall more deeply in love with our spiritual family in heaven and as a result devotion and prayer to God our loving Father may increase.

"Each of the elders held a harp and gold bowls filled with incense, which are the prayers of the holy ones."
(Rev. 5:8)

*****

I would like to give thanks to the many Priests, Deacons, and Seminarians at the Pontifical North American College who have helped in so many ways to provide information for this book. I would also like to thank in a special way my Bishop, William Callahan, my Vocation Director, Father Alan Wierzba, and all the wonderful souls in my diocese who have made it possible for me to study in Rome. Also I give many thanks to my parents and my family for their constant love and support through every stage of my life. Finally, I give thanks to God for His countless blessings and for the greatest gift in my life that of my Faith.

*****

Note to the Reader

This work is divided into three sections.

Part I: Twelve Walks in Rome
Lists over sixty churches in Rome and places them into twelve manageable walks. Each of the churches are notable for their historical, devotional, and architectural importance.

Part II: First Class Relics in Rome and Beyond
Provides detailed information regarding the location of relics in Rome and around the world. A special emphasis is placed upon the saints found on the liturgical calendar.

Part III: Devotional Guide to the City of Rome
This section organizes the saints by their feast days to highlight places of devotion in Rome. It follows the liturgical calendar and locates places of veneration for each saint throughout the year.

Index
Alphabetical listing of the saints with corresponding page numbers.

Note from the Author

One cannot help but to appreciate Christ's indispensable role in leading a person to sanctity. Every saint has a different story but all share the one fundamental truth that they were saved through Christ's ever-abundant grace. A saint, therefore, gives us hope for they show us the path to God.

During the last four years I have been blessed to visit about two-thirds of the over four-hundred churches listed in this book. I have done my best to provide accurate and reliable information. However, I am sure that there is much more to include. Therefore, I look forward to any suggestions or corrections that may be useful in improving the content.

Travelling

A few comments with regard to travelling. Most European cities are quite safe for tourists and pilgrims. However, always check local travel advisories before entering a new city. This will help to prevent any wandering into dangerous neighborhoods. Always be watchful for pickpockets especially around train stations and other high traffic areas. Use caution when travelling alone and especially at night. For cities outside of Europe and America use extra caution. One should be aware that social and cultural norms may be different.

Table of Contents

PART I

Twelve Walking Tours

For The Pilgrim In
Rome

Region #1
The Forum & The Aventine Hill

The Forum was the cultural and religious center of ancient Rome. The now ruined temples and monuments testify to the greatness of this once all-powerful city. Rising just to the west of these ruins is the Capitoline Hill upon which is the *Victor Emmanuel II Monument*. This monument goes by several official names but is often just simply dubbed the *Wedding Cake* to describe its rather ostentatious appearance. It was completed in the early 20th century to celebrate the unification of Italy. Ever since the Middle Ages this hill has served as the center of Rome's civic life. The beautiful *Piazza del Campidoglio* and its surrounding palazzi, designed in part by Michelangelo, demonstrate its historic importance. The Aventine Hill located just south of this area also has a rich history. It is known in particular for its many important Christian churches including *Santa Sabina*.

San Giorgio in Velabro

Begin this walking tour at the church of *Santa Francesca Romana* located just west of the Colosseum. After your visit head west along the Via dei Fori Imperiali to reach the church of *Santi Cosma e Damiano*. From here continue as before until you reach the very large *Victor Emmanuel II Monument*. Upon reaching this monument walk so as to go up and behind this building. One can either follow the road or take the staircase. At the top you will enter the *Piazza del Campidoglio*. From here there is access to the church of *Santa Maria in Aracoeli*. After visiting this church descend the Capitoline Hill from the exit located in the southeast corner of the piazza. Along the descent you will find a lookout with an amazing view of the entire Forum area. Continue south until you reach the church of *San Giorgio in Velabro*. Should you have time several other churches in this area are also worthy of a visit including: *Santa Maria in Cosmedin, Santa Maria della Consolazione, San Nicola in Carcere,* and *Sant'Anastasia*. However, don't expend too much energy since you will still need to climb the Aventine Hill to finish the last stage of this walk. On top of this hill is the historic church of *Santa Sabina* and also the very famous keyhole with a stunning view of *St Peter's Basilica*. This keyhole is located within a gate just 500 feet south of *Santa Sabina* as one walks to the church of *Sant'Anselmo*. The gate is the entrance to the headquarters of the Knights of Malta. You will probably find tourists lining up in front of it for a view.

The following churches are listed according to the order of the suggested route. The total distance is about 1.7 miles. To walk will probably take about 4 hours if one visits each of the churches. The churches are generally open from 7AM-1PM and from 4PM-7PM. *San Giorgio in Velabro* may not be open as frequently.

Santa Francesca Romana (Saint Frances of Rome)
Piazza di Santa Francesca Romana 4
†This church is next to the Roman Forum.
†The remains of St Frances of Rome (d. 1440) are in the crypt below the main sanctuary. Her skeleton is vested in the habit of the Oblate Sisters.
†To the right of the sanctuary is the tomb of Pope Gregory XI (d. 1378). He returned the papal seat to Rome after the exile in Avignon. St Catherine of Siena (d. 1380) was instrumental in persuading him to return. A relief depicting her involvement can be seen on the tomb.
†Two flagstones within the right transept of the church are said to bear the imprints of the knees of St Peter. According to a legend the magician, Simon Magus, levitated in the Roman Forum to demonstrate that his powers were superior to those of Peter. In response, Peter fell to the ground in prayer causing the knee imprints on the stone. Simon Magus then immediately fell to his death.

Santi Cosma e Damiano (Saints Cosmas and Damian)
Via dei Fori Imperiali 1
†This church is located next to the Roman Forum.
†The mosaic within the apse depicts Christ at his Second Coming. This masterpiece, created in the 6th century, was originally intended to be viewed from a greater distance. In the 17th century, however, the church was restored and the floor raised about 25 feet to its present location. Thus the mosaic is now much closer than it was intended. Beneath an altar in the lower church are relics of Saints Cosmas and Damian.

Santa Maria in Aracoeli (Our Lady in Aracoeli)
Piazza del Campidoglio 4
†This church is on top of the Capitoline Hill.
†Relics of St Helena, the mother of Constantine, rest in the left transept.
†Twelve paintings in the upper nave depict events from the life of the Blessed Virgin Mary. The gilded ceiling honors the Christian victory obtained at the Battle of Lepanto.

San Giorgio in Velabro (Saint George in Velabro)
Via del Velabro 19
✝This church is just east of Tiber Island.
✝Part of the skull of St George rests beneath the main altar.

Santa Sabina (Saint Sabina)
Piazza Pietro d'Illiria 1
✝This church is located on the Aventine Hill just south of Circo Massimo.
✝In 1219 St Dominic and his friars received permission to move into this church. Three years later, on June 5, 1222, the church was given in perpetuity to the Dominican Order by Pope Honorius III. Today it serves as the Order's General Curia. The room in which St Dominic lived has been converted into a chapel and can be visited with permission. Also in the garden, visible from the narthex, is an orange tree that is said to have been planted by St Dominic himself.
✝The first chapel on the left side of the nave is dedicated to St Dominic. Within this chapel is a polished black stone that the Devil is said to have thrown at St Dominic.
✝St Thomas Aquinas lived here when he opened a house of studies at *Santa Sabina* to teach theology to Dominican students in 1265. It was also around this time that he began to write the *Summa Theologica*.
✝One of the oldest depictions of the crucifixion in Christian art is located on the uppermost left panel of the left entrance door. This wooden door dates back to the year 430 AD. (Note: This is not the entrance off of the street but the entrance from the narthex.)

Region #2
Trastevere

The oldest Christian church to be found in Rome, *Santa Maria in Trastevere*, is located within this region. Historical documents show that this church traces its history back to a house church founded by Pope St Callistus I in 220 AD and that the foundation for the present church was constructed in the 340s. At the base of the sanctuary in this church an even older tradition is remembered by a memorial marker that says in Latin 'Fons Olei' which translated to English means 'Oil Fountain.' Tradition holds that at this very spot for one entire day in the year 38 BC a fountain of oil gushed out from the ground. Its flow was so intense that a small river was created that reached all the way to the Tiber River. Later Christians saw this as a sign that foreshadowed the coming of Christ.

Santa Maria in Trastevere

Begin your route at the beautiful little church of *Santa Maria della Scala* on the north end of Trastevere. From here follow the narrow and twisting streets south until you reach *Santa Maria in Trastevere*. After an ample visit at this historic church continue southeast along Via di San Francesco a Ripa until you reach the church of *San Francesco d'Assisi a Ripa*. After a brief visit in this church head northeast along Via della Luce to *Santa Cecilia in Trastevere*. On this part of the route the streets widen and the buildings lose their grandeur; however, once you reach the church of *Santa Cecilia in Trastevere* you will be pleasantly rewarded with one of the most beautiful churches in all of Rome. After visiting this church head northwest on Via dei Genovesi until you reach the church of *San Crisogono*. From here walk along the busy Viale di Trastevere in the direction of the Tiber River. Upon reaching the river turn right and continue in this direction until you reach Tiber Island. The final church of this walk, *San Bartolomeo all'Isola*, will be on your right as you enter the island. Finally the church of *San Pancrazio*, which is not listed on this route, is also worthy of a visit and is located just one mile to the west of this route.

The following churches are listed according to the order of the suggested route. The total distance is about 1.5 miles. To walk will probably take about 3 hours if one visits each of the churches. The churches are generally open from 7AM-1PM and from 4PM-7PM.

Santa Maria della Scala (Our Lady at the Steps)
Piazza della Scala 23
†The right foot of St Teresa of Avila (d. 1582) rests within this church in a beautiful chapel to the left of the main sanctuary. It was gifted to this church in 1617. (This chapel is not visible from the nave of the church and it is rarely open to the public. However, if one kindly asks the sacristan access may be granted. If the sacristan is not present he or she can be called at the neighboring convent door.)
†A miraculous image of the Blessed Virgin Mary entitled *Madonna della Scala* is also venerated in the left transept.

Santa Maria in Trastevere (Our Lady in Trastevere)
Via della Paglia 14 / Piazza Santa Maria in Trastevere
✝This church is dedicated to the Assumption of The Blessed Virgin Mary. A painting of the Assumption by Domenico Zampieri can be seen in the middle of the coffered wooden ceiling.
✝Relics of the two popes, St Callistus I (d. 222) and St Cornelius (d. 253), rest under the main altar of this church. These relics are joined by others in particular those of the priest and martyr St Calepodius (d. 232).

San Francesco d'Assisi a Ripa (Saint Francis of Assisi in Ripa)
Piazza San Francesco d'Assisi 88
✝St Francis of Assisi (d. 1226) stayed within a room in this church during a visit to Rome. Within this room is a stone that is said to have been used by him as a pillow.

Santa Cecilia in Trastevere (Saint Cecilia in Trastevere)
Piazza di Santa Cecilia 22
✝This church is built over the ruins of the house that St Cecilia had lived in prior to her martyrdom.
✝In 821 the body of St Cecilia was exhumed from the *Catacombs of San Callisto* by Pope St Paschal I (d. 824) and returned to this church. Today her remains rest within the crypt under the main altar
✝The recumbent statue of St Cecilia below the main altar was completed by Stefano Maderno in the late 16th century. A gash on her neck recalls the miraculous events surrounding her martyrdom. Tradition claims that St Cecilia was condemned to execution first by drowning and then by decapitation. Both attempts failed. The second method, however, left her greatly wounded. The executioner struck her neck three times with a sword but being unable to sever her head fled in fear. She survived for three days, offered all she had to the poor, and then expired.

San Crisogono (Saint Chrysogonus)
Piazza Sonnino 44
✝Part of the skull of St Chrysogonus, a Roman martyr, rests beneath the main altar of this church. Also within a side chapel are the remains of Blessed Anne Marie Taigi (d. 1837).

San Bartolomeo all'Isola (Saint Bartholomew on the Island)
Piazza San Bartolomeo, Tiber Island
✝The Holy Roman Emperor, Otto III, began building *San Bartolomeo all'Isola* in 998 to honor his friend St Adalbert (d. 997) who had been recently martyred. An arm of St Adalbert is currently enshrined in the chapel to the left of the main sanctuary. It rests within a little metal box placed under the altar of this chapel.
✝Relics of the apostle, St Bartholomew, rest within the red porphyry basin that supports the main altar.
✝Enshrined in each of the side altars are relics of recent martyrs from around the world.
✝This church also housed the relics of St Paulinus of Nola (d. 431) for about 1000 years until they were transferred to the Italian city of Nola in 1909.

San Pancrazio (Saint Pancras)
Piazza San Pancrazio 5/D
✝This church is west of Trastevere and borders the Villa Doria Pamphili Park. It was built on the site of St Pancras' tomb.
✝In 1798 a general under Napoleon Bonaparte invaded Rome and established the Roman Republic. During this time intruders entered the church of *San Pancrazio* and severely damaged the remains of St Pancras. His head, which was kept in the *Basilica of St John Lateran* from 850 to 1966, fortunately was left untouched. In 1966 Pope Paul VI returned this relic to *San Pancrazio*. It now rests within a reliquary bust on the right side of the nave.
✝Additionally, a few relics of St Pancras and other early church martyrs are said to rest within the porphyry urn that makes up the base of the altar in the main sanctuary.

Region #3
St Peter's Basilica

Within *St Peter's Basilica* are buried many prominent saints and about 100 of the 264 deceased popes. The following are those that are celebrated on the Roman Catholic Liturgical Calendar. They are listed in the order that they are found within the basilica when one tours the basilica in a counter-clockwise direction. Also the following image marks with a dot the rough location of each chapel.

Floor Plan of St Peter's Basilica

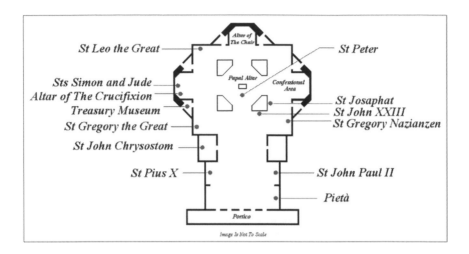

Right Side Of The Nave

Saint John Paul II, pope
Chapel of St Sebastian – Located on the right side of the nave just after Michelangelo's statue of the Pietà.

✝In 2011 the remains of St John Paul II (d. 2005) were removed from the crypt of this basilica and placed within the altar of this chapel. Since this basilica is visited by thousands of people every day the tomb is roped off to provide a small area of prayer. Access to this area is granted if one asks to pray at the tomb.

Saint Gregory Nazianzen, bishop and doctor
Altar of Our Lady of Succour – Located on the right side of the nave just after the entrance to the confessional area.

✝Beneath this altar are some relics of St Gregory Nazianzen. In 2004 a major part of these relics were returned to the Ecumenical Patriarch of Constantinople.

Saint John XXIII, pope
Altar of St Jerome – Located on the right side of the nave at the base of the first column.
†The body of St John XXIII (d. 1963) rests under this altar. He is known in particular for announcing the opening of the Second Vatican Council.

Saint Josaphat, bishop and martyr
Altar of St Basil – Located within the confessional area on the back side of the first column.
†The remains of St Josaphat rest below this altar. During the early part of the 17th century he valiantly tried to bring Christians within the Polish-Lithuanian Kingdom of Eastern Europe into full communion with Church of Rome. As a result of his efforts he suffered martyrdom in 1623.

Relics Associated With St Peter

Saint Peter, apostle
†Tradition holds that St Peter was crucified upside down in the middle of Nero's Circus. The *Altar of The Crucifixion*, located in the left transept of *St Peter's Basilica*, is very close to the actual site where this crucifixion took place.
†The bones of St Peter are in the confessio below the Papal Altar and his jawbone can be seen on the Scavi tour.
†Tradition also holds that within the large bronze chair located above the *Altar of the Chair* in the apse of the church is a second smaller chair made out of wood. This second chair is said to consist of fragments from the original Episcopal chair that St Peter once sat in.

Left Side Of The Nave

Saint Leo the Great, pope and doctor
Altar of St Leo the Great – Located in the far left corner of the left transept.
†The remains of St Leo the Great (d. 461) rest under this altar.
†St Leo was known both for his exemplar defense of orthodox theology and for his efforts in halting the advance of the Barbarian tribes. A marble relief of his important meeting with Attila the Hun is placed above this altar.

Saints Simon and Jude, apostles

St Joseph's Altar – Located in the left transept where the Blessed Sacrament is reserved.
✝Relics of the two apostles, St Simon and St Jude, rest under this altar.

Saint Luke, evangelist & Saint Sebastian, martyr

Treasury Museum – Located within the hallway leading to the sacristy.
✝Many important artifacts are within this museum. Of special importance are the following relics of St Luke and St Sebastian.
✝A silver reliquary bust is said to contain the head of St Luke. This reliquary dates back to the 14th century and the relic is said to have come from Constantinople. However, this same relic is also said to be located in the *Cathedral of St Vitus* in Prague, Czech Republic. A recent study on the relics of St Luke was conducted at the request of Archbishop Antonio Mattiazzo of Padua in 1998. This study seems to suggest that the authentic relic of St Luke's head is the one within the *Cathedral of St Vitus*.
✝Also placed within a glass-sided reliquary is the skull of St Sebastian. Before its placement in this museum this skull was located in the Roman church of *Santi Quattro Coronati*.

Saint Gregory the Great, pope and doctor

Altar of St Gregory the Great – Located within the left transept near the entrance to the sacristy.
✝Relics of St Gregory the Great (d. 604) rest below this altar. The mosaic above this altar recounts a Eucharistic miracle attributed to him.

Saint John Chrysostom, bishop and doctor

Chapel of the Immaculate Conception
✝Also known as the Wedding Chapel or the Chapel of the Choir.
✝This is the third chapel on the left side of the nave.
✝Some relics of St John Chrysostom (d. 407) rest below the altar within this chapel. In 2004 a major part of these relics were returned to the Ecumenical Patriarch of Constantinople.

Saint Pius X, pope

Presentation Chapel – Located on the left side of the nave between the Baptistry and the Wedding Chapel.
✝The body of St Pius X (d. 1914) rests under the altar in this chapel. He is known in particular for lowering the age of First Communion to the Age of Reason.

Region #4
Basilica of St John Lateran

The region that surrounds the *Basilica of St John Lateran* touches upon the very beginnings of the Christian faith. So many of the relics found here go back to the earliest disciples and even to Christ himself. *Santa Croce in Gerusalemme* and *Scala Santa* preserve many relics from Christ's very own passion and death. The *Basilica of St John Lateran* has twelve striking statues of the apostles lining the nave. And finally the *Basilica of San Clemente* has relics of several first century saints who lived and evangelized just a generation after Christ walked the earth.

Basilica of St John Lateran

Begin your route at *Santa Croce in Gerusalemme* on the eastern end of this region. After visiting this church head west along Viale Carlo Felice. Please note that the large statue of St Francis of Assisi (d. 1226) that is described later is along this street. Continue until you reach the *Basilica of St John Lateran* and *Scala Santa*. After visiting these churches continue west along Via dei Santi Quattro to visit *Santi Quattro Coronati* and the *Basilica of San Clemente*. From here turn south onto Via Celimontana. Take this street until Via di San Paolo della Croce which will bring you to the quiet church of *Santi Giovanni e Paolo*.

The following churches are listed according to the order of the suggested route. The total distance is about 1.5 miles. To walk will probably take about 4 hours if one visits each of the churches. The churches are generally open from 7AM-1PM and from 4PM-7PM. The *Basilica of St John Lateran* is open from 7AM - 7PM and does not close during the pranzo hour.

Santa Croce in Gerusalemme (Holy Cross in Jerusalem)
Piazza di Santa Croce in Gerusalemme 12
✝This church is east of the *Basilica of St John Lateran*.
✝Found here are relics of the True Cross brought to Rome by St Helena in 325.
✝These relics include: the Titulus Crucis (This is the sign that hung over the head of Christ and that declared him to be the King of the Jews), a Crucifixion nail, a fragment of the True Cross, two thorns from the Crown of Thorns, the greater part of the sponge used to give Christ vinegar, a piece of the cross from the good thief (St Dismas), and a bone from the index finger of St Thomas the Apostle.
✝This chapel can be accessed by the staircase on the left side of the sanctuary.

Basilica of St John Lateran
Piazza San Giovanni in Laterano 4
†Positioned above the Papal Altar of this church are two busts of St Peter and St Paul. According to tradition the skulls or parts of the skulls of St Peter and St Paul are within these busts. Also located within the Papal Altar is a wooden table that St Peter and many of the earliest popes are said to have celebrated the Eucharist upon.
†Located to the left of the Papal Altar is another very ancient table. This table rests above the altar where the Blessed Sacrament is reserved. It is placed directly behind a bronze relief of the Last Supper. Tradition claims that it was upon this table that Jesus and the apostles celebrated the Last Supper.
†Within a small park just outside of this basilica is a large statue of St Francis (d. 1226). He is depicted facing the façade of the basilica with his arms outstretched. If one stands behind this statue at a certain distance it looks as if St Francis is holding up the church. This recalls the dream of Pope Innocent III in 1209 when he saw the church being supported by St Francis.

Scala Santa (Holy Steps)
Across from the *Basilica of St John Lateran*
†This building was originally the Papal Palace from the time of Constantine until the move to Avignon in 1313.
†It contains 28 marble steps that were originally located at Pilate's house in Jerusalem. St Helena brought these steps to Rome. These are believed to be the same steps that Christ walked upon during his Passion.
†Within the chapel at the top of the steps is a very ancient image of the Lord called the *Acheropita* which means, "Not made by the hand of man." One tradition credits St Luke with the painting of this image and an angel with providing the finishing touches.

Santi Quattro Coronati (Four Holy Crowned Ones)
Piazza dei Santi Quattro Coronati 20
†This church is east of the Colosseum.
†For centuries the skull of St Sebastian was venerated within the crypt of this church. Signage at an altar on the left side of the nave continues to indicate its presence. However, at some point in the last century the skull was removed. It can now be found within a reliquary in the Treasury Museum of *St Peter's Basilica*.

Basilica di San Clemente (Basilica of Saint Clement)
Via Labicana 95 / Piazza San Clemente
✝This church is east of the Colosseum. Below the present 12th century basilica are three additional levels. The first two can be visited. These consist of an ancient Christian church and an even older pagan temple. A fourth stratum even further below preserves the remnants of some buildings that were destroyed by a fire during the reign of Emperor Nero (d. 68).
✝A chapel on the right side of the nave is dedicated to Saints Cyril (d. 869) and Methodius (d. 885). The extant remains of St Cyril rest within the altar of this chapel.
✝Also the remains of St Ignatius of Antioch (d. 107) and of St Clement I (d. 97) rest below the main altar.
✝Tradition claims that St Cyril discovered some bones and an anchor while he was in Crimea. These were believed to be the relics of St Clement I. St Cyril then carried these relics to Rome where they were placed in the *Basilica of San Clemente*.

Santi Giovanni e Paolo (Saints John and Paul)
Piazza dei Santi Giovanni e Paolo 13
✝This church is south of the Colosseum.
✝St Paul of the Cross (d. 1775) is buried under the altar in the large side chapel on the right side of the nave. Upon request one can visit the room in which he died in the monastery adjacent to the church.
✝Located beneath this church is a complex of well preserved ancient Roman houses. Among these is an ancient house church. These ruins can be visited.

Region #5
Quirinale

Within the Quirinale region you will experience the hustle and bustle of normal Roman life. Seldom will you find a quaint and picturesque little side street. Despite this the region still offers its own unique beauty and is marked by several very important churches.

Begin this walking route at *Santa Maria degli Angeli* just off of Piazza della Repubblica. After a visit to this large church continue northwest to *Santa Maria della Vittoria*. Near this church are several other churches worthy of a visit including *Santa Susanna* and *San Bernardo alle Terme*. After visiting these churches head southwest along Via XX Settembre and Via del Quirinale to reach *Sant'Andrea al Quirinale*. Also worth a visit along this street is the beautiful piazza in front of the Quirinale. The final church on this route, *San Lorenzo in Panisperna*, can be visited by heading southeast on Via Milano.

Santa Susanna

The following churches are listed according to the order of the suggested route. The total distance is about 1 mile. To walk will probably take about 2.5 hours if one visits each of the churches. The churches are generally open from 7AM-1PM and from 4PM-7PM. *San Lorenzo in Panisperna* is generally open only for Mass on Sunday.

Santa Maria degli Angeli (Our Lady of the Angels)
Piazza della Repubblica
✝This church is at Piazza della Repubblica. It is a very spacious church built over the Baths of Diocletian.
✝Many angels are depicted within this church. Located near the entrance are two angels gracefully supporting shell-shaped holy water fonts. In the main sanctuary is a 16th century painting that depicts seven angels surrounding the Blessed Virgin Mary. An additional pair of sculpted angels then surround this painting.

Santa Maria della Vittoria (Our Lady of the Victory)
Via XX Settembre 17
✝This church is north of Piazza della Repubblica.
✝Located here is Gian Lorenzo Bernini's famous sculpture entitled *The Ecstasy of St Teresa.*

Sant'Andrea al Quirinale (Saint Andrew at the Quirinale)
Via del Quirinale 29
✝This church is south of the Barberini metro stop. It was designed by Gian Lorenzo Bernini.
✝The remains of St Stanislaus Kostka (d. 1568), a young Jesuit novice who died in Rome at the age of seventeen, rest here. The room in which he died has been converted into a chapel and can be visited by asking the sacristan.

San Lorenzo in Panisperna (Saint Lawrence in Panisperna)
Via Panisperna 90
✝This church is west of the *Basilica of St Mary Major*. It is often closed during the week. However, it is always open for the faithful during Sunday liturgies.
✝This church rests over the spot of St Lawrence's martyrdom (d. 258). A chapel built under the porch marks where it occurred. Within this chapel is the oven that was used to roast St Lawrence alive.
✝Within the church the second chapel on the left side of the nave is dedicated to St Bridget (d. 1373). Her body was originally buried in this chapel before being moved to Sweden. She used to beg for alms for the poor outside of this church and prayed before the crucifix by the main altar.

Region #6
Piazza Navona

The area around Piazza Navona is known for its charming streets, its beautiful architecture, and its delightful shops. A sense of mystery envelops the area. Therefore, do not be alarmed if you suddenly get off course and lose a sense of where you are. In fact this is to be expected. A few wrong turns will no doubt only allow you to see more of this beautiful area!

Sant'Agnese in Agone

Start your excursion at *Sant'Agnese in Agone*. From here head south on Via della Cuccagna until you reach *San Pantaleo*. After visiting this church continue along the busy Corso Vittorio Emanuele until you reach *Chiesa Nuova*. If you feel confident you can also walk along the more picturesque street of Via del Governo Vecchio to reach *Chiesa Nuova*. From here head north until you get to Via dei Coronari and the church of *San Salvatore in Lauro*. Finally, walk back towards Piazza Navona to visit both *Sant'Agostino* and *San Luigi dei Francesi*.

The following churches are listed according to the order of the suggested route. The total distance is about 1 mile. To walk will probably take about 2.5 hours if one visits each of the churches. The churches are generally open from 7AM-1PM and from 4PM-7PM.

Sant'Agnese in Agone (Saint Agnes in Agone)
Piazza Navona
✝According to tradition St Agnes was martyred at this location in 304 AD. A relic of her skull is present in a chapel located to the left of the main sanctuary.

San Pantaleo (Saint Pantaleon)
Piazza San Pantaleo / Piazza dei Massimi 4
✝This church is located along the Corso Vittorio Emanuele.
✝The relics of St Joseph Calasanz (d. 1648) rest under the main altar of this church. His rooms can be visited in the adjacent convent.
✝St Joseph Calasanz is uniquely known for setting up the first free public school in modern Europe. During his lifetime it was highly controversial to educate the poor. Some thought that it would only leave the poor more dissatisfied with their lowly tasks in society. Education was not seen as an opportunity for advancement. St Joseph Calasanz nevertheless persevered and was eventually appreciated and honored for his work.

Chiesa Nuova (The New Church)
Via del Governo Vecchio 134
✝This church is located along the Corso Vittorio Emanuele.
✝The body of St Philip Neri (d. 1595) is enshrined in the left transept. His private rooms can be visited on certain days of the week. They are located in the right wall of the left transept. St Philip Neri spent the last 12 years of his life at *Chiesa Nuova*.
✝In 1597 this church received the skulls of Saints Nereus and Achilleus. They rest within reliquaries in the sacristy and are sometimes brought out for public veneration on May 12th.
✝The additional remains of Saints Nereus and Achilleus are said to rest within a porphyry urn under the main altar of this church. In 1870 they were stolen from the church of *Santi Nereo e Achilleo*; however, they were later recovered and are now said to rest here.

San Salvatore in Lauro (Holy Savior in Lauro)
Piazza San Salvatore in Lauro 15
†This church is west of Piazza Navona.
†Some relics of St Padre Pio (d. 1968) are kept within a side chapel in this church. This includes both a vial of blood from his stigmata and a stole. A second chapel contains a small bone fragment from an arm of St Jude the Apostle.

Sant'Agostino (Saint Augustine)
Piazza Sant'Agostino
†This church is near Piazza Navona.
†Relics of St Monica (d. 387), the mother of St Augustine, rest within the Blessed Sacrament Chapel just to the left of the main sanctuary.
†Near the entrance of the church is a statue of the Blessed Virgin Mary called *Madonna del Parto* which literally means *Our Lady of Childbirth*. Expectant mothers often come to pray in front of this statue to ask for Mary's intercession for a safe pregnancy. So great has the devotion been over the years that the silver foot of the statue has begun to wear away. (This is also a wonderful statue to visit on Mother's Day in order to give thanks to our own mothers.)
†Also in the first chapel on the left side of the nave is a painting by Caravaggio entitled *Madonna dei Pellegrini* which means *Our Lady of the Pilgrims*.

San Luigi dei Francesi (Saint Louis of the French)
Piazza San Luigi dei Francesi 5
†This church is near Piazza Navona.
†This church is known for its paintings. The most famous being *The Calling of St Matthew* by Caravaggio located in the *Contarelli Chapel*. This is the last chapel on the left side of the nave. The other two paintings in this chapel are also attributed to Caravaggio and are entitled *The Martyrdom of St Matthew* and *The Inspiration of St Matthew*.

Region #7
Piazza di Spagna

Piazza di Spagna is one of the most picturesque places in Rome. At the top of the Spanish Steps is the late Renaissance church of *Santissima Trinità dei Monti* and at the base of these steps in the middle of Piazza di Spagna is the *Colonna dell'Immacolata*. This column was dedicated in 1857 to honor the recently declared dogma of the Immaculate Conception. The four Old Testament prophets encircling the base of this column (Moses, Isaiah, David, & Ezekiel) each gave prophecies that alluded to a virgin birth.

Santissima Trinità dei Monti

From the church of *Santissima Trinità dei Monti* cut across on Via delle Carrozze to visit the large church of *San Carlo al Corso*. After visiting this church walk south along the Via del Corso until you reach Via della Mercede. Turn left to visit *San Silvestro in Capite*. From here head south to *Santa Maria in Via* where you can quench your thirst with a cold drink of water from a miraculous well. Finally continue to the east to visit *Sant'Andrea delle Fratte* and *Santa Maria della Concezione*.

The following churches are listed according to the order of the suggested route. The total distance is about 1.25 miles. To walk will probably take about 3.5 hours if one visits each of the churches. The churches are generally open from 7AM-1PM and from 4PM-7PM.

Santissima Trinità dei Monti (Most Holy Trinity of the Mounts)
Piazza della Trinità dei Monti
✝This church is at the top of the Spanish Steps.
✝Within the various side chapels in this church are many distinguished pieces of religious art. Among these are *The Assumption of the Virgin* and *The Deposition of Christ* by Daniele da Volterra and *The Flagellation of Jesus* by Louis Vincent Leon Pallière.
✝Also a painting of Our Lady called *Mater Admirabilis* is preserved within the convent chapel. St Therese of the Child Jesus (d. 1897) knelt in front of this painting during her visit to Rome and beseeched God for the grace to enter the convent at the age of 15. To visit this chapel enter the door at the *Instituto Del Sacro Cuore*. This door is not reached by the staircase to the church but by a second staircase on the left side.

San Carlo al Corso (Saint Charles on the Corso)
Via del Corso 437
✝This church is near the Spanish Steps.
✝The dedication for this church is to the great 16th century Archbishop of Milan, St Charles Borromeo. A relic of his heart rests within a reliquary in an altar located behind the main sanctuary.

San Silvestro in Capite (Saint Sylvester in Capite)
Piazza San Silvestro
✝This church is near the Spanish Steps.
✝A relic of the skull of St John the Baptist rests within the chapel to the left of the main entrance. The authenticity is uncertain since this same relic is said to be located at a number of other places throughout the world including the *Cathedral of Amiens* in France, the *Residenz Museum* in Munich, Germany, and the *Umayyad Mosque* in Damascus, Syria.
✝The remains of St Sylvester I (d. 335) rest in the confessio below the main altar. Also a work from 1688 depicting the legend of St Sylvester I baptizing Constantine can be seen in the apse vault.

Santa Maria in Via (Our Lady of the Way)
Via del Mortaro 24
†This church is near the Spanish Steps.
†On September 26, 1256 a miraculous icon of the Blessed Virgin Mary appeared at this location. It was found painted on a stone and floating upon the water of an overflowing well. The first chapel on the right side of the nave preserves this miraculous well and icon. Cups are normally provided so that pilgrims can drink some of the water from this well.

Sant'Andrea delle Fratte (Saint Andrew of the Bushes)
Via Sant'Andrea delle Fratte 1
†This church is near the Spanish Steps.
†The third altar on the left side of the nave is where the Blessed Virgin Mary appeared to Ratisbonne, an agnostic Jew, in 1842. Ratisbonne converted on the spot. In 1918 St Maximilian Mary Kolbe (d. 1941) offered his first Mass in this very same chapel.
†The two masterfully sculpted angels on either side of the main sanctuary were created by Gian Lorenzo Bernini. They were originally designed for *Ponte Sant'Angelo*; however, they were deemed too beautiful to be placed outside.

Santa Maria della Concezione (Our Lady of the Immaculate Conception)
Via Veneto 27
†This church is just north of the Barberini metro stop.
†Relics of St Justin the Martyr (d. 165) rest under the altar within the choir chapel. Kindly ask the sacristan for access. The remains of St Justin the Martyr were temporarily transferred in 1992 to the parish church of *San Giustino a Centocelle* in Rome; however, they have now been returned to this church.
†The bones of nearly 4,000 Capuchin friars are located in the crypt.

Region #8
Pantheon

The *Pantheon* has existed for over 2000 years. Despite its great age its dome remains the largest unreinforced concrete dome in the entire world. The building itself was originally designed as a temple to honor all of the ancient Roman gods. However, after the collapse of the Western Roman Empire it was consecrated as a Christian place of worship in 609 AD. Pilgrims can still to this day attend Mass here on weekends and holy days.

Pantheon

Begin this walking tour at the *Pantheon*. From here head south to visit *Santa Maria sopra Minerva*. One can typically leave *Santa Maria sopra Minerva* through a door located to the left of the main sanctuary in the front of the church. This will exit upon Via di Sant'Ignazio. Head left on this street to visit the church of *Sant'Ignazio*. From here continue west along Via in Aquiro to visit *La Maddalena*. Finally, proceed north along Via di Campo Marzio to reach *San Lorenzo in Lucina*.

The following churches are listed according to the order of the suggested route. The total distance is about 1 mile. To walk will probably take about 2.5 hours if one visits each of the churches. The churches are generally open from 7AM-1PM and from 4PM-7PM. The *Pantheon*, however, will remain open during the pranzo hour.

Pantheon / Santa Maria dei Martiri (Our Lady of the Martyrs)
Piazza della Rotonda
✝This ancient temple was converted into a Christian church in the year 609. It now honors the Blessed Virgin Mary and the Christian martyrs.

Santa Maria sopra Minerva (Our Lady Above Minerva)
Piazza della Minerva 42
✝This church is near the Pantheon.
✝The body of St Catherine of Siena rests under the main altar. She spent the last two years of her life in Rome before her passing in 1380. A devotional chapel made out of the room where she died can be visited by entering the sacristy. Originally this room was located a few blocks away at Via Santa Chiara, 14. However, in the 1630s it was reconstructed and brought here.
✝To the left of the main altar is Michelangelo's famous statue of Christ the Redeemer. A bit further left near the *Frangipane Chapel* is the tomb of Fra Angelico (d. 1455).

Sant'Ignazio (Saint Ignatius)
Via del Caravita 8/a
✝This church is east of the Pantheon.
✝The remains of St Aloysius Gonzaga (d. 1591) rest under the altar in the right transept. His rooms are next to the church and can be visited by appointment.
✝The body of St Robert Bellarmine (d. 1621), a prominent cardinal and theologian of the Counter-Reformation, rests under the altar in the third chapel on the right side of the nave.
✝The remains of St John Berchmans (d. 1621), the patron saint of altar servers, rest under the altar in the left transept.

La Maddalena (The Magdalene)
Piazza della Maddalena 53
✝This church is just north of the Pantheon.
✝In the chapel in the right transept is a miraculous crucifix that is said to have spoken to St Camillus de Lellis.
✝In the third chapel on the right side of the nave are the remains of St Camillus de Lellis. He lived in the adjacent monastery and died here in 1614. His rooms can be visited by asking the sacristan. One of these rooms has been transformed into a chapel and contains the relic of his heart.

San Lorenzo in Lucina (Saint Lawrence in Lucina)
Via in Lucina 16/a
✝This church is north of the Pantheon.
✝The grill used to burn St Lawrence (d. 258) is preserved under the altar in the first chapel on the right side of the nave.

Region #9
Outside Of The Aurelian Walls

St Sebastian

The following churches and catacombs are located outside of the Aurelian Walls that surround the ancient city of Rome; therefore, they are a bit difficult to reach. Nevertheless, they are rich in history and are definitely worth a visit. In fact, most of these places came into existence during the first few centuries of the church and are intimately connected to the lives of St Peter, St Paul, and the other martyrs.

The churches and catacombs listed on the following pages are placed in no particular order. They are all a considerable distance from the city center; therefore, one will need to use public transportation to reach them. However, the *Catacombs of San Callisto, San Sebastiano Fuori Le Mura,* and *Domine Quo Vadis* are all within one mile of each other and a walk between these places once they are reached by public transportation is easy to do. The churches are generally open from 7AM-1PM and from 4PM-7PM. *Saint Paul Outside the Walls* is open from 7AM-7PM.

Tre Fontane (The Three Fountains)

Via Acque Salvie 1

✝This shrine is located south of the Aurelian Walls. It can be reached by the Metro. Take the B Line and exit at the Laurentina stop. Then walk 0.5 miles on Via Laurentina to the shrine. One can also reach the shrine with the 761 bus.

✝There are three churches located at this shrine. The one located on the backside of the property, called *San Paolo alle Tre Fontane*, is believed to mark the spot of St Paul's martyrdom. Legend says that after St Paul was decapitated his head bounced three times and with each bounce a fountain of water sprang up. Three grated areas along the eastern wall of this church cover up the locations of these three fountains. Also within this church is the column to which St Paul was bound and the table upon which he died.

✝Another church on this property, *Santa Maria Scala Coeli*, is believed to mark the spot of St Paul's imprisonment prior to his martyrdom. This is the first church on the right as one enters. A crypt below the main sanctuary of this church marks the spot where St Paul was imprisoned.

Catacombs of San Callisto

Via Appia Antica 110/126

✝These catacombs are located south of the Aurelian Walls. They can be reached with the 118 or the 218 bus.

✝St Sixtus II (d. 258), St Pontian (d. 235), St Fabian (d. 250), St Cornelius (d. 253) and a number of other early popes were originally buried here. The remains of St Sixtus II were later moved to *San Sisto Vecchio*, the remains of St Fabian to *San Sebastiano Fuori Le Mura*, and the remains of St Cornelius to *Santa Maria in Trastevere*.

✝St Cecilia was also buried in these catacombs. In 821 her remains were removed and taken to *Santa Cecilia in Trastevere*.

✝Finally, it was at this location in the year 258 that Roman soldiers burst into a chapel and arrested St Sixtus II and four other deacons while they were celebrating the liturgy. St Lawrence (d. 258) was not present for this arrest; however, a legend holds that St Lawrence was able to speak to St Sixtus just before the pope was martyred. In this conversation St Sixtus prophetically stated, "You shall follow me in three days." St Lawrence then in three days went on to suffer his own martyrdom by being burnt alive on a gridiron.

San Sebastiano Fuori Le Mura (Saint Sebastian Outside the Walls)
Via Appia Antica 136
✝This church is south of the Aurelian Walls. It can be reached with the 118 or the 218 bus.
✝St Sebastian (d. 288) was originally buried in the catacombs located under this church. At some point, however, his remains were removed. Some of these remains are now located within an urn in a chapel on the left side of the nave. This is the chapel with the very impressive statue of St Sebastian created by Giuseppe Giorgetti.
✝Directly across from this chapel on the right side of the nave is a reliquary chapel that contains the column to which St Sebastian was tied and an arrow that pierced his flesh. Also within this same reliquary chapel are some small relics said to be from St Peter, St Paul, St Andrew, and a number of other saints including the pope, St Fabian (d. 250). St Fabian was originally buried in the *Catacombs of San Callisto* but later his remains were moved to this church.
✝This church has an ancient tradition connecting it to St Peter and to St Paul. The *Depositio Martyrum* shows that in the year 258 pilgrims came to *San Sebastiano Fuori Le Mura* on June 29th, the Feast Day of Saints Peter and Paul, to honor these two great saints. Therefore, it is presumed that at one time this church housed the remains of both St Peter and St Paul.
✝Tradition also claims that within the catacombs located under this church St Philip Neri (d. 1595) experienced such an enlargement of his heart due to a supernatural infusion of God's love that two of his ribs cracked.

Domine Quo Vadis (Lord, Where Are You Going?)
Via Appia Antica
✝This church is south of the Aurelian Walls. It can be reached with the 118 or the 218 bus.
✝This is the location where Christ allegedly appeared to St Peter as he was fleeing Rome. Upon seeing the Lord, St Peter asked, "Domine, Quo Vadis?" (Lord, where are you going?) to which Jesus replied, "I am going to Rome to be crucified again." Spurred on by this encounter St Peter returned to Rome where he became a martyr.

Basilica of St Paul Outside the Walls
Via Ostiense 186
†This basilica can be reached by the Metro. Take the B Line and exit at the *Basilica di San Paolo* stop.
†St Paul is buried in the confessio. Above his tomb are the chains that had been used to imprison him prior to his martyrdom. These chains were placed in this prominent location in 2008.
†Also a crucifix that is said to have spoken to St Bridget in 1370 is in the Blessed Sacrament Chapel.
†Lining the nave are 266 medallions depicting every pope from the last 2000 years.

Sant'Agnese Fuori le Mura (Saint Agnes Outside the Walls)
Via S Agnese 315
†This church is northeast of the Aurelian Walls and is located on Via Nomentana. It can be reached with the 60, 84, or 90 bus.
†The bones of St Agnes (d. 304) rest in the crypt under the main sanctuary.

San Lorenzo fuori le Mura (Saint Lawrence Outside the Walls)
Piazzale del Verano 3
†This church is east of the Aurelian Walls. It can be reached by a number of buses or trams.
†The remains of St Lawrence (d. 258), St Stephen, and St Justin lie in the confessio below the main altar. (Note: The relics are labeled as St Justin the Presbyter. Therefore, it is likely that this is not St Justin the Martyr.)
†A marble stone slab beneath the choir floor is said to be the stone on which St Lawrence was placed after his execution. Also enshrined in this lower area is the body of Blessed Pius IX (d. 1878).

Region #10
Fontana di Trevi

Trevi Fountain

This short route includes three churches just to the south of the Trevi Fountain. Despite being brief, this route allows one to visit two of the apostles, a miraculous crucifix, and a Marian grotto.

The following churches are listed according to the order of the suggested route. The total distance is about 1/3 of a mile. To walk will probably take about 1.5 hours if one visits each of the churches. The churches are generally open from 7AM-1PM and from 4PM-7PM. *Santa Rita da Cascia alle Vergini* may not be open as frequently.

Santa Rita da Cascia alle Vergini (Saint Rita of Cascia at the Vergini)
Via del Umiltà 83B
✝ This church is just south of the Trevi Fountain.
✝ A grotto honoring Our Lady of Lourdes is found within a small room immediately on the left after entering.

Santi Apostoli (Holy Apostles)
Piazza dei Santi Apostoli 51
✝ This church is just east of Piazza Venezia.
✝ Relics of St Philip and St James the Less rest within the confessio of this church. During the 6th century they were transferred from Constantinople to Rome by Pope Pelagius I (d. 561). In 1873, as excavations commenced below the central altar, their relics were unearthed. They were then carefully examined and repositioned within the confessio where they rest today.
✝ Also the painting above the main altar depicts the martyrdom of St Philip and St James the Less. It was completed by Domenico Maria Muratori in the early 18th century.

San Marcello al Corso (Saint Marcellus on the Corso)
Piazza di San Marcello 5
✝ This church is north of Piazza Venezia.
✝ A fire on the night of May 22, 1519 destroyed most of this church. Only the outer walls and a 15th century wooden crucifix survived. This miraculous crucifix can now be found in the fourth chapel on the right side of the nave. A relic of the true cross is also preserved within this chapel in a reliquary.

Region #11
Basilica of St Mary Major

The *Basilica of St Mary Major* was constructed in honor of the Blessed Virgin Mary by Pope Sixtus III shortly after the Council of Ephesus. It replaced an earlier church that had been built by Pope Liberius in the 4th century. At this council the church solemnly declared that the Blessed Virgin Mary was the Mother of God to protect against the Christological heresies that attacked the full divinity of Jesus. Thus this Marian dogma helped to strengthen the doctrine that Jesus was both fully human and fully divine. This region, therefore, being anchored by this great basilica is steeped in tradition and many of its relics go back to beginnings of the church.

Sacro Cuore di Gesu a Castro Pretorio

Begin this route at *Sacro Cuore di Gesu a Castro Pretorio* located not far from the northeast exit of the Termini train station. After visiting this church continue west on Via Urbana to visit *Santa Pudenziana*. From here it is a short walk to the *Basilica of St Mary Major*. After an ample visit to this great basilica depart and head south to visit both *Santa Prassede* and *Santuario della Madonna del Perpetuo Soccorso*. From these churches continue south on Via Merulana until you reach Viale del Monte Oppio. Turn right on this street to visit *San Martino ai Monti*. After visiting this church continue west on Viale del Monte Oppio which will turn to the right and become Via delle Sette Sale. This quiet road will lead you directly to *San Pietro in Vincoli*. Finally head north and cut across Via Cavour to visit *Santa Maria ai Monti*.

The following churches are listed according to the order of the suggested route. The total distance is about 1.5 miles. To walk will probably take about 5 hours if one visits each of the churches. The churches are generally open from 7AM-1PM and from 4PM-7PM. *Sacro Cuore di Gesu a Castro Pretorio* & *Santa Pudenziana*, may not be open as frequently. The *Basilica of St Mary Major* is open from 7AM - 7PM and does not close during the pranzo hour.

Sacro Cuore di Gesu a Castro Pretorio
(Sacred Heart of Jesus at Castro Pretorio)
Via Marsala 42
✝This church is near the Termini Train Station. It was built by St John Bosco and finished in 1887. The church continues to be served by the Salesians.
✝St John Bosco (d. 1888) celebrated Mass at the altar in the left transept. It was at this altar that he profoundly realized that his life had fulfilled the vision he had as a youth.
✝In the museum to the right of the main sanctuary are various relics. One reliquary contains a bone fragment of St John Bosco. Also upon request one can visit the rooms of St John Bosco.

Santa Pudenziana (Saint Pudentiana)
Via Urbana 160
✝This church is west of the *Basilica of St Mary Major*.
✝It is believed that St Peter lodged here while he was in Rome. The house in which he stayed was owned and provided for by St Pudens, a Roman Senator. Since early Christians did not have public places for worship it is also presumed that St Peter celebrated Mass here. Remnants from the ancient wooden altar used for these Masses are said to be preserved in the chapel dedicated to him on the left side of the main sanctuary.

Basilica of St Mary Major
Piazza di Santa Maria Maggiore 42
✝Some relics of St Matthias rest within the porphyry urn that makes up the base of the Papal Altar. Also in the confessio below this altar are five pieces of wood believed to be from the crib of Jesus Christ.
✝The remains of St Jerome (d. 420) were brought to this basilica in the 12ᵗʰ century. There is some doubt as to their exact location. They either rest under the Papal Altar within the main body of the church or within the confessio in the right transept.
✝Within the *Pauline Chapel* in the left transept is a miraculous image of the Blessed Virgin Mary entitled *Protectress of the Roman People*. Tradition credits St Luke for the creation of this image.

Santa Prassede (Saint Praxedes)
Via di Santa Prassede 9 / Via San Martino ai Monti
✝This church is just south of the *Basilica of St Mary Major*.
✝In a chapel on the right side of the nave is said to be the Pillar of Christ's scourging. Its authenticity, however, is doubtful since the quality of its marble seems to be too good for the punishment of criminals. A more realistic specimen is venerated in the *Church of the Holy Sepulchre* in Jerusalem.

Santuario della Madonna del Perpetuo Soccorso
(Sanctuary of Our Lady of Perpetual Help)
Via Merulana 26
✝This church is just south of the *Basilica of St Mary Major*. It is dedicated to St Alphonsus Liguori (d. 1787).
✝A miraculous image of the Blessed Virgin Mary entitled *Our Lady of Perpetual Help* is above the main altar.

San Martino ai Monti (Saint Martin at the Hills)

Viale Monte Oppio 28

✝This church is south of the *Basilica of St Mary Major*.

✝The greater part of the remains of St Martin I (d. 655) were transferred from Crimea to this church in Rome. They now rest in the confessio below the main altar. This confessio also houses the relics of many other saints taken from the *Catacombs of Priscilla*.

✝A tradition claims that the pope, St Sylvester I (d. 335), and many other bishops met here to prepare for the Council of Nicaea. They then reconvened at this same church after the Council to announce the newly formulated Nicene Creed. Constantine was in attendance for this. The large painting on the left side of the nave created in 1640 recalls one of these meetings. However, this tradition is often tied to the 'Symmachian Forgeries' thus throwing some doubt on its credibility. Nevertheless, it does seem probable that some agreement was achieved between Constantine and St Sylvester I that allowed for the success of the Council of Nicaea.

San Pietro in Vincoli (Saint Peter in Chains)

Piazza San Pietro in Vincoli 4/a

✝This church is near the Cavour metro stop.

✝A tradition claims that St Peter was condemned and imprisoned near this site. Venerated within the confessio are the chains of St Peter. A tradition holds that these chains are a result of the chains from St Peter's imprisonment in Jerusalem coming into contact with the chains from St Peter's imprisonment in Rome. Miraculously these two chains were fused into the one inseparable chain that is now found in the confessio.

✝Michelangelo's famous statue of Moses is on the right side of the nave.

✝Within the crypt are said to rest the remains of the seven Jewish brothers who lost their lives in 2 Maccabees 7. They were acquired in the 6th century by Pope Pelagius I.

Santa Maria ai Monti (Our Lady at the Hills)

Via della Madonna dei Monti 41

✝This church is near the Cavour metro stop.

✝This church was built due to a miraculous discovery of an image of the Blessed Virgin Mary in a nearby Poor Clare convent that had fallen into ruins. To celebrate this great find Pope Gregory XIII (d. 1585) commissioned the building of this church. This miraculous image is now placed above the main altar.

Region #12
Campo de' Fiori

The region near Campo de' Fiori has a rich faith history beginning with the early martyrs and culminating in the late 16th and early 17th centuries with the construction of the three great preaching churches: *Il Gesu, Chiesa Nuova*, and *Sant'Andrea della Valle*.

Il Gesu

Begin your route at *San Giovanni Battista dei Fiorentini*. This church borders the Tiber River and is just east of the Vatican. From this church continue east along the Corso Vittorio Emanuele until you reach *Sant'Andrea della Valle*. From here head southwest to reach *San Girolamo della Carità* and *Santa Brigida a Campo de' Fiori*. This route will take you through the markets of Campo de' Fiori. After visiting these churches continue east along Via dei Giubbonari to reach *San Carlo ai Catinari*. From this church cross the relatively busy street called Via Arenula and then follow Via Funari until you reach *Santa Maria in Campitelli*. After visiting this church cut across until you once again come to the Corso Vittorio Emanuele and the church called *Il Gesu*.

The following churches are listed according to the order of the suggested route. The total distance is about 1.5 miles. To walk will probably take about 4 hours if one visits each of the churches. The churches are generally open from 7AM-1PM and from 4PM-7PM. *San Girolamo della Carità* & *Santa Brigida a Campo de' Fiori* may not be open as frequently.

San Giovanni Battista dei Fiorentini
(Saint John the Baptist of the Florentines)
Via Acciaioli 2
†This church is just east of the Vatican. It is next to the Tiber River and the Corso Vittorio Emanuele.
†St Philip Neri (d. 1595) became rector of this church in 1564. He also founded the Congregation of the Oratory at this church.
†A relic of St Mary Magdalene's foot rests in a shrine to the left of the main sanctuary.

Sant'Andrea della Valle (Saint Andrew of the Valley)
Piazza Vidoni 6 / Piazza Sant'Andrea della Valle
†This church is located along the Corso Vittorio Emanuele. Prior to the construction of this church in the 17th century a small church dedicated to St Sebastian was located here. Tradition claims that this ancient church rested upon a sewer from which the body of St Sebastian (d. 288) was recovered following his martyrdom. Today a remnant of this ancient church is partially preserved within a niche found in the first chapel on the left side of the nave.
†Also the third chapel on the left side of the nave is dedicated to St Sebastian. The altarpiece within this chapel was painted by Giovanni de' Vecchi in 1614.
†The second chapel on the right side of the nave is dedicated to Our Lady of Sorrows. A reproduction of Michelangelo's Pietà is located within this chapel.
†The large paintings in the sanctuary depict the martyrdom of St Andrew.

San Girolamo della Carità (Saint Jerome of Charity)

Via di Monserrato 62/a

✝This church is near Piazza Farnese.

✝This church was built on the site of the house of St Paula. Tradition claims that St Jerome (d. 420) lived in this house when he was secretary to Pope St Damasus I (d. 384).

✝St Philip Neri (d. 1595) lived here from 1551 to 1583.

✝In the left transept is a spectacular chapel honoring St Philip Neri. A marble statue of the saint is surrounded by a gilded frame. The ceiling also opens up revealing a small domed space filled with further statues of angels.

Santa Brigida a Campo de' Fiori (Saint Bridget at the Field of Flowers)

Piazza Farnese 96

✝This church is at Piazza Farnese.

✝Following the death of her husband, St Bridget of Sweden devoted herself completely to a life of prayer and service. After founding the *Bridgettine Sisters* in Sweden she felt compelled to visit Rome in order to seek official approval for her community. Her visit resulted in her permanently remaining in the city for the next twenty-four years until her passing in 1373. Today a few of her relics rest within this Bridgettine convent which still to this day is occupied by members of her community. Her body was returned to Sweden shortly after her death.

San Carlo ai Catinari (Saint Charles at the Catinari)

Piazza Benedetto Cairoli 117

✝This church is near the Largo di Torre Argentina.

✝A chapel in the right transept preserves a copy of the miraculous image of the Blessed Virgin Mary entitled *Mother of Divine Providence*. The original is located in a Barnabite church in Trastevere.

✝On February 3rd several relics of St Blaise are presented within this church for veneration. Of special note is a reliquary which contains a bone from the throat of St Blaise. This relic is used to bless the throats of the faithful.

Santa Maria in Campitelli (Our Lady in Campitelli)
Piazza di Campitelli 9
† This church is near the Jewish quarter.
† The body of St John Leonardi (d. 1609) is enshrined in the second chapel on the left side of the nave.

Il Gesu (The Jesus)
Via degli Astalli 16
† This church is located along the Corso Vittorio Emanuele. It honors a number of Jesuit saints.
† St Ignatius of Loyola (d. 1556), the founder of the Jesuits, is buried under the altar in the left transept. His rooms are located in the Generalate next to the church and may be visited.
† An arm of St Francis Xavier (d. 1552) rests within a reliquary above the altar in the right transept. With this arm he baptized thousands of individuals in India and the Far East.
† The remains of St Peter Faber (d. 1546), an early companion of St Ignatius, are also located here. They are said to rest below the main entrance to this church having been placed here when the church was built in the 16th century. During the placement of these relics it was impossible to separate the bones of St Peter Faber from the bones of other individuals; therefore, his bones are buried together with theirs.

PART II

First Class Relics

For The Saints Found On The Roman Catholic Liturgical Calendar

** ** ** ** ** ** ** **

St Peter's Basilica

First Class Relics In Rome

(For The Saints On The Roman Catholic Liturgical Calendar)

Adalbert, bishop and martyr
Agnes, virgin and martyr
Aloysius Gonzaga, religious
Bartholomew, apostle
Blaise, bishop and martyr
Bridget, religious
Callistus I, pope and martyr
Camillus de Lellis, priest
Catherine of Siena, virgin and doctor
Cecilia, virgin and martyr
Charles Borromeo, bishop
Clement I, pope and martyr
Cornelius, pope and martyr
Cosmas and Damian, martyrs
Cyril, monk
Damasus I, pope
Fabian, pope and martyr
Frances of Rome, religious
Frances Xavier Cabrini, virgin
Francis Xavier, priest
George, martyr
Gregory Nazianzen, bishop and doctor
Gregory the Great, pope and doctor
Ignatius of Antioch, bishop and martyr
Ignatius of Loyola, priest
James the Less, apostle
Jerome, priest and doctor
John Baptist de la Salle, priest
John Chrysostom, bishop and doctor
John I, pope and martyr
John XXIII, pope
John Leonardi, priest
John Paul II, pope

John the Baptist, martyr
Josaphat, bishop and martyr
Joseph Calasanz, priest
Justin, martyr
Lawrence, deacon and martyr
Leo the Great, pope and doctor
Luke, evangelist
Marcellinus and Peter, martyrs
Martin I, pope and martyr
Mary Magdalene
Matthias, apostle
Monica
Nereus and Achilleus, martyrs
Pancras, martyr
Paul, apostle
Paul of the Cross, priest
Peter, apostle
Peter Faber, priest
Peter Julian Eymard, priest
Philip, apostle
Philip Neri, priest
Pius V, pope
Pius X, pope
Polycarp, bishop and martyr
Robert Bellarmine, bishop and doctor
Sebastian, martyr
Simon and Jude, apostles
Sixtus II, pope and martyr
Stephen, first martyr
Sylvester I, pope
Teresa of Jesus, virgin and doctor
Thomas, apostle

Adalbert, bishop and martyr (April 23rd) and Bartholomew, apostle (August 24th)

St Adalbert [Wojciech in Polish] (d. 997) (Relics: Rome, Italy; Prague, Czech Republic; Gniezno, Poland)

St Bartholomew (Relics: Rome, Italy; Benevento, Italy; Lipari, Sicily; Frankfurt, Germany)

According to the *Roman Martyrology* St Bartholomew suffered martyrdom in the Roman province of Armenia. It is recorded that he was first skinned alive and then put to death by decapitation. Five centuries later and half-way across the Mediterranean his relics were found in Lipari, Sicily. Most likely they arrived here through normal means; however, a pious tradition contends that this transfer occurred miraculously. This tradition claims that the sarcophagus of St Bartholomew was thrown into the sea by infidels. It then floated upon the water until it finally and miraculously came to the shores of the tiny island of Lipari. Regardless, how the relics arrived they remained on this island until the middle of the 9th century. At this time they were transferred to Benevento, Italy and then in the latter part of the 10th century they were brought to Rome by the Holy Roman Emperor, Otto III, where they were interred in the church of *San Bartolomeo all'Isola* on Tiber Island. This final transfer, however, is contested by the city of Benevento which continues to claim possession of the true relics of St Bartholomew.

San Bartolomeo all'Isola (Saint Bartholomew on the Island)
Piazza San Bartolomeo, Tiber Island
✝An arm of St Adalbert is currently enshrined in the chapel to the left of the main sanctuary. It rests within a little metal box placed under the altar of this chapel.
✝Relics of the apostle, St Bartholomew, rest within the red porphyry basin that supports the main altar.

Agnes, virgin and martyr (January 21st)

Agnes, virgin and martyr (January 21ˢᵗ)

St Agnes (d. 304, Rome, Italy) (Relics: Rome, Italy)

Sant'Agnese in Agone
(Saint Agnes in Agone)
Piazza Navona
✝According to tradition St Agnes was martyred at this location in 304 AD. A relic of her skull is present in a chapel located to the left of the main sanctuary.

Sant'Agnese Fuori le Mura
(Saint Agnes Outside the Walls)
Via S Agnese 315
✝This church is northeast of the Aurelian Walls and is located on Via Nomentana.
✝The bones of St Agnes rest in the crypt under the main sanctuary.

Aloysius Gonzaga, religious (June 21ˢᵗ) and Robert Bellarmine, bishop and doctor (September 17ᵗʰ)

St Aloysius Gonzaga (d. 1591, Rome, Italy) (Relics: Rome, Italy; Castiglione delle Stiviere, Italy)

St Robert Bellarmine (d. 1621, Rome, Italy) (Relics: Rome, Italy)

Sant'Ignazio (Saint Ignatius)
Via del Caravita 8/a
✝This church is east of the Pantheon.
✝The remains of St Aloysius Gonzaga rest under the altar in the right transept. His rooms are next to the church and can be visited by appointment.
✝The body of St Robert Bellarmine, a prominent cardinal and theologian of the Counter-Reformation, rests under the altar in the third chapel on the right side of the nave.
✝The remains of St John Berchmans (d. 1621), the patron saint of altar servers, rest under the altar in the left transept.

Blaise, bishop and martyr (February 3rd)

St Blaise (d. 316, Armenia) (Relics: Rome, Italy; Maratea, Italy; Dubrovnik, Croatia)

San Carlo ai Catinari
(Saint Charles at the Catinari)
Piazza Benedetto Cairoli 117
✝This church is near the Largo di Torre Argentina. It is dedicated to St Blaise as its full name *Santi Biagio e Carlo ai Catinari* indicates.
✝On February 3rd several relics of St Blaise are presented within this church for veneration. Of special note is a reliquary which contains a bone from the throat of St Blaise. This relic is used to bless the throats of the faithful.
✝The second chapel on the right side of the nave is also dedicated to St Blaise.

Bridget, religious (July 23rd)

St Bridget (d. 1373, Rome, Italy) (Relics: Rome, Italy; Vadstena, Sweden)

Santa Brigida a Campo de' Fiori
(Saint Bridget at the Field of Flowers)
Piazza Farnese 96
✝This church is at Piazza Farnese.
✝Following the death of her husband, St Bridget of Sweden devoted herself completely to a life of prayer and service. After founding the Bridgettine Sisters in Sweden she felt compelled to visit Rome in order to seek official approval for her community. Her visit resulted in her permanently remaining in the city for the next twenty-four years until her passing in 1373. Today a few of her relics rest within this Bridgettine convent which still to this day is occupied by members of her community. Her body was returned to Sweden shortly after her death.

Callistus I, pope and martyr (October 14th) and Cornelius, pope and martyr (September 16th)

St Callistus I (d. 222, Rome, Italy) (Relics: Rome, Italy)

St Cornelius (d. 253, Civitavecchia, Italy) (Relics: Rome, Italy; Aachen, Germany)

St Cornelius died in the Italian city of Civitavecchia in 253 AD. His remains were then transferred south to Rome and placed in the *Catacombs of San Callisto* on the Appian Way. Five centuries later his relics, along with those of St Callistus I, were transferred to the Roman church of *Santa Maria in Trastevere* by Pope Adrian I (772-795). Pope Gregory IV (827-844) then had their remains placed under the main altar of this same church during his pontificate. From here a tradition claims that the remains of both St Cornelius and the bishop, St Cyprian, were transferred to Compiègne, France. Some of the sources conflict, however, with regard to this tradition. For instance, the *Martyrology of Ado* mentions the transfer of St Cyprian but not the transfer of St Cornelius. As a result two separate traditions have arisen with regard to St Cornelius' relics. The Roman tradition holds that some of his relics still remain under the main altar in *Santa Maria in Trastevere*. In the 18th century some of these relics were transferred to the Roman church of *Santi Celso e Giuliano*. A sarcophagus with these relics can still be found in this church. On the other hand the highly venerated relic of St Cornelius' head in the *Kornelimünster Abbey* near Aachen, Germany demonstrates that the purported transfer of his relics to Compiègne in the 9th century may also have credence.

Santa Maria in Trastevere (Our Lady in Trastevere)
Via della Paglia 14 / Piazza Santa Maria in Trastevere
†This church is located in Trastevere.
†Relics of the two popes, St Callistus I and St Cornelius, rest under the main altar of this church. These relics are joined by others in particular those of the priest and martyr St Calepodius (d. 232).

Santi Celso e Giuliano (Saints Celsus and Julian)
Vicolo del Curato 12 / Via del Banco Santo Spirito
†This church is located across the Tiber River from *Castel Sant'Angelo*. The main entrance to the church is on Via del Banco Santo Spirito.
†Some relics of St Cornelius were transferred to this church in the 18th century. These relics are located in an urn to the right of the main entrance.

Camillus de Lellis, priest (July 18th)*

St Camillus de Lellis (d. 1614, Rome, Italy) (Relics: Rome, Italy)

La Maddalena (The Magdalene)
Piazza della Maddalena 53
✝This church is just north of the Pantheon.
✝In the chapel in the right transept is a miraculous crucifix that is said to have spoken to St Camillus de Lellis.
✝In the third chapel on the right side of the nave are the remains of St Camillus de Lellis. He lived in the adjacent monastery and died here in 1614. His rooms can be visited by asking the sacristan. One of these rooms has been transformed into a chapel and contains the relic of his heart.

Catherine of Siena, virgin and doctor (April 29th)

St Catherine of Siena (d. 1380, Rome, Italy) (Relics: Rome, Italy; Siena, Italy; Venice, Italy)

Santa Maria sopra Minerva (Our Lady Above Minerva)
Piazza della Minerva 42
✝This church is near the Pantheon.
✝The body of St Catherine of Siena rests under the main altar. She spent the last two years of her life in Rome before her passing in 1380. A devotional chapel made out of the room where she died can be visited by entering the sacristy. Originally this room was located a few blocks away at Via Santa Chiara, 14. However, in the 1630s it was reconstructed and brought here.

Monastero della Madonna del Rosario a Monte Mario
(Monastery of Our Lady of the Rosary at Monte Mario)
Via Alberto Cadlolo 51
✝This monastery is on Monte Mario northwest of the Aurelian Walls.
✝The left hand of St Catherine of Siena rests within the church at this monastery.

Cecilia, virgin and martyr (November 22nd)

St Cecilia (d. Sicily) (Relics: Rome, Italy)

Santa Cecilia in Trastevere
(Saint Cecilia in Trastevere)
Piazza di Santa Cecilia 22

✝This church is in the southern part of Trastevere. It is built over the ruins of the house that St Cecilia had lived in prior to her martyrdom.

✝In 821 the body of St Cecilia was exhumed from the *Catacombs of San Callisto* by Pope St Paschal I (d. 824) and returned to this church. Today her remains rest within the crypt under the main altar.

✝The recumbent statue of St Cecilia below the main altar was completed by Stefano Maderno in the late 16th century. A gash on her neck recalls the miraculous events surrounding her martyrdom. Tradition claims that St Cecilia was condemned to execution first by drowning and then by decapitation. Both attempts failed. The second method, however, left her greatly wounded. The executioner struck her neck three times with a sword but being unable to sever her head fled in fear. She survived for three days, offered all she had to the poor, and then expired.

Charles Borromeo, bishop (November 4th)

St Charles Borromeo (d. 1584, Milan, Italy) (Relics: Rome, Italy; Milan, Italy)

San Carlo al Corso (Saint Charles on the Corso)
Via del Corso 437

✝This church is near the Spanish Steps.

✝The dedication of this church is to the great 16th century Archbishop of Milan, St Charles Borromeo. A relic of his heart rests within a reliquary in an altar located behind the main sanctuary.

Clement I, pope and martyr (November 23rd), Cyril, monk (February 14th), and Ignatius of Antioch, bishop and martyr (October 17th)

St Clement I (d. 97) (Relics: Rome, Italy)

St Cyril (d. 869, Rome, Italy) (Relics: Rome, Italy)

St Ignatius of Antioch (d. 107, Rome, Italy) (Relics: Rome, Italy)

St Cyril is believed to have discovered both the anchor and the relics of St Clement I in Crimea in 861 AD. St Cyril then brought these relics to Rome during his visit in 868 AD. He died in Rome a year later. His brother, St Methodius, wished to return the body of St Cyril to his homeland in Thessalonica; however, Pope Adrian II would not allow this. As a result the body of St Cyril was kept in Rome and buried in the *Basilica of San Clemente*, the same church where he had deposited the relics of St Clement I a year prior. The remains of St Cyril remained in this church until their removal and disappearance during the French establishment of the Roman Republic in the late 18th century. In the 1960's, a fortunate discovery by an Irish Dominican led to the retrieval of a small relic of St Cyril. This relic is now within this church as noted below.

Basilica di San Clemente (Basilica of Saint Clement)
Via Labicana 95 / Piazza San Clemente
†This church is east of the Colosseum.
†The remains of St Clement I and of St Ignatius of Antioch rest beneath the main altar. On the feast of St Clement I a reliquary bust containing his skull is festively carried in procession through the streets of Rome.
†A chapel on the right side of the nave is dedicated to Saints Cyril and Methodius (d. 885). The relic of St Cyril found in the 1960's rests within the altar of this chapel.

Cosmas and Damian, martyrs (September 26th)

Saints Cosmas and Damian (d. 287, Syria) (Relics: Rome, Italy; Munich, Germany)

Santi Cosma e Damiano
(Saints Cosmas and Damian)
Via dei Fori Imperiali 1
✝This church is located next to the Roman Forum.
✝Relics of Saints Cosmas and Damian rest under the altar in the lower church. Each year for the feast of Saints Cosmas and Damian these relics are brought out for public veneration.

Damasus I, pope (December 11th)

St Damasus I (d. 384, Rome, Italy) (Relics: Rome, Italy)

San Lorenzo in Damaso (Saint Lawrence in Damaso)
Piazza della Cancelleria 1
✝This church is at the *Palazzo della Cancelleria* near Campo de' Fiori. It is believed to have been founded in the very home of St Damasus I whose remains now rest under the main altar.

Fabian, pope and martyr and Sebastian, martyr (January 20th)

St Fabian (d. 250, Rome, Italy) (Relics: Rome, Italy)

St Sebastian (d. 288, Rome, Italy) (Relics: Rome, Italy)

A major part of the relics of St Gregory the Great and the body of St Sebastian are said to have been taken to Soissons, France in 826 AD. Alban Butler in *The Lives of the Fathers, Martyrs, and Other Principal Saints* claims that in 1564 these relics were stolen and thrown into a ditch by Calvinists. This tradition then maintains that some of these desecrated relics were recovered and subsequently placed into surrounding churches in that area. Despite this tradition the veneration of their relics in Rome has been maintained for centuries.

San Sebastiano Fuori Le Mura
(Saint Sebastian Outside the Walls)
Via Appia Antica 136
†This church is south of the Aurelian Walls.
†The last chapel on the right side of the nave is dedicated to the pope, St Fabian. Also a reliquary chapel near the center of the church on the right side of the nave contains relics of the saint. St Fabian was originally buried in the *Catacombs of San Callisto* but later his remains were moved to this church. Also within this same chapel are the column to which St Sebastian was tied, an arrow that pierced his flesh, and some small relics from a number of other saints including St Peter, St Paul, and St Andrew.
†Directly across from this chapel and on the left side of the nave is a chapel dedicated to St Sebastian. St Sebastian was originally buried in the catacombs located under this church. At some point, however, his remains were removed. Some of these remains are now located within an urn in this chapel below the very impressive statue of St Sebastian created by Giuseppe Giorgetti.
†This church has an ancient tradition connecting it to St Peter and to St Paul. The *Depositio Martyrum* shows that in the year 258 pilgrims came to *San Sebastiano Fuori Le Mura* on June 29th, the Feast Day of Saints Peter and Paul, to honor these two great saints. Therefore, it is presumed that at one time this church housed the remains of both St Peter and St Paul.
†Tradition also claims that within the catacombs located under this church St Philip Neri (d. 1595) experienced such an enlargement of his heart due to a supernatural infusion of God's love that two of his ribs cracked.

St Peter's Basilica
Treasury Museum
†The skull of St Sebastian is placed within a glass-sided reliquary in this museum.

Santi Quattro Coronati (Four Holy Crowned Ones)
Piazza dei Santi Quattro Coronati 20
†This church is east of the Colosseum.
†For centuries the skull of St Sebastian was venerated within the crypt of this church. Signage at an altar on the left side of the nave continues to indicate its presence. However, at some point in the last century the skull was removed. It can now be found within a reliquary in the Treasury Museum of *St Peter's Basilica* as previously noted.

Frances of Rome, religious (March 9th)

St Frances of Rome (d.
1440, Rome, Italy)
(Relics: Rome, Italy)

**Santa Francesca
Romana** (Saint Frances
of Rome)
Piazza di Santa Francesca
Romana 4
✝This church is next to
the Roman Forum.

✝The remains of St Frances of Rome are in the crypt below the main
sanctuary. Her skeleton is vested in the habit of the Oblate Sisters.
✝To the right of the sanctuary is the tomb of Pope Gregory XI (d. 1378). He
returned the papal seat to Rome after the exile in Avignon. St Catherine of
Siena (d. 1380) was instrumental in persuading him to return. A relief
depicting her involvement can be seen on the tomb.

Frances Xavier Cabrini, virgin (November 13th)*

St Frances Xavier Cabrini (d. 1917, Chicago, Illinois, USA) (Relics: New
York City, New York, USA; Chicago, Illinois, USA; Rome, Italy; Codogno,
Italy; Sant'Angelo Lodigiano, Italy)

Chiesa del Santissimo Redentore e Santa Francesca Cabrini
(Church of the Most Holy Redeemer and St Frances Cabrini)
Via Sicilia 215
✝This church is north of Piazza della Repubblica.
✝The skull of St Frances Xavier Cabrini rests within this church. It is placed
within a statue of her likeness that reposes within an urn on the right side of
the nave.

Francis Xavier, priest (December 3rd), Ignatius of Loyola, priest (July 31st), and Peter Faber, priest

St Francis Xavier (d. 1552, Shangchuan Island, China) (Relics: Rome, Italy; Goa, India; Antwerp, Belgium)

St Ignatius of Loyola (d. 1556, Rome, Italy) (Relics: Rome, Italy)

St Peter Faber (d. 1546, Rome, Italy) (Relics: Rome, Italy)

Il Gesu (The Jesus)
Via degli Astalli 16
✝This church is located along the Corso Vittorio Emanuele. It honors a number of Jesuit saints.

✝An arm of St Francis Xavier rests within a reliquary above the altar in the right transept. With this arm he baptized thousands of individuals in India and the Far East.

✝St Ignatius of Loyola, the founder of the Jesuits, is buried under the altar in the left transept. His rooms are located in the Generalate next to the church and may be visited.

✝The remains of St Peter Faber (d. 1546), an early companion of St Ignatius, are also located here. They are said to rest below the main entrance to this church having been placed here when the church was built in the 16th century. During the placement of these relics it was impossible to separate the bones of St Peter Faber from the bones of other individuals; therefore, his bones are buried together with theirs.

George, martyr (April 23ʳᵈ)

St George (d. 303, Lydda, Palestine) (Relics: Lod, Israel; Rome, Italy)

San Giorgio in Velabro
(Saint George in Velabro)
Via del Velabro 19
✝This church is just east of Tiber Island.
✝Part of the skull of St George rests beneath the main altar.

✝History is filled with legends surrounding this early Christian martyr. The most famous involves him slaying a dragon. Critical research in the last century has upheld the existence of St George; however, it has cast doubts upon many of his legendary accounts. (Note: Other shrines throughout the world also claim to have the relic of his skull.)

Gregory Nazianzen, bishop and doctor (January 2ⁿᵈ)

St Gregory Nazianzen (d. 389, Cappadocia) (Relics: Rome, Italy; Istanbul, Turkey; Mount Athos, Greece; Lisbon, Portugal)

The body of St Gregory Nazianzen was first buried near his hometown in Cappadocia and then later transferred to Constantinople. In the 8ᵗʰ century his remains were removed from Constantinople and brought to Rome by a group of Basilian nuns who were escaping the Iconoclastic persecutions in the East. These nuns were given residence in the Campo Marzio district just north of the Pantheon in Rome. They then placed the remains of St Gregory Nazianzen within their church.

St Peter's Basilica
Altar of Our Lady of Succour
✝Located on the right side of the nave just after the entrance to the confessional area.
✝Beneath this altar are some relics of St Gregory Nazianzen. In 2004 a major part of these relics were returned to the Ecumenical Patriarch of Constantinople.

Santa Maria della Concezione in Campo Marzio
(Our Lady of the Conception in Campo Marzio)
Piazza Campo Marzio 45
✝This church is north of the Pantheon.
✝As noted previously Basilian nuns brought the relics of St Gregory Nazianzen to Rome in the 8th century. They were kept in Rome at Campo Marzio and eventually placed within this church.
✝With the exception of one arm the remains of St Gregory Nazianzen were transferred to *St Peter's Basilica* in 1580. This arm remained at *Santa Maria della Concezione* as compensation and was eventually placed in the nearby church of *San Gregorio*. This relic, however, is not accessible to the general public since *San Gregorio* is the church used by the Deputies of the Italian Parliament.

Gregory the Great, pope and doctor (September 3rd)

St Gregory the Great (d. 604, Rome, Italy) (Relics: Rome, Italy)

A major part of the relics of St Gregory the Great and the body of St Sebastian are said to have been taken to Soissons, France in 826 AD. Alban Butler in *The Lives of the Fathers, Martyrs, and Other Principal Saints* claims that in 1564 these relics were stolen and thrown into a ditch by Calvinists. This tradition then maintains that some of these desecrated relics were recovered and subsequently placed into surrounding churches in that area. Despite this tradition the veneration of their relics in Rome has been maintained for centuries.

St Peter's Basilica
Altar of St Gregory the Great
✝Located within the left transept near the entrance to the sacristy.
✝Relics of St Gregory the Great rest below this altar. The mosaic above this altar recounts a Eucharistic miracle attributed to him.

Jerome, priest and doctor (September 30th), Matthias, apostle (May 14th), and Pius V, pope (April 30th)

St Jerome (d. 420,
Bethlehem, Judea)
(Relics: Rome, Italy)

St Matthias (Relics:
Rome, Italy; Trier,
Germany)

St Pius V (d. 1572, Rome,
Italy) (Relics: Rome,
Italy)

St Helena is said to have acquired the relics of St Matthias in the 4th century. These relics were then distributed to both Rome, Italy and Trier, Germany.

Basilica of St Mary Major
Piazza di Santa Maria Maggiore 42

✝Some relics of St Matthias rest within the porphyry urn that makes up the base of the Papal Altar. Also in the confessio below this altar are five pieces of wood believed to be from the crib of Jesus Christ.

✝Enshrined within the large chapel in the right transept is the body of St Pius V. His remains rest within an urn on the left side of this chapel.

✝The remains of St Jerome were brought to this basilica in the 12th century. There is some doubt as to their exact location. They either rest under the Papal Altar within the main body of the church or within the confessio in the right transept.

John Baptist de la Salle, priest (April 7ᵗʰ)

St John Baptist de la Salle (d. 1719, Rouen, France) (Relics: Rome, Italy)

Casa Generalizia dei Fratelli delle Scuole Cristiane
(Generalate of the Brothers of Christian Schools)
Via Aurelia 476
†Located west of the Vatican.
†The remains of St John Baptist de la Salle were transferred here in 1937. They now rest in the sanctuary of the church.
†During the early 18ᵗʰ century he founded a community of consecrated laymen commonly referred to as the Christian Brothers. This community pioneered many educational reforms within France.

John Chrysostom, bishop and doctor (September 13ᵗʰ)

St John Chrysostom (d. 407, NE Turkey) (Relics: Rome, Italy; Florence, Italy; Istanbul, Turkey; Moscow, Russia; Mount Athos, Greece)

St Peter's Basilica
Chapel of the Immaculate Conception
†Also known as the Wedding Chapel or the Chapel of the Choir.
†This is the third chapel on the left side of the nave.
†Some relics of St John Chrysostom rest below the altar within this chapel. In 2004 a major part of these relics were returned to the Ecumenical Patriarch of Constantinople.

John I, pope and martyr (May 18ᵗʰ)

St John I (d. 526, Ravenna, Italy) (Relics: Rome, Italy)

St Peter's Basilica
†St John I reigned as pope for less than three years. During his brief papacy he ardently supported orthodoxy despite intense pressures exerted by the Arian ruler of Italy, King Theodoric. Eventually the king had him arrested. Due to the poor treatment that he received while imprisoned he passed away in 526 AD. His body now rests in the crypt of this basilica.

John Leonardi, priest (October 9th)

St John Leonardi (d. 1609, Rome, Italy) (Relics: Rome, Italy)

Santa Maria in Campitelli
(Our Lady in Campitelli)
Piazza di Campitelli 9
†This church is near the Jewish quarter.
†The body of St John Leonardi is enshrined in the second chapel on the left side of the nave.

John Paul II, pope (October 22nd)

St John Paul II (d. 2005, Rome, Italy) (Relics: Rome, Italy)

St Peter's Basilica
Chapel of St Sebastian
†Located on the right side of the nave just after Michelangelo's statue of the Pietà.
†In 2011, in preparation for his beatification, the remains of St John Paul II were removed from the crypt of this basilica and placed within the altar of this chapel. Since thousands of people visit this basilica every day the tomb is roped off to provide a small area of prayer. Access is granted if one asks to pray at the tomb.

John the Baptist, martyr (June 24th, August 29th) and Sylvester I, pope (December 31st)

St John the Baptist (Relics: Rome, Italy; Florence, Italy; Siena, Italy; Amiens, France; Munich, Germany; Damascus, Syria)

St Sylvester I (d. 335) (Relics: Rome, Italy)

San Silvestro in Capite
(Saint Sylvester in Capite)
Piazza San Silvestro
†This church is near the Spanish Steps.
†A relic of the skull of St John the Baptist rests within the chapel to the left of the main entrance. The authenticity is uncertain since this same relic is said to be located at a

number of other places throughout the world including *the Cathedral of Amiens* in France, the *Residenz Museum* in Munich, Germany, and the *Umayyad Mosque* in Damascus, Syria.
†The remains of St Sylvester I rest in the confessio below the main altar. They were transferred to this church in the 8th century from the *Catacombs of Priscilla*. On his feast day a relic of his skull is brought out for veneration.
†Depicted within the apse vault above the main altar is the popular legend of St Sylvester I baptizing Constantine.

John XXIII, pope (October 11th)

St John XXIII (d. 1963,
Rome, Italy) (Relics:
Rome, Italy)

St Peter's Basilica
Altar of St Jerome
✝Located on the right side
of the nave at the base of
the first column.
✝The body of St John
XXIII rests under this
altar. He is known in

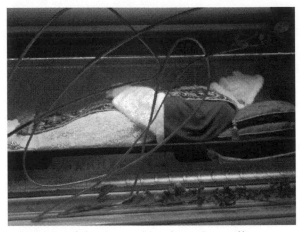

particular for announcing the opening of the Second Vatican Council.

Josaphat, bishop and martyr (November 12th)

St Josaphat (d. 1623, Vitebsk, Russia) (Relics: Rome, Italy)

St Peter's Basilica
Altar of St Basil
✝Located within the confessional area on the back side of the first column.
✝The remains of St Josaphat rest below this altar. During the early part of the
17th century he valiantly tried to bring Christians within the Polish-Lithuanian
Kingdom of Eastern Europe into full communion with Church of Rome. As a
result of his efforts he suffered martyrdom in 1623.

Joseph Calasanz, priest (August 25th)

St Joseph Calasanz (d. 1648, Rome, Italy) (Relics: Rome, Italy)

San Pantaleo (Saint Pantaleon)
Piazza San Pantaleo / Piazza dei Massimi 4
†This church is along the Corso Vittorio Emanuele.
†The relics of St Joseph Calasanz rest under the main altar of this church. His rooms can be visited in the adjacent convent.
†St Joseph Calasanz is known for setting up the first free public school in modern Europe. During his lifetime it was highly controversial to educate the poor. Some thought that it would only leave the poor more dissatisfied with their lowly tasks in society. Education was not seen as an opportunity for advancement. St Joseph Calasanz nevertheless persevered and was eventually appreciated and honored for his work.

Justin, martyr (June 1st)

St Justin (d. 165, Rome, Italy) (Relics: Rome, Italy; Sacrofano, Italy)

Santa Maria della Concezione
(Our Lady of the Immaculate Conception)
Via Veneto 27
†This church is near Piazza Barberini.
†Relics of St Justin the Martyr rest under the altar within the choir chapel. Kindly ask the sacristan for access. The remains of St Justin the Martyr were temporarily transferred in 1992 to the parish church of *San Giustino a Centocelle* in Rome; however, they have now been returned to this church.
†The bones of nearly 4,000 Capuchin friars are located in the crypt.

Lawrence, deacon and martyr (August 10^(th)) and Stephen, first martyr (December 26^(th))

St Lawrence (d. 258,
Rome, Italy) (Relics:
Rome, Italy)

St Stephen (Relics: Rome,
Italy)

**San Lorenzo fuori le
Mura** (Saint Lawrence
Outside the Walls)
Piazzale del Verano 3
✝This church is east of the
Aurelian Walls.

✝The remains of St Lawrence, St Stephen, and St Justin lie in the confessio
below the main altar. (Note: The relics are labeled as St Justin the Presbyter.
Therefore, it is likely that this is not St Justin the Martyr.)
✝A marble stone slab beneath the choir floor is said to be the stone on which
St Lawrence was placed after his execution. Also enshrined in this lower area
is the body of Blessed Pius IX (d. 1878).

Leo the Great, pope and doctor (November 10^(th))

St Leo the Great (d. 461, Rome, Italy) (Relics: Rome, Italy)

St Peter's Basilica
Altar of St Leo the Great
✝Located in the far left corner of the left transept.
✝The remains of St Leo the Great rest under this altar.
✝St Leo was known both for his exemplar defense of orthodox theology and
for his efforts in halting the advance of the Barbarian tribes. A marble relief of
his important meeting with Attila the Hun is placed above this altar.

Luke, evangelist (October 18th)

St Luke (Relics: Rome, Italy; Padua, Italy; Prague, Czech Republic; Thebes, Greece)

St Peter's Basilica
Treasury Museum
✝A silver reliquary bust within this museum is said to contain the head of St Luke. This reliquary dates back to the 14th century and the relic is said to have come from Constantinople. However, this same relic is also said to be located in the _Cathedral of St Vitus_ in Prague, Czech Republic. A recent study on the relics of St Luke was conducted at the request of Archbishop Antonio Mattiazzo of Padua in 1998. This study seems to suggest that the authentic relic of St Luke's head is the one within the _Cathedral of St Vitus_.

Marcellinus and Peter, martyrs (June 2nd)

Saints Marcellinus and Peter (d. 304, Rome, Italy) (Relics: Rome, Italy; Seligenstadt, Germany)

Santi Marcellino e Pietro (Saints Marcellinus and Peter)
Via Merulana 162
✝This church is near the _Basilica of St John Lateran_.
✝Relics of Saints Marcellinus and Peter are preserved within the main altar of this church. Typically on their feast day they are brought out and exposed for public veneration. A large painting depicting their martyrdom is also placed above the main altar.

Martin I, pope and martyr (April 13th)

St Martin I (d. 655, Chersonesus Taurica or 'Cherson/Kherson', Ukraine)
(Relics: Rome, Italy)

Pope Martin I was exiled to Crimea in 654 AD by Emperor Constans II. The
pope ardently opposed the heresy of Monothelitism and the emperor's attempt
to halt debates over it. As a result, he suffered exile and death in Crimea.

San Martino ai Monti (Saint Martin at the Hills)
Viale Monte Oppio 28
✝This church is south of the *Basilica of St Mary Major*.
✝The greater part of the remains of St Martin I were transferred from Crimea
to this church in Rome. They now rest in the confessio below the main altar.
This confessio also houses the relics of many other saints taken from the
Catacombs of Priscilla.
✝A tradition claims that the pope, St Sylvester I (d. 335), and many other
bishops met here to prepare for the Council of Nicaea. They then reconvened
at this same church after the Council to announce the newly formulated Nicene
Creed. Constantine was in attendance for this. The large painting on the left
side of the nave created in 1640 recalls one of these meetings. However, this
tradition is often tied to the 'Symmachian Forgeries' thus throwing some doubt
on its credibility. Nevertheless, it does seem probable that some agreement
was achieved between Constantine and St Sylvester I that allowed for the
success of the Council of Nicaea.

Mary Magdalene (July 22nd)

St Mary Magdalene (Relics: Rome, Italy; Plan-d'Aups-Sainte-Baume, France;
Saint-Maximin-La-Sainte-Baume, France; Vézelay, France)

San Giovanni Battista dei Fiorentini
(Saint John the Baptist of the Florentines)
Via Acciaioli 2
✝This church is just east of the Vatican. It is next to the Tiber River and the
Corso Vittorio Emanuele.
✝A relic of St Mary Magdalene's foot rests in a shrine to the left of the main
sanctuary. Also the chapel in the left transept is dedicated to her.

Monica (August 27th)

St Monica (d. 387, Ostia, Italy) (Relics: Rome, Italy)

Sant'Agostino
(Saint Augustine)
Piazza Sant'Agostino
✝This church is near Piazza Navona.
✝Relics of St Monica, the mother of St Augustine, rest within the Blessed
Sacrament Chapel just to the left of the main sanctuary.

Nereus and Achilleus, martyrs (May 12th) and Philip Neri, priest (May 26th)

Saints Nereus and Achilleus (d. 4th
century) (Relics: Rome, Italy)

St Philip Neri (d. 1595, Rome, Italy)
(Relics: Rome, Italy)

Chiesa Nuova (The New Church)
Via del Governo Vecchio 134
✝This church is located along the
Corso Vittorio Emanuele.
✝The body of St Philip Neri is enshrined in the left transept of this church.
His private rooms can be visited on
certain days of the week. They are
located in the right wall of the left
transept. St Philip Neri spent the last 12
years of his life at _Chiesa Nuova_.
✝In 1597 this church received the skulls of Saints Nereus and Achilleus. They
rest within reliquaries in the sacristy and are sometimes brought out for public
veneration on May 12th.
✝The additional remains of Saints Nereus and Achilleus are said to rest within
a porphyry urn under the main altar of this church. In 1870 they were stolen
from the church of _Santi Nereo e Achilleo_; however, they were later recovered
and are now said to rest here.

Pancras, martyr (May 12th)

St Pancras (d. 4th century) (Relics: Rome, Italy)

San Pancrazio
(Saint Pancras)
Piazza San Pancrazio 5/D
✝This church is west of Trastevere and was built on the site of St Pancras' tomb.
✝In 1798 a general under Napoleon Bonaparte invaded Rome and established the Roman Republic. During this time intruders entered the church of *San Pancrazio* and severely damaged the remains of St Pancras. His head, which was kept in the *Basilica of St John Lateran* from 850 to 1966, fortunately was left untouched. In 1966 Pope Paul VI returned this relic to *San Pancrazio*. It now rests within a reliquary bust on the right side of the nave.
✝Additionally, a few relics of St Pancras and other early church martyrs are said to rest within the porphyry urn that makes up the base of the altar in the main sanctuary.

Paul, apostle (January 25th, June 29th)

(Relics: Rome, Italy; Valletta, Malta)

Basilica of St Paul Outside the Walls
Via Ostiense 186
✝St Paul is buried in the confessio of this church. Above his tomb are the chains that had been used to imprison him prior to his martyrdom. These chains were placed in this prominent location in 2008.
✝Also the main altar in the left transept is dedicated to the Conversion of St Paul. The painting above this altar, completed by Vincenzo Camuccini, depicts this event.

Basilica of St John Lateran
Piazza San Giovanni in Laterano 4
†Positioned above the Papal Altar of this church are two busts of St Peter and St Paul. According to tradition the skulls or parts of the skulls of St Peter and St Paul are within these busts. Also located within the Papal Altar is a wooden table that St Peter and many of the earliest popes are said to have celebrated the Eucharist upon.
†Located to the left of the Papal Altar is another very ancient table. This table rests above the altar where the Blessed Sacrament is reserved. It is placed directly behind a bronze relief of the Last Supper. Tradition claims that it was upon this table that Jesus and the apostles celebrated the Last Supper.

Paul of the Cross, priest (October 20th)*

St Paul of the Cross (d. 1775, Rome, Italy) (Relics: Rome, Italy)

Santi Giovanni e Paolo
(Saints John and Paul)
Piazza dei Santi Giovanni e Paolo 13
†This church is south of the Colosseum.
†St Paul of the Cross is buried under the altar in the large side chapel on the right side of the nave. Upon request one can visit the room in which he died in the monastery adjacent to the church.
†Located beneath this church is a complex of well preserved ancient Roman houses. Among these is an ancient house church. These ruins can be visited.

Peter, apostle (February 22nd, June 29th)

(Relics: Rome, Italy)

St Peter's Basilica

✝Tradition holds that St Peter was crucified upside down in the middle of Nero's Circus. The *Altar of The Crucifixion*, located in the left transept of *St Peter's Basilica*, is very close to the actual site where this crucifixion took place.

✝The bones of St Peter are in the confessio below the Papal Altar and his jawbone can be seen on the Scavi tour.

✝Tradition also holds that within the large bronze chair located above the *Altar of the Chair* in the apse of the church is a second smaller chair made out of wood. This second chair is said to consist of fragments from the original Episcopal chair that St Peter once sat in.

Basilica of St John Lateran

Piazza San Giovanni in Laterano 4

✝As noted previously above the Papal Altar are two busts of St Peter and St Paul. According to tradition the skulls or parts of the skulls of St Peter and St Paul are within these busts.

Peter Julian Eymard, priest (August 2nd)

St Peter Julian Eymard (d. 1868, La Mure, France) (Relics: Rome, Italy; Paris, France)

Chiesa San Claudio (Church of Saint Claudius)
Via del Pozzetto 160
†This church is near the Spanish Steps.
†A relic of St Peter Julian Eymard is placed within a statue of his likeness that rests within an urn on the right side of the nave.
†This church is managed by priests from the *Congregation of the Blessed Sacrament* which St Peter Julian Eymard founded in 1856.

Philip and James, apostles (May 3rd)

St James the Less – The cousin of the Lord and the son of Alphaeus. (d. 62) (Relics: Rome, Italy; Jerusalem, Israel)

St Philip – (Relics: Rome, Italy; Florence, Italy)

Santi Apostoli (Holy Apostles)
Piazza dei Santi Apostoli 51
†This church is just east of Piazza Venezia.
†Relics of St Philip and St James the Less rest within the confessio of this church. During the 6th century they were transferred from Constantinople to Rome by Pope Pelagius I (d. 561). In 1873, as excavations commenced below the central altar, their relics were unearthed. They were then carefully examined and repositioned within the confessio where they rest today.
†Also the painting above the main altar depicts the martyrdom of St Philip and St James the Less. It was completed by Domenico Maria Muratori in the early 18th century.

Pius X, pope (August 21ˢᵗ)

St Pius X (d. 1914, Rome, Italy) (Relics: Rome, Italy)

St Peter's Basilica
Presentation Chapel
✝Located on the left side of the nave between the Baptistry and the Wedding Chapel.
✝The body of St Pius X rests under the altar in this chapel. He is known in particular for lowering the age of First Communion to the Age of Reason.

Polycarp, bishop and martyr (February 23ʳᵈ)

St Polycarp (d. 155, Smyrna) (Relics: Rome, Italy)

Sant'Ambrogio della Massima
(Saint Ambrose)
Via San Ambrogio 3
✝This church is located west of Piazza Venezia near the Fontana delle Tartarughe. It is set behind some buildings and is not easy to notice from the street. It is not open often.
✝The relics of St Polycarp are set in a marble memorial stone under the main altar.
✝Tradition also holds that this church rests on land that was formerly the location of a house owned by St Ambrose's father and occupied by his older sister.

Simon and Jude, apostles (October 28th)

St Simon (Relics: Rome, Italy)

St Jude (Relics: Rome, Italy; Chicago, Illinois, USA)

St Peter's Basilica
St Joseph's Altar
✝Located in the left transept where the Blessed Sacrament is reserved.
✝Relics of the two apostles, St Simon and St Jude, rest under this altar.

San Salvatore in Lauro (Holy Savior in Lauro)
Piazza San Salvatore in Lauro 15
✝This church is west of Piazza Navona.
✝A small bone fragment from an arm of St Jude rests within a side chapel in this church.

Sixtus II, pope and martyr (August 7th)

St Sixtus II (d. 258, Rome, Italy) (Relics: Rome, Italy)

San Sisto Vecchio (Old Saint Sixtus)
Piazzale Numa Pompilio 8
✝This church is south of the Colosseum.
✝The relics of St Sixtus II were moved from the *Catacombs of San Callisto* to this church. A small stone located within the wall on the left side of the nave marks their location.
✝Pope Honorius III gave this church to the Dominican order with the issue of a Papal Bull dated December 3, 1218. This was the first Dominican monastery in Rome.
✝The Miracle of the Bread attributed to St Dominic occurred within the refectory of this monastery. Upon request this room can be visited.

Teresa of Jesus, virgin and doctor (October 15th)

St Teresa (d. 1582, Alba de Tormes, Spain) (Relics: Rome, Italy; Avila, Spain; Alba de Tormes, Spain)

Santa Maria della Scala (Our Lady at the Steps)
Piazza della Scala 23
✝This church is located in Trastevere.
✝The right foot of St Teresa of Avila rests within this church in a beautiful chapel to the left of the main sanctuary. It was gifted to this church in 1617. (This chapel is not visible from the nave of the church and it is rarely open to the public. However, if one kindly asks the sacristan access may be granted. If the sacristan is not present he or she can be called at the neighboring convent door.)

Thomas, apostle (July 3rd)

St Thomas (Relics: Rome, Italy; Ortona, Italy; Mylapore, India)

Santa Croce in Gerusalemme (Holy Cross In Jerusalem)
Piazza di Santa Croce in Gerusalemme 12
✝This church is east of the *Basilica of St John Lateran*.
✝A bone from the index finger of St Thomas the Apostle is located here. It is said that this is the same finger that he inserted into the side of the Risen Christ.
✝Also found here are relics of the True Cross brought to Rome by St Helena in 325. These relics include: the Titulus Crucis (This is the sign that hung over the head of Christ and that declared him to be the King of the Jews), a Crucifixion nail, a fragment of the True Cross, two thorns from the Crown of Thorns, the greater part of the sponge used to give Christ vinegar, and a piece of the cross from the good thief (St Dismas).
✝This chapel can be accessed by the staircase on the left side of the sanctuary.

First Class Relics In Italy

(For The Saints Found On The Roman Catholic Liturgical Calendar)

** ** ** ** ** ** ** **

Assisi, Italy

First Class Relics In Italy

(For The Saints On The Roman Catholic Liturgical Calendar)

Northern Italy
Near Venice
Athanasius, bishop and doctor
Catherine of Siena, virgin and doctor
Francis de Sales, bishop and doctor
Lucy, virgin and martyr
Mark, evangelist
Nicholas, bishop
Near Padua
Anthony of Padua, priest and doctor
Josephine Bakhita, virgin
Luke, evangelist
Near Milan
Aloysius Gonzaga, religious
Ambrose, bishop and doctor
Angela Merici, virgin
Anthony Zaccaria, priest
Augustine, bishop and doctor
Charles Borromeo, bishop
Columban, abbot
Eusebius of Vercelli, bishop
Frances Xavier Cabrini, virgin
Gianna Beretta Molla*
Jerome Emiliani, priest
John Bosco, priest
Pier Giorgio Frassati (Blessed)*
Near Bologna
Anne, mother of The Virgin Mary
Apollinaris, martyr
Dominic, priest
Peter Chrysologus, bishop and doctor
Peter Damian, bishop and doctor

Central Italy
Near Rome
Benedict, abbot
Bonaventure, bishop and doctor
Justin, martyr
Maria Goretti, virgin and martyr
Scholastica, virgin
Thomas Aquinas, priest and doctor

Central Italy
Near Florence
Andrew, apostle
Bernardine of Siena, priest
Catherine of Siena, virgin and doctor
Clare, virgin
Elizabeth Ann Seton, religious
Francis of Assisi
Gemma Galgani*
John Chrysostom, bishop and doctor
John the Baptist, martyr
Mary Magdalene de Pazzi, virgin
Philip, apostle
Rita of Cascia, religious
Romuald, abbot

Southern Italy
Near Naples
Alphonsus Liguori, bishop and doctor
Andrew, apostle
Bartholomew, apostle
Cajetan, priest
Gregory VII, pope
Januarius, bishop and martyr
Matthew, apostle and evangelist
Paulinus of Nola, bishop
Philomena, martyr*
Calabria & Sicily
Agatha, virgin and martyr
Bartholomew, apostle
Blaise, bishop and martyr
Bruno, priest
Francis of Paola, hermit
Louis
Paulinus of Nola, bishop
Adriatic Coast of Italy
Nicholas, bishop
Pio of Pietrelcina, priest
Thomas, apostle
Timothy, bishop

Note: The Saints marked with an (*) are not on the
Roman Catholic Liturgical Calendar.

Northern Italy
Near Venice

Athanasius, bishop and doctor (May 2nd)

St Athanasius (d. 373, Alexandria, Egypt) (Relics: Venice, Italy; Cairo, Egypt)

San Zaccaria (Saint Zacharias)
Campo San Zaccaria
30122 Venice, Italy
✝The remains of St Athanasius and St Zacharias, the father of St John the Baptist, are enshrined on the right side of the nave.
✝Saint Athanasius was a passionate defender of orthodoxy during the Arian crisis in the 4th century. As a result, he suffered exile on numerous occasions. Nevertheless, by the end of his life he was able to return to

Alexandria and died in peace surrounded by his clergy at the age of seventy-seven. It is unclear how his relics arrived in Venice.

Catherine of Siena, virgin and doctor (April 29th)

St Catherine of Siena (d. 1380, Rome, Italy) (Relics: Rome, Italy; Siena, Italy; Venice, Italy)

Santi Giovanni e Paolo (Saints John and Paul)
Castello 6363
30122 Venice, Italy
✝A relic of the foot of St Catherine of Siena rests near the *Chapel of St Dominic* on the right side of nave.

Francis de Sales, bishop and doctor (January 24th)

St Francis de Sales (d. 1622, Lyon, France) (Relics: Treviso, Italy; Annecy, France)

Monastero della Visitazione
(Monastery of the Visitation)
Via G. B. Mandruzzato 22
31100 Treviso, Italy
✝During the French Revolution the Visitation nuns transferred the heart of St Francis de Sales from Lyon, France to Treviso, Italy. Today this relic remains in Treviso and rests within the church at this monastery. The relic is located on the right side of the nave. If the relic is not visible kindly ask a nun to raise the protective screen.

Lucy, virgin and martyr (December 13th)

St Lucy (d. 304, Syracuse, Sicily) (Relics: Syracuse, Sicily; Venice, Italy)

Several different traditions account for the translation of St Lucy's remains. The first claims that the Duke of Spoleto, Faroald II, transferred her remains to a small city in central Italy. From here they were taken to Metz, France by Otto I in 972 AD. This tradition then seems to end here as the whereabouts of these relics are unknown today. A separate tradition claims that the Byzantine General, Giorgio Maniace, transferred the relics in 1038 AD from Syracuse to Constantinople. With the fall of Constantinople in 1204 these relics were then transferred to Venice, Italy. They remained here throughout the following centuries occasionally being transferred to different churches within the city. In 1860 they were brought to their present location within the parish church of *San Geremia*. Since this final transfer, however, her remains have been desecrated on two separate occasions. The most recent occurred in November of 1981 when two individuals stole the body of St Lucy from this church. Gratefully one month later her body was returned to this church on her feast day.

San Geremia (Saint Jeremiah)
Sestiere Cannaregio 290
30131 Venice, Italy
✝The body of St Lucy is enshrined in this church on the side opposite the church entrance. Her remains rest within a beautiful glass-sided urn set within a golden casket.

Mark, evangelist (April 25ᵗʰ)

St Mark (d. Alexandria, Egypt) (Relics: Venice, Italy; Cairo, Egypt; Reichenau, Germany)

Basilica di San Marco
(Saint Mark's Basilica)
Piazza San Marco
30124 Venice, Italy
✝In 828 two Venetian merchants stole the relics of St Mark from Alexandria and brought them

to Venice. A popular legend holds that the relics were hid in a barrel of pork so that they would not be discovered. These relics are now located beneath the main altar of this church. The Pala d'Oro is located just behind this altar on the back side of the retable.

Nicholas, bishop (December 6th)

St Nicholas (d. 350, Myra, Turkey) (Relics: Bari, Italy; Venice, Italy)

In 1993 a small grave was found on Gemiler Island east of Rhodes. Historians believe that the body of St Nicholas was originally buried in this grave and then subsequently transferred to Myra. From Myra the

bones of St Nicholas were stolen by Italian merchants in 1087 and taken to the two Italian cities of Bari and Venice. The merchants from Bari raided the tomb first and in their haste they took only the large bone fragments. The Venetian merchants came later and took the remaining smaller bone fragments. A scientific study in 1992 confirmed that both collections are from the same skeleton.

San Nicolo al Lido (Saint Nicholas at the Lido)
Riviera San Nicolo
30126 Venice, Italy
✝Small bone fragments of St Nicholas rest within this church. They are placed within a beautiful funerary monument located in the main sanctuary. Three statues placed above this monument depict St Nicholas and two other saints whose relics are also preserved here.

Northern Italy
Near Padua

Anthony of Padua, priest and doctor (June 13th)

St Anthony of Padua (d. 1231, Padua, Italy) (Relics: Padua, Italy)

Basilica di Sant'Antonio da Padova
(Basilica of Saint Anthony of Padua)
Piazza del Santo 11
35123 Padova, Italy

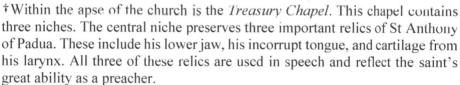

✝The tomb of St Anthony of Padua rests within a chapel on the left side of the nave. His tomb was opened in 1981 and contains the bones of the saint.
✝Within the apse of the church is the *Treasury Chapel*. This chapel contains three niches. The central niche preserves three important relics of St Anthony of Padua. These include his lower jaw, his incorrupt tongue, and cartilage from his larynx. All three of these relics are used in speech and reflect the saint's great ability as a preacher.

Josephine Bakhita, virgin (February 8th)

St Josephine Bakhita (d. 1947, Schio, Italy) (Relics: Schio, Italy)

Chiesa della Sacra Famiglia – Suore Canossiane
(Church of the Holy Family – Canossian Sisters)
Via Fusinato 51
36015 Schio, Italy

✝St Josephine Bakhita began her life as a slave in Sudan. After gaining her freedom she became a nun in Italy and spent the last 45 years of her life in this Canossian convent. Her body now rests under the main altar of this church.

Luke, evangelist (October 18th)

St Luke (Relics: Rome,
Italy;   Padua,   Italy;
Prague, Czech Republic;
Thebes, Greece)

St Luke is believed to
have died in Thebes,
Greece during the latter
part of the first century.
Records then indicate
the transfer of his rem-
ains to Constantinople in
the fourth century. From

here one theory suggests that his remains were transferred to Padua during the
Iconoclastic persecutions in the 8th century. Documented proof of their
presence in Padua surfaces by the year 1177 when a tomb is unearthed next to
Santa Giustina bearing the symbols of St Luke. Papal recognition of these
relics followed soon after.

Abbazia Santa Giustina (Abbey of Saint Justina)
Via Giuseppe Ferrari 2A
35123 Padova, Italy
✝The body of St Luke rests within the left transept of this church. A recent
study upon these relics was conducted at the request of Archbishop Antonio
Mattiazzo of Padua in 1998. This study determined that these relics are of an
individual that would fit the description of St Luke.
✝A decorated tomb within the right transept of this church is dedicated to St
Matthias. Apart from the beautiful inscription upon the tomb which in Latin
reads "Sors cecidit super Mathiam" the church provides no signage to support
the presence of the apostle's relics within the tomb. This is somewhat striking
since directly across from his tomb the church explains in great detail the relics
of St Luke. Some, nevertheless have argued that these relics of St Matthias
were brought to Padua in the 8th century at about the same time as the arrival
of St Luke's relics. This tradition, however, conflicts with the even older
tradition of St Helena who in the 4th century is said to have acquired the relics
of St Matthias and distributed them to both Rome, Italy and Trier, Germany.

Northern Italy
Near Milan

Aloysius Gonzaga, religious (June 21ˢᵗ)

St Aloysius Gonzaga (d. 1591, Rome, Italy) (Relics: Rome, Italy; Castiglione delle Stiviere, Italy)

Il Santuario di San Luigi Gonzaga
(The Sanctuary of Saint Aloysius Gonzaga)
Via Cesare Battisti 1
46043 Castiglione delle Stiviere, Italy
✝St Aloysius Gonzaga was raised in this city at his family's castle. Despite this lofty upbringing he decided to renounce his worldly inheritance in favor of a life as a Jesuit. During his formation in Rome he was never lacking in charity and often spent many hours caring for the sick. On one such occasion he himself contracted the plague. Shortly thereafter at the tender age of twenty-three he passed away. His skull was eventually given to one of his brothers and returned to his family's castle. Today this relic rests above the main altar of the church located here.

Ambrose, bishop and doctor (December 7ᵗʰ)

St Ambrose (d. 397, Milan, Italy) (Relics: Milan, Italy)

Basilica di Sant'Ambrogio (Basilica of Saint Ambrose)
Piazza Sant'Ambrogio 15
20123 Milan, Italy
✝St Ambrose was the bishop of this city for over 20 years. It was during this time that St Augustine (d. 430) heard St Ambrose's powerful preaching and became attracted to the Christian faith. Today the body of St Ambrose, dressed in white pontifical vestments, rests within an urn in the crypt of this church. Lying beside his remains are the bodies of two additional saints, the martyrs Gervasius and Protasius.

Angela Merici, virgin (January 27th)

St Angela Merici (d. 1540, Brescia, Italy) (Relics: Brescia, Italy)

Chiesa di Sant'Angela Merici (Church of Saint Angela Merici)
Via Francesco Crispi 23
25121 Brescia, Italy
✝The remains of St Angela Merici rest within this church in a chapel on the right side of the nave. The original church that housed her relics was destroyed during World War II on March 2, 1945. The present sanctuary was built over this destroyed church.

Anthony Zaccaria, priest (July 5th)

St Anthony Zaccaria (d. 1539, Cremona, Italy) (Relics: Milan, Italy)

San Barnaba (Saint Barnabas)
Via della Commenda 5
20122 Milan, Italy
✝In this city St Anthony Zaccaria founded the *Congregation of the Regular Clerks of St Paul* commonly referred to as the *Barnabites*.
✝St Anthony Zaccaria's short life was marked by great compassion for the poor and an equally strong desire to share the Word of God. Just prior to his canonization in 1897 his remains were placed within the crypt of this church. Today some of these remains still rest within this church. They are placed within the statue of his likeness that rests below the main altar of this church. A majority of his relics, however, have been distributed to other Barnabite communities throughout the world.

Augustine, bishop and doctor (August 28th)

St Augustine (d. 430, Annaba, Algeria) (Relics: Pavia, Italy; Annaba, Algeria)

Upon his death St Augustine was buried in the ancient city of Hippo in Northern Africa. A few decades later, due to the growing persecution of Christians in that area, his remains were transferred to Sardinia. In 720 AD Sardinia itself became unsafe; therefore, his remains were again moved. This time they were brought to Pavia, Italy.

San Pietro in Ciel D'Oro (Saint Peter in the Heavens of Gold)
Piazza San Pietro in Ciel D'Oro
27100 Pavia, Italy
✝The remains of St Augustine rest within a glass-sided urn located within the large funerary monument in the main sanctuary of this church.
✝Boethius is also buried in this church. His tomb rests within the crypt and is labeled S. Severini Boetii.

Benedict, abbot (July 11th)

St Benedict (b. 480, Norcia, Italy) (d. 547, Monte Cassino, Italy) (Relics. Monte Cassino, Italy; Saint-Benoît-sur-Loire, France; Brescia, Italy)

Duomo Nuovo (The New Cathedral)
Piazza Paolo VI
25121 Brescia, Italy
✝An arm bone of St Benedict rests within this church. It is placed in front of the beautiful funerary monument dedicated to St Apollonio on the right side of the nave. Around the year 759 this relic was given to a Benedictine community in Leno, located just south of Brescia. During the 15th century it was transferred to Brescia.
✝Recently this bone has been rigorously studied in an attempt to authenticate the relics in either Monte Cassino or Saint-Benoît-sur-Loire. Documentation shows that this bone came from Montecassino in 759. This late date provides evidence that at least some relics of the saint were still preserved in Montecassino following the alleged theft in the 7th century. On the other hand, recent studies seem to indicate that the physical characteristics of this bone from Brescia do not match the Montecassino source.

Charles Borromeo, bishop (November 4th)

St Charles Borromeo (d.
1584, Milan, Italy)
(Relics: Rome, Italy;
Milan, Italy)

Duomo di Milano
(Cathedral of Milan)
Piazza del Duomo 18
20122 Milan, Italy
†The remains of St
Charles Borromeo rest
within the crypt of this
church. Access to this
crypt is located on the right side of the main sanctuary. St Charles was a greatly
beloved bishop of this city during the late 16th century.
†Located below this church is an ancient baptistery. It was here that St
Ambrose baptized St Augustine in 387 AD.

Columban, abbot (November 23rd)

St Columban (d. 615, Bobbio, Italy) (Relics: Bobbio, Italy)

Abbazia di Bobbio (Bobbio Abbey)
Piazza Santa Fara
29022 Bobbio, Italy
†As a young man St Columban's apostolic zeal carried him away from his
native Ireland first to England and then to France where he attracted many
followers to his apostolic mission. Eventually he moved to Italy and was given
a tract of land near Bobbio. It was here that he spent the last years of his life.
His remains now rest within a sarcophagus in the crypt of this church.

Eusebius of Vercelli, bishop (August 2ⁿᵈ)

St Eusebius of Vercelli (d. 371, Vercelli, Italy) (Relics: Vercelli, Italy)

Cattedrale di Vercelli (Cathedral of Vercelli)
Piazza S. Eusebio
13100 Vercelli, Italy
✝This church is dedicated to St Eusebius of Vercelli. During his life he strenuously opposed the heresy of Arianism. In 355 AD at a synod in Milan his refusal to accept Arianism led to his exile. During this time he suffered greatly especially at the hands of an Arian bishop in Syria. Some years later he was granted his freedom and eventually returned to Vercelli.
✝An altar on the left side of the nave contains an urn with the remains of St Eusebius.

Frances Xavier Cabrini, virgin (November 13ᵗʰ)*

St Frances Xavier Cabrini (d. 1917, Chicago, Illinois, USA) (Relics: New York City, New York, USA; Chicago, Illinois, USA; Rome, Italy; Codogno, Italy; Sant'Angelo Lodigiano, Italy)

Centro di Spiritualità Santa Francesca Cabrini (Center of Spirituality)
Via Giosuè Carducci 50
26845 Codogno, Italy
✝Nine years before arriving in America St Frances Xavier Cabrini founded the *Institute of Missionaries of the Sacred Heart of Jesus* in this city. Today a small museum located at this center wonderfully preserves this event. Also located here is the relic of St Frances' heart. It rests within the convent chapel just to the right of the main sanctuary. It is best to call ahead prior to visiting to reserve a tour.

Basilica di Sant'Antonio Abate e Santa Francesca Cabrini
(Basilica of St Anthony the Abbot and St Frances Cabrini)
Via Umberto I
Sant'Angelo Lodigiano, Italy
✝Construction of this beautiful church began in 1928 and was completed ten years later. A bone from St Frances Xavier Cabrini rests within a marble altar in the chapel dedicated in her name.
✝St Frances Xavier Cabrini was also born in this city. Her childhood home is reconstructed into a museum and can be visited.

Gianna Beretta Molla

St Gianna Beretta Molla (d. 1962) (Relics: Mesero, Italy)

Santuario Santa Gianna Beretta Molla
(Sanctuary of Saint Gianna Beretta Molla)
Piazza Europa 2
20010 Mesero, Italy
✝This church honors the memory of St Gianna Beretta Molla. A chapel on the right side of the nave preserves some artifacts from her life.
✝Located just a few blocks north of this shrine, just off Via Kennedy, is the tomb of St Gianna Beretta Molla. She is buried next to her husband in a small edifice within the parish cemetery.

Basilica di San Martino (Basilica of Saint Martin)
Via Roma 39
20013 Magenta, Italy
✝St Gianna Beretta Molla was born in this city and baptized in this church. It was also here that she married her husband, Pietro Molla. A wonderful exhibit in the left transept displays pictures from her wedding day.

Jerome Emiliani, priest (February 8th)

St Jerome Emiliani (d.
1537, Somasca di
Vercurago, Italy)
(Relics: Somasca di
Vercurago, Italy)

**Santuario di San
Girolamo Emiliani**
(Sanctuary of Saint
Jerome Emiliani)
Via alla Basilica 1
23808 Vercurago, Italy

✝This church honors the
memory of St Jerome Emiliani. It was here in this city that he founded the
Somascan Fathers with the primary mission of caring for orphans. During his
feast on February 8th the Somascan Fathers present to the faithful an urn
containing his skull. His bones rest behind a grate placed upon a wall within
the chapel dedicated to him on the right side of the nave.

✝The spot where St Jerome Emiliani died is preserved within a small chapel
located just a short walk from the church. Also of note is the small sanctuary
called the *Valletta* located along a path that rises above this town. Further along
this same path is an abandoned fortress called the *Rocca dell'Innominato*
which provides an amazing view of both the Southern Alps and of Italy's
northern lakes.

John Bosco, priest (January 31st)

St John Bosco (d. 1888, Turin, Italy) (Relics: Turin, Italy)

Basilica di Maria Ausiliatrice (Basilica of Mary Our Helper)
Piazza Maria Ausiliatrice 27
10512 Torino, Italy

✝St John Bosco founded the Salesian community at this location and later in
1868 completed this magnificent basilica. Relics of St John Bosco now rest
within the chapel dedicated to him on the right side of the nave. Some of his
relics are also periodically put on tour throughout the world. Also within this
church are the remains of St Dominic Savio, a very saintly youth who studied
under St John Bosco.

Pier Giorgio Frassati

Blessed Pier Giorgio
Frassati (d. 1925, Turin,
Italy) (Relics: Turin,
Italy)

Duomo di Torino
(Turin Cathedral)
Via XX Settembre 87
10122 Turin, Italy
†Blessed Pier Giorgio
Frassati is buried in the
third chapel on the left
side of the nave.

†Also kept in this church is the Holy Shroud of Turin. Unfortunately, it is not
often presented for public veneration. The last opportunity occurred during the
spring of 2015.

Northern Italy
Near Bologna

Anne, mother of The Blessed Virgin Mary (July 26th)

(Relics: Apt, France; Bologna, Italy; Sainte-Anne d'Auray, France; Sainte-Anne de Beaupré, Quebec, Canada; Vienna, Austria)

Cattedrale di San Pietro
(Cathedral of Saint Peter)
Via Indipendenza 7
40126 Bologna, Italy
✝The head of St Anne is said to rest within a reliquary in the second chapel on the right side of the nave.
✝In 1435 the King of England, Henry VI, gave this relic to the city of Bologna after their bishop, Blessed Nicolò Albergati, smoothed relations between England and France during the 100 Years' War.

Apollinaris, bishop and martyr (July 20th)

St Apollinaris (d. 1st
century, Ravenna,
Italy) (Relics:
Ravenna, Italy;
Remagen, Germany;
Düsseldorf, Germany)

**Basilica di
Sant'Apollinare in
Classe**
(Basilica of Saint
Apollinaris in Classe)
Via Romea Sud 224
48124, Classe Ravenna, Italy

✝The bones of St Apollinaris rest within the main altar of this church.

✝A debate arose in Ravenna during the 12th century whether the true relics of
St Apollinaris rested within the *Basilica di Sant'Apollinare Nuovo* or within
the *Basilica di Sant'Apollinare in Classe*. After examining the evidence Pope
Alexander III determined that the authentic relics rested within the *Basilica di
Sant'Apollinare in Classe*. An empty tomb within this church dated from 1173
AD preserves the memory of this declaration. This empty tomb is located
below the small marble altar placed in the center of the nave. The bones of St
Apollinaris were transferred to the main altar within the sanctuary in the 18th
century.

Dominic, priest (August 8th)

St Dominic (d. 1221, Bologna,
Italy) (Relics: Bologna, Italy)

Basilica di San Domenico
(Basilica of Saint Dominic)
Piazza San Domenico
40124 Bologna, Italy
✝The remains of St Dominic rest
within this church in an exquisite
tomb called the *Arca di San
Domenico*. This tomb is placed in
a large side chapel on the right side
of the nave. The relic of St
Dominic's skull is enshrined
within a reliquary on the backside
of this tomb.

Peter Chrysologus, bishop and doctor (July 30th)

St Peter Chrysologus (d. 450, Imola, Italy) (Relics: Imola, Italy)

Cattedrale di San Cassiano (Cathedral of Saint Cassian)
Piazza Duomo 1
40026 Imola, Italy
✝St Peter Chrysologus was born in this city in 406 AD. He eventually became
the Bishop of Ravenna and was known for his outstanding homilies. One
hundred seventy-six of these homilies survive to this day.
✝The remains of St Peter Chrysologus rest within an altar in the crypt of this
church. Kindly ask the sacristan for access. The relics of St Peter Chrysologus
are within the altar to the left. The more prominent central altar preserves a
few bone fragments from the martyr St Cassian.

Peter Damian, bishop and doctor (February 21ˢᵗ)

St Peter Damian (d. 1072, Faenza, Italy) (Relics: Faenza, Italy)

Duomo di Faenza
(Faenza Cathedral)
Piazza XI Febbraio
48018 Faenza, Italy

✝St Peter Damian was born in the nearby town of Ravenna yet always retained a strong connection to Faenza. It was here that he studied early in life and later where he founded a hermitage and a monastery. He was known in life as a reformer, a scholar, and a diplomat. He died in Faenza and his remains were interred in a monastery within this city. In 1826 they were transferred to the cathedral where they rest today. They can be found solemnly displayed within an urn in the sixth chapel on the left side of the nave.

Central Italy
Near Florence

Andrew, apostle (November 30th), John Chrysostom, bishop and doctor (September 13th), John the Baptist, martyr (June 24th, August 29th), and Philip, apostle (May 3rd)

St Andrew (Relics: Amalfi, Italy; Florence, Italy; Patras, Greece; Edinburgh, Scotland; Cologne, Germany; Kiev, Ukraine)

St John Chrysostom (d. 407, NE Turkey) (Relics: Rome, Italy; Florence, Italy; Istanbul, Turkey; Moscow, Russia; Mount Athos, Greece)

St John the Baptist (Relics: Rome, Italy; Florence, Italy; Siena, Italy; Amiens, France; Munich, Germany; Damascus, Syria)

St Philip (Relics: Rome, Italy; Florence, Italy)

Duomo di Firenze
(Florence Cathedral)

✝Relics of the following four saints are said to be within the sacristy of this church.

✝The skull of St John Chrysostom (Acquired in 1360), an arm of St Andrew the Apostle (Acquired in the 14th century), an arm of St Philip the Apostle (Acquired in 1205), and a finger of St John the Baptist (Acquired in 1419).

✝It is said that this is the same finger that St John the Baptist used to point at Jesus when he proclaimed, "Behold the Lamb of God."

Cattedrale di Santa Maria Assunta
(Cathedral of Our Lady Assumed)
Piazza del Duomo 8
53100 Siena, Italy
✝In May of 1464 Pope Pius II presented to this church the right arm of St John the Baptist. This relic now rests on the left side of the nave behind the *Chapel of St John the Baptist*. Each year this relic is presented for public veneration prior to the saint's feast day on June 24th.

Bernardine of Siena, priest (May 20th)

St Bernardine of Siena (d. 1444, d. L'Aquila, Italy)
(Relics: L'Aquila, Italy)

Basilica di San Bernardino (Basilica of Saint Bernardine)
Via San Bernardino
67100 L'Aquila, Italy
✝On April 6, 2009 an earthquake hit the Italian city of L'Aquila and severely damaged the *Basilica of San Bernardino*. As a result the relics of St Bernardine of Siena were removed from this church. At present they rest within a church dedicated to St Bernardine of Siena at Piazza d'Armi along Via Ugo Piccinini in L'Aquila. However, once the necessary repairs to the basilica are completed the relics will be returned to their original resting place within the basilica.

Gemma Galgani

St Gemma Galgani (d. 1903, Lucca, Italy)
(Relics: Lucca, Italy)

Monastero/Santuario di Santa Gemma
(Monastery/Sanctuary of Saint Gemma)
Via Tiglio 271
55100 Lucca, Toscana, Italy

†The body of St Gemma Galgani is enshrined beneath the main altar of this church. As a young woman she strongly desired to become a nun; however, her poor health prevented her from fulfilling this wish. Nevertheless, God bestowed upon her many incredible graces by uniting her to his passion and cross. At the age of twenty-one she received the stigmata and later she would go on to experience the scourging and the crowning of thorns. She embraced all of these sufferings for the conversion of sinners. At the age of twenty-five she passed away on the afternoon of Holy Saturday after a long fight with tuberculosis.

Mary Magdalene de Pazzi, virgin (May 25th)

St Mary Magdalene de Pazzi (d. 1607, Florence, Italy) (Relics: Florence, Italy)

Monastero di Santa Maria Maddalena dei Pazzi a Careggi
(Monastery of Saint Mary Magdalene de Pazzi at Careggi)
Via di Careggi / Via dei Massoni
50139 Florence, Italy
†The remains of St Mary Magdalene de Pazzi are located in the main sanctuary of the church at this monastery.

Catherine of Siena, virgin and doctor (April 29th)

St Catherine of Siena (d. 1380, Rome, Italy)
(Relics: Rome, Italy; Siena, Italy; Venice, Italy)

Basilica di San Domenico
(Basilica of Saint Dominic)
Piazza San Domenico
53100 Siena, Italy

†The head of St Catherine of Siena rests within a chapel on the right side of the nave.
†Also a finger of the saint is venerated within a reliquary case just to the right of this chapel. This relic has traditionally been used to impart a blessing on the Italian military.

Santuario di Santa Caterina (Sanctuary of Saint Catherine)
Via Costa di Sant'Antonio 6
53100, Siena, Italy
†This church is built over the family home of St Catherine of Siena. She was born and raised at this location.

Clare, virgin (August 11th)

St Clare (d. 1253, Assisi, Italy) (Relics: Assisi, Italy)

Basilica di Santa Chiara
(Basilica of Saint Clare)
Piazza Santa Chiara
06081 Assisi, Italy
✝The remains of St Clare are enshrined within the crypt of this church.
✝Also within the large chapel on the right side of this church is the *San Damiano Crucifix* that spoke to St Francis of Assisi. (This is the chapel where Morning Prayer and Evening Prayer are prayed.)

Elizabeth Ann Seton, religious (January 4th)*

St Elizabeth Ann Seton (d. 1821, Emmitsburg, Maryland, USA) (Relics: Emmitsburg, Maryland, USA)

Livorno, Italy holds a special place for St Elizabeth Ann Seton as it was here that she was introduced to the Catholic Faith after her husband's illness and death.

Parrocchia Santa Elisabetta Anna Seton
(Church of Saint Elizabeth Ann Seton)
Piazza Giovanni Maria Lavagna 15
57125 Livorno, Italy
✝William, the husband of St Elizabeth Ann Seton, is buried under a small gravestone in front of this church.

Francis of Assisi (October 4th)

St Francis (d. 1226, Assisi, Italy) (Relics: Assisi, Italy)

Basilica di San Francesco D'Assisi
(Basilica of Saint Francis of Assisi)
Piazza San Francesco 2
06081 Assisi, Italy
✝St Francis is buried in the crypt of this church.

Chiesa Nuova (The New Church)
Piazza Chiesa Nuova
06081 Assisi, Italy
✝This church preserves part of the house where St Francis grew up. This includes the small room where he was temporarily imprisoned by his father.

San Damiano (Saint Damian)
Via San Damiano 85
06081 Assisi, Italy
✝It was at this church that the *San Damiano Crucifix* miraculously spoke to St Francis the words, "Go repair my church which you see is falling into ruins."
✝Later this church was given to St Clare. A room inside marks the location where she died in 1253.

Eremo delle Carceri (Hermitage of the Prisons)
Via Eremo delle Carceri
06081 Assisi, Italy
✝St Francis would often come here for extended silent prayer.

Rita of Cascia, religious (May 22nd)

St Rita of Cascia (d. 1457, Cascia, Italy) (Relics: Cascia, Italy)

Santuario di Santa Rita da Cascia (Sanctuary of Saint Rita of Cascia)
Viale Santa Rita 13
06043 Cascia, Italy
✝The body of St Rita of Cascia is enshrined on the left side of the nave of this church. She was a wife and mother who later in life upon her husband's death joined an Augustinian convent. In marriage she suffered greatly from her abusive husband. Thus today she is the patroness for all who suffer from abusive relationships.

Romuald, abbot (June 19th)

St Romuald (d. 1027, Val di Castro, Italy) (Relics: Fabriano, Italy)

Chiesa di Santi Biagio e Romualdo (Church of Saints Blaise and Romuald)
Piazza Daniele Manin 12
60044 Fabriano, Italy
✝St Romuald was originally buried near the monastic cell in which he died in Val di Castro. In 1466 his body was found incorrupt; therefore, in 1481 his remains were brought to the nearby city of Fabriano. Today his relics rest within the crypt of this church.

The Seven Holy Founders of the Servite Order (February 17th)

In 1233 seven young
Florentine men gathered
together to begin the
Servite community. They
first gathered in a house in
the outskirts of Florence
near the convent of the
Friars Minor at La
Camarzia. Later they
moved eleven miles north
of Florence to Monte
Senario.

Rita of Cascia, religious (May 22nd)

St Rita of Cascia (d. 1457, Cascia, Italy) (Relics: Cascia, Italy)

Santuario di Santa Rita da Cascia (Sanctuary of Saint Rita of Cascia)
Viale Santa Rita 13
06043 Cascia, Italy

✝The body of St Rita of Cascia is enshrined on the left side of the nave of this church. She was a wife and mother who later in life upon her husband's death joined an Augustinian convent. In marriage she suffered greatly from her abusive husband. Thus today she is the patroness for all who suffer from abusive relationships.

Romuald, abbot (June 19th)

St Romuald (d. 1027, Val di Castro, Italy) (Relics: Fabriano, Italy)

Chiesa di Santi Biagio e Romualdo
(Church of Saints Blaise and Romuald)
Piazza Daniele Manin 12
60044 Fabriano, Italy

✝St Romuald was originally buried near the monastic cell in which he died in Val di Castro. In 1466 his body was found incorrupt; therefore, in 1481 his remains were brought to the nearby city of Fabriano. Today his relics rest within the crypt of this church.

The Seven Holy Founders of the Servite Order (February 17th)

In 1233 seven young
Florentine men gathered
together to begin the
Servite community. They
first gathered in a house in
the outskirts of Florence
near the convent of the
Friars Minor at La
Camarzia. Later they
moved eleven miles north
of Florence to Monte
Senario.

Central Italy
Near Rome

Benedict, abbot (July 11*th*) and Scholastica, virgin (February 10*th*)

St Benedict (b. 480, Norcia, Italy) (d. 547, Monte Cassino, Italy) (Relics: Monte Cassino, Italy; Saint-Benoît-sur-Loire, France; Brescia, Italy)

St Scholastica (b. 480, Norcia, Italy) (d. 547, Monte Cassino, Italy) (Relics: Monte Cassino, Italy; Juvigny-sur-Loison, France)

It is uncertain if the relics of Saint Benedict and Saint Scholastica are still at Monte Cassino or if they were moved in the seventh century to Saint-Benoît-sur-Loire, France.

Abbazia di Montecassino (Abbey of Monte Cassino)
Via Montecassino
03043 Cassino, Italy
†The remains of St Benedict and St Scholastica are said to rest under the main altar of the church at this monastery. Following the tragic destruction of this church during World War II the relics were exhumed and analyzed. This study, conducted in 1950, did not produce conclusive evidence to either confirm or deny the authenticity of these relics.

Monastero di San Benedetto (Saint Benedict's Monastery)
Via Reguardati 22
06046 Norcia, Italy
†This monastery is built over the house where St Benedict and St Scholastica were born.

Monastero di San Benedetto (Saint Benedict's Monastery)
Piazzale San Benedetto
00028 Subiaco, Roma, Italia
†Subiaco is where St Benedict lived as a hermit. It is also from this city that he began establishing monasteries. In total he spent 25 years of his life in this city.

Bonaventure, bishop and doctor (July 15th)

St Bonaventure (d. 1274, Lyon, France) (Relics: Bagnoregio, Italy)

Cattedrale San Bonaventura (Cathedral of Saint Bonaventure)
Piazza Cavour
01022 Bagnoregio, Italy
✝The only remaining relic of St Bonaventure, his right arm, rests within a chapel on the right side of the nave of this church. This relic was brought to Bagnoregio in 1491 as a gift since the saint's birth home is in the nearby hill city of Civita di Bagnoregio. This transfer was providential because a little less than a century later, in 1562, his tomb in Lyon, France was plundered by French Huguenots and his remains were burned in the public square. During this event his incorrupt head was preserved; however, several centuries later during the French Revolution it disappeared and has remained missing ever since.

Justin, martyr (June 1st)

St Justin (d. 165, Rome, Italy) (Relics: Rome, Italy; Sacrofano, Italy)

Santi Giovanni Battista e Biagio
(Saint John the Baptist and Saint Blaise)
Piazza San Biagio 10 / Via di Mezzo
00060 Sacrofano, Italy
✝This church is located about 10 miles north of Rome.
✝Some bones of St Justin the Martyr are said to rest in an urn under the main altar.
✝Note: The parish *San Giovanni Battista e Biagio* has two churches in the center of Sacrofano. The larger church with a piazza claims to have some small relics of St Blaise. The smaller church, which is located in the historic part of the city and is simply called *Chiesa di San Giovanni Battista*, has the relics of St Justin the Martyr.

Catherine of Siena, virgin and doctor (April 29th)

St Catherine of Siena (d.
1380, Rome, Italy)
(Relics: Rome, Italy;
Siena, Italy; Venice, Italy)

**Basilica di San
Domenico**
(Basilica of Saint
Dominic)
Piazza San Domenico
53100 Siena, Italy
✝The head of St Catherine
of Siena rests within a

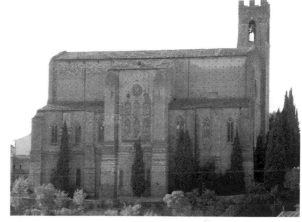

chapel on the right side of the nave.
✝Also a finger of the saint is venerated within a reliquary case just to the right
of this chapel. This relic has traditionally been used to impart a blessing on the
Italian military.

Santuario di Santa Caterina (Sanctuary of Saint Catherine)
Via Costa di Sant'Antonio 6
53100, Siena, Italy
✝This church is built over the family home of St Catherine of Siena. She was
born and raised at this location.

Clare, virgin (August 11th)

St Clare (d. 1253, Assisi, Italy) (Relics: Assisi, Italy)

Basilica di Santa Chiara
(Basilica of Saint Clare)
Piazza Santa Chiara
06081 Assisi, Italy
✝The remains of St Clare are enshrined within the crypt of this church.
✝Also within the large chapel on the right side of this church is the *San Damiano Crucifix* that spoke to St Francis of Assisi. (This is the chapel where Morning Prayer and Evening Prayer are prayed.)

Elizabeth Ann Seton, religious (January 4th)*

St Elizabeth Ann Seton (d. 1821, Emmitsburg, Maryland, USA) (Relics: Emmitsburg, Maryland, USA)

Livorno, Italy holds a special place for St Elizabeth Ann Seton as it was here that she was introduced to the Catholic Faith after her husband's illness and death.

Parrocchia Santa Elisabetta Anna Seton
(Church of Saint Elizabeth Ann Seton)
Piazza Giovanni Maria Lavagna 15
57125 Livorno, Italy
✝William, the husband of St Elizabeth Ann Seton, is buried under a small gravestone in front of this church.

Francis of Assisi (October 4th)

St Francis (d. 1226, Assisi, Italy)
(Relics: Assisi, Italy)

Basilica di San Francesco D'Assisi
(Basilica of Saint Francis of Assisi)
Piazza San Francesco 2
06081 Assisi, Italy
✝St Francis is buried in the crypt of this church.

Chiesa Nuova (The New Church)
Piazza Chiesa Nuova
06081 Assisi, Italy
✝This church preserves part of the house where St Francis grew up. This includes the small room where he was temporarily imprisoned by his father.

San Damiano (Saint Damian)
Via San Damiano 85
06081 Assisi, Italy
✝It was at this church that the *San Damiano Crucifix* miraculously spoke to St Francis the words, "Go repair my church which you see is falling into ruins."
✝Later this church was given to St Clare. A room inside marks the location where she died in 1253.

Eremo delle Carceri (Hermitage of the Prisons)
Via Eremo delle Carceri
06081 Assisi, Italy
✝St Francis would often come here for extended silent prayer.

Gemma Galgani

St Gemma Galgani (d. 1903, Lucca, Italy)
(Relics: Lucca, Italy)

Monastero/Santuario di Santa Gemma
(Monastery/Sanctuary of Saint Gemma)
Via Tiglio 271
55100 Lucca, Toscana, Italy
✝The body of St Gemma Galgani is
enshrined beneath the main altar of this
church. As a young woman she strongly
desired to become a nun; however, her poor
health prevented her from fulfilling this
wish. Nevertheless, God bestowed upon
her many incredible graces by uniting her
to his passion and cross. At the age of
twenty-one she received the stigmata and

later she would go on to experience the scourging and the crowning of thorns.
She embraced all of these sufferings for the conversion of sinners. At the age
of twenty-five she passed away on the afternoon of Holy Saturday after a long
fight with tuberculosis.

Mary Magdalene de Pazzi, virgin (May 25ᵗʰ)

St Mary Magdalene de Pazzi (d. 1607, Florence, Italy) (Relics: Florence, Italy)

Monastero di Santa Maria Maddalena dei Pazzi a Careggi
(Monastery of Saint Mary Magdalene de Pazzi at Careggi)
Via di Careggi / Via dei Massoni
50139 Florence, Italy
✝The remains of St Mary Magdalene de Pazzi are located in the main sanctuary
of the church at this monastery.

Maria Goretti, virgin and martyr (July 6th)

St Maria Goretti (d. 1902, Le Ferriere / Ferriere di Conca, Italy) (Relics: Nettuno, Italy)

Santuario di Nettuno (Sanctuary of Nettuno) Viale Matteotti 00048, Nettuno, Italy
†This church is located next to the sea.
†The remains of St Maria Goretti rest below the main altar in the lower chapel of this church.

Casa del Martírio di Santa Maria Goretti
(House of Saint Maria Goretti's Martyrdom)
†This is where St Maria Goretti was martyred. It is in the small town of Le Ferriere which is 11 kilometers outside of Nettuno.

Thomas Aquinas, priest and doctor (January 28th)

St Thomas Aquinas (b. 1225, Roccasecca, Italy) (d. 1274, Fossanova, Italy)
(Relics: Toulouse, France; Aquino, Italy; Naples, Italy)

Cattedrale di Aquino (Cathedral of Aquino)
Piazza San Tommaso d'Aquino
03031 Aquino, Italy
✝In 1963 the Archbishop of Toulouse, Gabriel Marie Garrone, gave to this church a small rib bone of St Thomas Aquinas. This relic is carried in procession every year on the evening of March 7th.

Parrocchia Santa Annunziata
(Parish of the Holy Annunciation)
Via della Chiesa 6
Roccasecca, Italy
✝This church is just below the castle where St Thomas Aquinas was born. Presently this castle is in a state of ruin. However, a nice boardwalk allows easy access to the area.

Abbazia di Fossanova (Abbey of Fossanova)
Via San Tommaso D'Aquino 1
04015 Priverno, Latina, Italy
✝St Thomas Aquinas was passing through this area on his way to the Council of Lyon. As he approached Fossanova he became deathly ill and was forced to stop. The monks at the *Abbey of Fossanova* took St Thomas in and cared for him until his death. For some years after his death his bones remained at this abbey and rested in the main sanctuary of the church. They were later moved in 1369 to Toulouse, France.

Southern Italy
Near Naples

Alphonsus Liguori, bishop and doctor (August 1st)

St Alphonsus Liguori (d. 1787, Pagani, Italy) (Relics: Pagani, Italy)

Basilica di Sant'Alfonso (Basilica of Saint Alphonsus)
Piazza Sant'Alfonso 1
84016 Pagani, Italy
✝A wooden statue of St Alphonsus Liguori rests under an altar to the left of the main sanctuary. This statue is so life like that at first glance one may think that the entire body of St Alphonsus Liguori is incorrupt. However, this is not the case. Some relics of the saint, nevertheless, are present. They rest on a silver carriage below the wooden statue.

Andrew, apostle (November 30th)

St Andrew (Relics: Amalfi, Italy; Florence, Italy; Patras, Greece; Edinburgh, Scotland; Cologne, Germany; Kiev, Ukraine)

Duomo di Sant'Andrea (Cathedral of Saint Andrew)
Piazza Duomo
84011 Amalfi, Italy
✝Tradition claims that St Andrew was martyred and buried in Patras, Greece. Later most of his relics were relocated to Constantinople. Following the sacking of this city in 1204 AD they were transferred to Amalfi, Italy and placed within this church. Most of these relics remain here today and are located within the crypt below the main altar.

Bartholomew, apostle (August 24th)

St Bartholomew (Relics: Rome, Italy; Benevento, Italy; Lipari, Sicily; Frankfurt, Germany)

According to the *Roman Martyrology* St Bartholomew suffered martyrdom in the Roman province of Armenia. It is recorded that he was first skinned alive and then put to death by decapitation. Five centuries later and half-way across the Mediterranean his relics were found in Lipari, Sicily. Most likely they arrived here through normal means; however, a pious tradition contends that this transfer occurred miraculously. This tradition claims that the sarcophagus of St Bartholomew was thrown into the sea by infidels. It then floated upon the water until it finally and miraculously came to the shores of the tiny island of Lipari. Regardless, how the relics arrived they remained on this island until the middle of the 9th century. At this time they were transferred to Benevento, Italy and then in the latter part of the 10th century they were brought to Rome by the Holy Roman Emperor, Otto III, where they were interred in the church of *San Bartolomeo all'Isola* on Tiber Island. This final transfer, however, is contested by the city of Benevento which continues to claim possession of the true relics of St Bartholomew.

Basilica di San Bartolomeo (Saint Bartholomew's Basilica)
Piazza Federico Torre
Benevento, Italy
✝As noted above the tradition in Benevento holds that the relics of St Bartholomew remain within this church. An exhibit near the front of the church portrays a recent analysis of these relics and provides support for this claim. Also a monument upon the side-wall recalls the 2001 declaration by St John Paul II which reopened the cult of St Bartholomew in this church.
✝The relics of St Bartholomew rest within a porphyry urn below the main altar. An additional bone fragment is placed within a bust of the saint. Twice a year, on August 24th and October 25th, the city celebrates his feast.

Cajetan, priest (August 7ᵗʰ)

St Cajetan (d. 1547,
Naples, Italy) (Relics:
Naples, Italy)

San Paolo Maggiore
(Saint Paul the Greater)
Piazza San Gaetano 76
80138 Naples, Italy

✝The remains of St Caj-
etan rest within a beautiful
tomb in the crypt of this
church. Access to this
crypt is through a door to the right of the double staircase that leads into the
church. St Cajetan was a religious reformer of the early 16ᵗʰ century. He and
several others founded the Theatines in 1524.

Gregory VII, pope (May 25ᵗʰ) and Matthew, apostle and evangelist (September 21ˢᵗ)

St Gregory VII (d. 1085, Salerno, Italy) (Relics: Salerno, Italy)

St Matthew (Relics: Salerno, Italy)

Duomo di Salerno
(Salerno Cathedral)
Via Duomo 1
84121 Salerno, Italy

✝Despite being the legitimate pope, St Gregory VII was forced out of Rome
in 1084 as a result of his ties to the Normans and the political pressures created
by the Holy Roman Emperor, Henry IV, and the antipope, Clement III. A year
later St Gregory VII died in Salerno as an exile. His remains now rest under
an altar in the right transept of this church.

✝The relics of St Matthew were brought to Salerno in 954 AD. A festival
honoring this translation occurs annually on May 6ᵗʰ. His relics are preserved
within the richly decorated crypt of this church.

Januarius, bishop and martyr (September 19th)

St Januarius [Gennaro in Italian] (d. 305)
(Relics: Naples, Italy)

Duomo di Napoli (Naples Cathedral)
Via Duomo 147
80138 Naples, Italy
✝St Januarius is most well known for the
liquefaction of his blood. This miracle occurs
annually on September 19th, December
16th, and the first Saturday in May.
✝The relics of St Januarius can be found in
three different locations within this church.
His blood, which is sealed in a reliquary, is
placed upon the altar in the second chapel on
the right side of the nave. This exquisite chapel also contains fifty-one silver
busts, each depicting a different saint. They were donated to this church by
various guilds and ecclesial institutions in the city. The bones of St Januarius
are found in the confessio below the main sanctuary. These bones, which are
visible, rest within a vase below the altar in this confessio. Finally, fragments
of his skull rest within a bust placed within an upper room of the museum
located next to this church.

*Joseph Moscati***

St Joseph Moscati (d. 1927, Naples, Italy) (Relics: Naples, Italy)

Gesù Nuovo (The New Jesus)
Piazza del Gesù Nuovo
80134 Naples, Italy
*The remains of St Joseph Moscati rest within a tomb placed within the second
chapel on the right side of the nave of this church. In life he was a medical
doctor and researcher who practiced great charity in his profession. In
particular he was known to never charge the poor for his services. A museum
just a short distance from his tomb preserves his memory. Within this museum
are both the bedroom in which he died and his study. Also preserved here are
many of the medical instruments that he used in life.

Paulinus of Nola, bishop (June 22nd)

St Paulinus of Nola (d. 431, Sicily) (Relics: Nola, Italy; Sutera, Sicily)

Cattedrale di Nola (Cathedral of Nola)
Piazza Duomo 1
80035 Nola, Italy
✝Annually on June 22nd crowds of people fill the square in front of this church to celebrate the feast of St Paulinus. A silver bust of the saint is processed into the crowd and eight festive obelisks and an ornamental wooden boat are blessed. The obelisks and boat harken back to a legendary story of the saint. It is said that as Barbarian tribes were invading Italy, St Paulinus offered to be taken captive in exchange for the return of a widow's son. This action of selfless love is said to have so impressed the leader of this invading party that he chose to grant St Paulinus his freedom. St Paulinus then returned to Italy and was warmly welcomed by the people of Nola.
✝Apart from this celebration relics of St Paulinus rest within this church in the fourth chapel on the left side of the nave.

Philomena, martyr

St Philomena (d. 304) (Relics: Mugnano del Cardinale, Italy)

The remains of St Philomena were found in 1802 in the *Catacombs of Priscilla* in Rome. In 1805 they were transferred to the following church in Mugnano del Cardinale, Italy.

Santuario di S. Filomena (Sanctuary of Saint Philomena)
Piazza Umberto 1
83027 Mugnano del Cardinale, Province of Avellino, Italy
✝The remains of St Philomena rest within this church in the second chapel on the left side of the nave. They are placed within a life-sized paper mache reproduction of her likeness that rests above the altar in this chapel.

Thomas Aquinas, priest and doctor (January 28ᵗʰ)

St Thomas Aquinas (b. 1225,
Roccasecca, Italy) (d. 1274,
Fossanova, Italy) (Relics: Toulouse,
France; Aquino, Italy; Naples,
Italy)

San Domenico Maggiore
(Saint Dominic the Greater)
Piazza San Domenico Maggiore 8
80134 Naples, Italy
✝St Thomas Aquinas lived in this
priory from 1272-1274. Preserved
within his cell is the miraculous
crucifix that exclaimed, "You have
written well of me, Thomas." Also
located here is a bone from his left
arm. Access to this cell is only given
by special permission.

Southern Italy
Calabria & Sicily

Agatha, virgin and martyr (February 5th)

St Agatha (d. 251, Catania, Sicily) (Relics: Catania, Sicily)

Chiesa di San Biagio / Sant'Agata alla Fornace
(Church of Saint Blaise / Saint Agatha at the Furnace)
Piazza Stesicoro
95124 Catania, Sicily, Italy
✝This church marks the spot of St Agatha's final suffering. It was here that she was placed into a furnace and martyred.

Duomo di Catania (Catania Cathedral)
Piazza del Duomo
95131 Catania, Sicily, Italy
✝The relics of St Agatha are located within the apse of this church in the *Chapel of St Agatha*. Unfortunately, this chapel is not accessible to the public. However, every year on February 4th and 5th the relics are brought out and the faithful are given the chance to participate in the procession of her relics through the streets of Catania.

Sant'Agata al Carcere (Saint Agatha at the Prison)
Via del Colosseo
95124 Catania, Sicily, Italy
✝This church is just behind the church of *Sant'Agata alla Fornace* (listed previously) and is considered to be the site of St Agatha's imprisonment. Also two lava slabs within this church show the imprints of St Agatha's little feet.

Bartholomew, apostle (August 24th)

St Bartholomew (Relics: Rome, Italy; Benevento, Italy; Lipari, Sicily; Frankfurt, Germany)

Cattedrale di San Bartolomeo (Saint Bartholomew's Cathedral)
Via del Concordato
Lipari, Sicily, Italy
✝A relic of the thumb of St Bartholomew rests within a silver arm reliquary in this church. This relic is exposed for veneration during feast days of the saint.

Blaise, bishop and martyr (February 3rd)

St Blaise (d. 316, Armenia) (Relics: Rome, Italy; Maratea, Italy; Dubrovnik, Croatia)

Basilica di San Biagio (Basilica of Saint Blaise)
Via Castello
Maratea, Italy
✝Relics of St Blaise were brought to this city in 732 AD and now rest within this church. They are located within a white marble urn located below a silver bust of the saint. Also of note is the large 68 foot tall statue of Christ the Redeemer that overlooks the sea just a short distance from this church.

Bruno, priest (October 6th)

St Bruno (d. 1101, Serra San Bruno, Italy) (Relics: Serra San Bruno, Italy)

Certosa di Serra San Bruno (Charterhouse of Serra San Bruno)
Via Santo Stefano 1
89822 Serra San Bruno, Italy
✝The remains of St Bruno rest within the main sanctuary of the church at this monastery. He lived here for ten years following the establishment of this monastery.

Francis of Paola, hermit (April 2nd)

St Francis of Paola (d. 1507, Plessis, France) (Relics: Paola, Italy)

Basilica di San Francesco di Paola
(Basilica of Saint Francis of Paola)
Largo San Francesco di Paola
87027 Paola, Italy

†In 1482 King Louis XI of France requested the presence of St Francis of Paola at his side as he neared death. St Francis was at first reluctant to accept the king's request because he did not want to leave his native Italy. However, upon the urging of Pope Sixtus IV he acquiesced. St Francis of Paola then remained in France for the next 25 years providing counsel to the French kings. He died in 1507 and was buried in Plessis. In 1562 his tomb was forcefully opened, his incorrupt body plundered, and the majority of his relics destroyed by French Huguenots. The few bones that escaped destruction were later taken to Paola, Italy. These bones now rest within this church.

Louis (August 25th)

St Louis (d. 1270, Tunis, Tunisia) (Relics: Monreale, Sicily; Saint-Denis, France)

In 1270 St Louis set out across the Mediterranean to begin the Eighth Crusade. Upon reaching the shores of Tunis his group met a number of setbacks. As they waited for reinforcements to fortify their position many within the group including St Louis caught dysentery and died. As the defeated crusaders returned to Europe they brought the remains of St Louis through Italy and France attracting many crowds of mourners along the way. His remains were then buried in *Saint-Denis Cathedral* in Paris, France. The Sicilian city of Monreale also continues to claim to have some of his relics.

Cattedrale di Monreale (Cathedral of Monreale)
Piazza Guglielmo II 1
90046 Monreale, Palermo, Sicily, Italy
†The innards of St Louis rest within an urn in the left transept of this church. These relics were acquired during the transfer of St Louis' body from Tunis to Paris.

Lucy, virgin and martyr (December 13th)

St Lucy (d. 304, Syracuse, Sicily) (Relics: Syracuse, Sicily; Venice, Italy)

The Sicilian city of Syracuse lost most of its relics of St Lucy through the transfers carried out by Faroald II and Giorgio Maniace during the 8th and the 11th centuries. Therefore, the following relics have been at various times returned to the city.

Duomo di Siracusa (Cathedral of Syracuse)
Piazza Duomo 5
96100 Syracuse, Sicily, Italy
✝In 1988 Syracuse received the left humerus bone of St Lucy from the Patriarch of Venice, Marco Cè. This relic now rests within a silver reliquary placed within the second altar on the right side of the nave of this church. A separate reliquary exposed only on special feasts contains two additional fragments from the left arm of St Lucy.
✝Also said to be preserved at this church are the robe, the veil, and the little shoes of the saint.
✝Finally, each year on December 13th and also on the first Sunday in May a statue of St Lucy is carried with much festivity through the streets of Syracuse. Within the chest of this statue, which was created by Pietro Rizzo in 1599, are three bone fragments from her ribs.

Basilica di Santa Lucia al Sepolcro
(Basilica of Saint Lucy at the Tomb)
Via Luigi Bignami 1
96100 Syracuse, Sicily, Italy
✝This church marks the spot where St Lucy was martyred.
✝Within the octagonal baptistery adjacent to this church is the grave where St Lucy was originally buried. Under the altar is a beautiful marble statue depicting the saint.

Paulinus of Nola, bishop (June 22nd)

St Paulinus of Nola (d. 431, Sicily) (Relics: Nola, Italy; Sutera, Sicily)

Santuario di San Paolino
(Sanctuary of Saint Paulinus)
Via Madonna del Monte
93010 Sutera, Sicily, Italy
✝Relics of St Paulinus of Nola are said to rest within an urn in this church. They are carried in procession annually on the Tuesday after Easter.
✝This shrine claims to have received its relics of St Paulinus of Nola in 1336. It is believed that they came from the remains that had been at *San Bartolomeo all'Isola* in Rome, Italy.

Southern Italy
Adriatic Coast of Italy

Nicholas, bishop (December 6th)

St Nicholas (d. 350, Myra, Turkey) (Relics: Bari, Italy; Venice, Italy)

In 1993 a small grave was found on Gemiler Island east of Rhodes. Historians believe that the body of St Nicholas was originally buried in this grave and then subsequently transferred to Myra. From Myra the bones of St Nicholas were stolen by Italian merchants in 1087 and taken to the two Italian cities of Bari and Venice. The merchants from Bari raided the tomb first and in their haste they took only the large bone fragments. The Venetian merchants came later and took the remaining smaller bone fragments. A scientific study in 1992 confirmed that both collections are from the same skeleton.

Basilica di San Nicolo (Basilica of Saint Nicholas)
Largo Abate Elia
70122 Bari, Italy
†Relics of St Nicholas rest within a small urn located under the altar in the crypt of this church.

Pio of Pietrelcina, priest (September 23rd)

St Pio of Pietrelcina (b. 1887, Pietrelcina, Italy; d. 1968, San Giovanni Rotondo, Italy) (Relics: San Giovanni Rotondo, Italy)

Chiesa San Pio (Church of Saint Padre Pio)
Piazzale Santa Maria Delle Grazie
71013 San Giovanni Rotondo, Italy
†The remains of St Padre Pio rest in the crypt below *Chiesa San Pio*. This is the large modern church located at the far end of the piazza. The entrance to the crypt is on the right side of this church.

†On the other end of the piazza is *Chiesa Santa Maria Delle Grazie.* This is where St Padre Pio celebrated Holy Mass and heard confessions for 52 years of his life. Immediately to the right of this church is a newer church that was built in 1959. Below these churches is a crypt where the remains of St Padre Pio had rested in the past. This location still attracts much veneration; however, his remains now rest below *Chiesa San Pio* as previously noted.

Thomas, apostle (July 3rd)

St Thomas (Relics: Rome, Italy; Ortona, Italy; Mylapore, India)

A tradition holds that in the 3rd century the bones of St Thomas the Apostle were taken from India and brought to Edessa, Turkey. These remains were then transferred to Ortona, Italy in 1258.

Basilica di San Tommaso Apostolo
(Basilica of Saint Thomas the Apostle)
Corso Giacomo Matteotti 35
66026 Ortona, Italy
†The relics of St Thomas the Apostle rest within a golden casket placed within a white marble altar located in the crypt of this church.

Timothy, bishop (January 26th)

St Timothy (Relics: Termoli, Italy)

Cattedrale di Termoli (Termoli Cathedral)
Piazza Duomo 1
86039 Termoli, Italy
†In 1945 the relics of St Timothy were rediscovered in this church beneath a marble tile that read, "Here rests Blessed Timothy disciple of the Apostle Paul." It is believed that they were buried here in 1239 and then over the following centuries forgotten.

First Class Relics Outside Of Italy

Spain & Portugal

** ** ** ** ** ** ** **

First Class Relics In Spain & Portugal

(For The Saints On The Roman Catholic Liturgical Calendar)

Anthony Mary Claret, bishop	John of God, religious
Elizabeth of Portugal	John of the Cross, priest and doctor
Gregory Nazianzen, bishop and doctor	Lawrence of Brindisi, priest and doctor
Isidore the farmer	Raymond of Penyafort, priest
Isidore, bishop and doctor	Teresa of Jesus, virgin and doctor
James, apostle	Vincent, deacon and martyr

Plaza de España – Seville, Spain

Anthony Mary Claret, bishop (October 24th)

St Anthony Mary Claret (d. 1870, Fontfroide, France) (Relics: Vic, Spain)

Casa d'Espiritualitat Claret
(Claretian House of Spirituality)
Rambla Sant Domènec 5
08500 Vic, Barcelona, Spain
†The remains of St Anthony Mary Claret rest within the crypt of the church at this retreat center. In 1849 he established the *Claretian Missionaries* in this city under their original title *The Missionary Sons of The Immaculate Heart of Mary*.

Elizabeth of Portugal (July 5th)*

St Elizabeth of Portugal (d. 1336, Coimbra, Portugal) (Relics: Coimbra, Portugal)

Mosteiro de Santa Clara a Nova
(New Monastery of Saint Clare)
Calçada de Santa Isabel / Alto de St^a Clara
3040-270 Coimbra, Portugal
†St Elizabeth of Portugal was both the Queen of Portugal and a great-niece of St Elizabeth of Hungary. In her kingdom she was known as the peacemaker since her efforts were critical in maintaining the peace between her husband and her son when they were battling against each other.
†The remains of St Elizabeth of Portugal currently rest within a casket above the main altar within the church at this convent. For ten years she was part of a Poor Clare community in this city.

Gregory Nazianzen, bishop and doctor (January 2nd) and Vincent, deacon and martyr* (January 23rd)

St Gregory Nazianzen (d. 389, Cappadocia) (Relics: Rome, Italy; Istanbul, Turkey; Mount Athos, Greece; Lisbon, Portugal)

St Vincent (d. 304, Valencia, Spain) (Relics: Lisbon, Portugal; Castres, France)

Sé Catedral de Lisboa
(Lisbon Cathedral)
Largo da Sé
1100-585 Lisbon, Portugal
†A tradition claims that relics of St Vincent were brought to Lisbon in 1175. It is uncertain, however, if these relics survived the devastating earthquake that hit this city in 1755. Nevertheless, there is within the Treasury of this church a reliquary chest which is said to contain some relics of St Vincent.
†Also placed within this Treasury Museum is a silver arm reliquary that contains the right arm bone of St Gregory Nazianzen.

Isidore* (May 15th)

St Isidore the Farmer (d. 1130, Madrid, Spain) (Relics: Madrid, Spain)

Parroquia de Nuestra Señora del Buen Consejo y San Isidoro
(Parish of Our Lady of Good Counsel and Saint Isidore)
Calle de Toledo 37
28005 Madrid, Spain
†The body of St Isidore is enshrined in the main sanctuary of this church. The remains of his wife, Maria de la Cabeza, also rest within this church. They were both peasant farm laborers who were known for their exceptional piety and humility.

Isidore, bishop and doctor (April 4th)

St Isidore (d. 636, Seville, Spain) (Relics: Leon, Spain; Murcia, Spain)

Basilica de San Isidoro (Basilica of Saint Isidore)
Plaza San Isidoro 4
24003 Leon, Spain
✝In 1063 the relics of St Isidore of Seville were transferred to this church. They now rest within a silver urn in the main sanctuary. During his life much of Roman society collapsed leaving academic institutions in disarray. During this time St Isidore used his great gifts as a scholar to preserve and pass on much of the ancient classical learning. He is considered by many as the most learned man of his age.

Catedral de Murcia (Cathedral of Murcia)
Plaza Cardenal Belluga 1
30001 Murcia, Spain
✝Some bones of St Isidore of Seville rest within a silver urn in the main sanctuary of this church. This urn holds remains from all four of the Cartagena saints: St Isidore of Seville, St Leander, St Fulgentius, and St Florentina.

James, apostle (July 25th)

St James the Greater – The brother of St John the Evangelist (d. 44) (Relics: Santiago de Compostela, Spain; Jerusalem, Israel)

Tradition holds that St James the Greater traveled to Spain soon after the death of Christ. During this time the Blessed Virgin Mary is said to have appeared to him as _Our Lady of the Pillar_. Subsequently he returned to Jerusalem where he was beheaded in 44 AD. According to tradition his relics were then returned to Spain either by angels or by Spanish disciples. The Armenian church of St James in Jerusalem, however, still claims to possess the relic of his head.

Catedral de Santiago de Compostela (Cathedral of St James of Compostela)
Praza do Obradoiro S/N
15705 Santiago de Compostela, La Coruna, Spain
✝For more than 1000 years pilgrims have walked along the famous _Camino de Santiago_ to visit the relics of St James the Greater in this church. In 2014 alone over 200,000 individuals made this pilgrimage. The relics of St James rest below the main sanctuary of this church within a small silver reliquary.

John of God, religious (March 8th)

St John of God (d. 1550, Granada, Spain) (Relics: Granada, Spain)

Basílica de San Juan de Dios
(Basilica of Saint John of God)
Calle San Juan de Dios 23
18001 Granada, Spain
†The remains of St John of God rest within a silver urn within the gilded Baroque altarpiece above the main altar. At the age of forty-two St John of God experienced a profound conversion which inspired him to dedicate himself totally to serving and caring for the hospitalized and the poor.

John of the Cross, priest and doctor (December 14th)

St John of the Cross (d. 1591, Ubeda, Spain) (Relics: Segovia, Spain; Ubeda, Spain)

Oratorio de San Juan de la Cruz /
Museo San Juan de la Cruz
(Oratory and Museum of Saint John of the Cross)
Calle Carmen 13
23400 Ubeda, Spain
†St John of the Cross died in this city. Shortly thereafter, his body was transferred to Segovia, Spain. In 1596 Pope Clement VIII agreed that some of his relics should be returned to Ubeda. These relics are now preserved within the sacristy of this church. Also within this church is the grave where his body originally rested before it was transferred to Segovia.

Monasterio de los Carmelitas Descalzos
(Monastery of the Discalced Carmelites)
Alameda de la Fuencisla
40003 Segovia, Spain
†The body of St John of the Cross rests within an ornate tomb in the church at this monastery. In life he was both a theologian and a mystic. His writings in these areas have made an enormous contribution to the modern understanding of the mystical experience.

Lawrence of Brindisi, priest and doctor (July 21ˢᵗ)

St Lawrence of Brindisi (d. 1619, Lisbon, Portugal) (Relics: Villafranca del Bierzo, Spain)

Monasterio de La Anunciada
(Monastery of the Annunciation)
Plaza Anunciada 1
24500 Villafranca del Bierzo, Spain
✝St Lawrence of Brindisi died in Lisbon, Portugal. Shortly thereafter, his body was transferred to Spain and brought to this city. His remains are now enshrined within this monastery.

Raymond of Penyafort, priest (January 7ᵗʰ)

St Raymond of Penyafort (d. 1275, Barcelona, Spain) (Relics: Barcelona, Spain)

Catedral de Santa Eulalia
(Cathedral of Saint Eulalia)
Plaça de la Seu
08002 Barcelona, Spain
✝St Raymond of Penyafort died in this city and his remains now rest within this church. During his life he codified the canons of the Catholic Church. As a result he is now honored as the patron saint of canon lawyers.

Teresa of Jesus, virgin and doctor (October 15ᵗʰ)

St Teresa (d. 1582, Alba de Tormes, Spain) (Relics: Rome, Italy; Avila, Spain; Alba de Tormes, Spain)

Convento de Santa Teresa
(Convent of Saint Teresa)
Plaza de la Santa 2
05001 Avila, Spain
✝This church is built over the home where St Teresa of Avila was born.

✝Within the gift shop, located outside of the church, are several prominent relics of St Teresa of Avila.

Monasterio de la Anunciación de Nuestra Señora de Carmelitas Descalzas / Madres Carmelitas Descalzas
(Discalced Carmelite Monastery of the Annunciation of Our Lady)
Plaza de Santa Teresa 3
37800 Alba de Tormes, Spain
✝While visiting various religious communities in the summer of 1582, St Teresa's health which was already weak began to worsen. Eventually she took to bed and passed away at Alba de Tormes. A great struggle then ensued between Avila and Alba de Tormes in regards to whom would receive her body. At one point her remains were transferred to Avila; however, shortly thereafter a Papal decree was issued and her body was returned to Alba de Tormes where it remains to this day within an urn above the main altar. Also preserved here, but separate from her body, are her heart and a bone from her arm.

First Class Relics Outside Of Italy

France

** ** ** ** ** ** ** **

First Class Relics In France
(For The Saints On The Roman Catholic Liturgical Calendar)

Anne, mother of The Virgin Mary
Anthony, abbot
Benedict, abbot
Bernadette*
Bernard, abbot and doctor
Catherine Laboure*
Chinese martyrs
Claude de la Colombiere*
Denis, bishop and martyr
Francis de Sales, bishop and doctor
Hilary, bishop and doctor
Jane Frances de Chantal, religious
John the Baptist, martyr
John Vianney, priest
Lazarus*
Louis

Louis Grignion de Montfort
Margaret Mary Alacoque, virgin
Martha
Martin of Tours, bishop
Mary Magdalene
Perpetua, martyr
Peter Julian Eymard, priest
Scholastica, virgin
Simon Stock*
Therese of the Child Jesus,
   virgin and doctor
Thomas Aquinas, priest and doctor
Vietnamese martyrs
Vincent, deacon and martyr
Vincent de Paul, priest
Vincent Ferrer, priest

Note: The Saints marked with an (*) are not on the Roman Catholic Liturgical Calendar.

Anne, mother of The Blessed Virgin Mary (July 26th)

(Relics: Apt, France; Bologna, Italy; Sainte-Anne d'Auray, France; Sainte-Anne de Beaupré, Quebec, Canada; Vienna, Austria)

Cathédrale Sainte-Anne / La Cathédrale d'Apt
(Saint Anne's Cathedral / Cathedral of Apt)
44 Place de la Cathédrale
84400 Apt, France
✝The first chapel on the left side of the nave is dedicated to St Anne. A reliquary niche within this chapel contains busts of several saints including St Anne.
✝It is uncertain how the relics of St Anne arrived in this church. Popular legend claims that they were brought by St Lazarus in the 1st century. However, it is more likely that they were transferred from the Holy Land to Constantinople and then brought to France after 1204 AD.

Sanctuaire Sainte-Anne d'Auray
(Sanctuary of Saint Anne of Auray)
9 Rue de Vannes
56400 Sainte-Anne d'Auray, France
✝A small chapel dedicated to St Anne was destroyed at this location in the 7th century. Ten centuries later it is said that St Anne began appearing to a simple villager and requested that a new church be built over this ancient chapel. A sanctuary was then built and a relic of St Anne was given to this church as a gift.

Anthony, abbot (January 17th)

St Anthony (d. 356, Mt. Colzim, Egypt) (Relics: Zaafarana, Egypt; Saint-Antoine l'Abbaye, France; Arles, France)

St Anthony requested to be buried secretly in an unmarked grave. Therefore, the exact location of his tomb is unknown. Nevertheless several traditions have arisen about his relics. One tradition holds that his tomb rests directly under *St Anthony's Monastery* in Egypt which was built close to where St Anthony had lived as a hermit. A second tradition holds that his tomb was discovered and that some of these relics were transported to France.

Saint-Antoine l'Abbaye (Abbey of Saint Anthony)
38160 Saint-Antoine l'Abbaye, France
†This abbey is located west of the city of Grenoble, France.
†Relics of St Anthony are said to have been transferred here around the 11th century.

L'Eglise Saint-Trophime (Church of Saint Trophime)
12 Rue du Cloître
13200 Arles, France
†Some relics of St Anthony are also said to rest in this church.

Benedict, abbot (July 11th) and Scholastica, virgin (February 10th)

St Benedict (b. 480, Norcia, Italy) (d. 547, Monte Cassino, Italy) (Relics: Monte Cassino, Italy; Saint-Benoît-sur-Loire, France; Brescia, Italy)

St Scholastica (b. 480, Norcia, Italy) (d. 547, Monte Cassino, Italy) (Relics: Monte Cassino, Italy; Juvigny-sur-Loison, France)

It is uncertain if the relics of Saint Benedict and Saint Scholastica were moved to Saint-Benoît-sur-Loire, France in the seventh century or if they still remain at Monte Cassino, Italy.

Abbaye de Fleury (Fleury Abbey)
1 Avenue de l'Abbaye
45730 Saint-Benoît-sur-Loire, France
†Tradition claims that during the latter part of the 7th century relics of St Benedict and St Scholastica were stolen from Montecassino and brought to this city in France. Today this is still a hotly debated issue with both shrines claiming to have the authentic relics. The relics located here rest within the crypt of the church.

L'église Saint-Denis (The Church of St Denis)
2 Rue Grande
55600 Juvigny-sur-Loison, France
†In the year 874 the relics of St Scholastica, which had been stolen from Montecassino as previously noted, were placed within the abbey located here. This abbey was later destroyed; however, the relics remain and are preserved within this church. They are processed annually during St Scholastica's feast in February.

Bernadette

St Bernadette (d. 1879, Nevers, France) (Relics: Nevers, France)

Couvent de Saint-Gildard
(Convent of Saint Gildard)
34 Rue Saint-Gildard
58000 Nevers, France
†The incorrupt body of St Bernadette is enshrined to the right of the main altar.

Bernard, abbot and doctor (August 20th)

St Bernard (d. 1153, Clairvaux, France) (Relics: Troyes, France)

Cathédrale de Troyes (Troyes Cathedral)
Place Saint-Pierre
10000 Troyes, France
†During the 13th century this church acquired an impressive collection of relics and artifacts that had been looted from the churches of Constantinople in 1204. During the French Revolution many of these relics and historic treasures were destroyed and the church itself was converted into a Temple of Reason. The church has since then been returned to sacred use and is known in particular for its expansive and impressive stained glass windows.
†One of the significant relics still preserved by this church is part of the skull of St Bernard. This relic can be found in the Treasury of this church.

Chinese and Vietnamese Martyrs (July 9th) (November 24th)

Honored on July 9th are 120 martyrs who died in China from the years 1648-1930. (Relics: Paris, France)

Honored on November 24th are 117 martyrs who died in Vietnam during the seventeenth, eighteenth, and nineteenth centuries. A further martyr, Blessed Andrew Phú Yên, was beatified in the year 2000. During these persecutions more than 100,000 Vietnamese Catholics lost their lives for their faith. (Relics: Paris, France; Penang, Malaysia)

Missions Etrangères de Paris (Foreign Missions of Paris)
128 Rue du Bac
75007 Paris, France
†This shrine preserves relics from a number of French missionaries who were martyred in Asia. Two of these martyrs, St Pierre Dumoulin-Borie and St Jean-Louis Bonnard, are among the 117 canonized Vietnamese martyrs. Also preserved here are some remains from Bishop Jean-Gabriel Dufresse who was martyred at the age of 64 in China.

Denis, bishop and martyr (October 9th) and Louis (August 25th)

St Denis (d. 3rd century, Paris, France) (Relics: Saint-Denis, France)

A sensational legend holds that after St Denis was beheaded he picked up his own head and miraculously carried it to the place where he wanted to be buried. Therefore, in art he is often depicted as holding his own head in his hands.

St Louis (d. 1270, Tunis, Tunisia) (Relics: Monreale, Sicily; Saint-Denis, France)

In 1270 St Louis set out across the Mediterranean to begin the Eighth Crusade. Upon reaching the shores of Tunis his group met a number of setbacks. As they waited for reinforcements to fortify their position many within the group including St Louis caught dysentery and died. As the defeated crusaders returned to Europe they brought the remains of St Louis through Italy and France attracting many crowds of mourners along the way. His remains were then buried in _Saint-Denis Cathedral_ in Paris, France. The Sicilian city of Monreale also continues to claim to have some of his relics.

Cathédrale de Saint-Denis (Cathedral of Saint Denis)
1 Place de la Legion d'Honneur
93200 Saint-Denis, France
✝Tradition claims that this church was erected over the tomb of St Denis.
✝For centuries the remains of St Louis also rested in this church. However, during the French Revolution these remains were destroyed. Only a finger was preserved.

Francis de Sales, bishop and doctor (January 24th) and Jane Frances de Chantal, religious (August 12th)

St Francis de Sales (d. 1622, Lyon, France) (Relics: Treviso, Italy; Annecy, France)

St Jane Frances de Chantal (d. 1641, Moulins, France) (Relics: Annecy, France)

Basilique de la Visitation (Basilica of the Visitation)
11 Avenue de la Visitation
74000 Annecy, France
✝The remains of St Francis de Sales and St Jane Frances de Chantal rest within two different sarcophagi near the communion rail at the base of the main sanctuary. St Francis de Sales is on the left and St Jane Frances de Chantal is on the right. Each sarcophagus is overlaid with a bronze relief depicting the saint's image.

Hilary, bishop and doctor (January 13th)

St Hilary (d. 368, Poitiers, France) (Relics: Poitiers, France)

L'Eglise Saint-Hilaire-le-Grand
(Church of Saint Hilary)
26 Rue Saint-Hilaire
86000 Poitiers, France
✝This church is built over the ancient tomb of St Hilary. In 1572 this tomb was plundered by French Huguenots and St Hilary's relics lost. Nearly a century later in 1657 a miraculous discovery of his relics was claimed in Le Puy, France. These relics were then transferred to Poitiers some years later. Today they are located within an ornate bronze reliquary in the crypt of this church.

John the Baptist, martyr (June 24ᵗʰ, August 29ᵗʰ)

St John the Baptist (Relics: Rome, Italy; Florence, Italy; Siena, Italy; Amiens, France; Munich, Germany; Damascus, Syria)

Cathédrale d'Amiens (Cathedral of Amiens)
30 Place Notre Dame
80000 Amiens, France
✝ Part of the skull of St John Baptist rests within this cathedral. The authenticity is uncertain since this skull is also said to be located at a number of other places throughout the world including *San Silvestro in Capite* in Rome, Italy, the *Residenz Museum* in Munich, Germany, and the *Umayyad Mosque* in Damascus, Syria.

John Vianney, priest (August 4ᵗʰ)

St John Vianney (d. 1859, Ars-sur-Formans, France) (Relics: Ars-sur-Formans, France)

Sanctuaire d'Ars
(Sanctuary of Ars)
451 Rue Jean Marie Vianney
01480 Ars-Sur-Formans, France
✝ The body of St John Vianney is enshrined in this church on the right side of the nave. His heart rests within a small chapel located just outside of this church.

Lazarus, Martha (July 29th), and Mary Magdalene (July 22nd)

St Lazarus (Relics: Marseille, France; Larnaca, Cyprus)

St Martha (Relics: Tarascon, France)

St Mary Magdalene (Relics: Rome, Italy; Plan-d'Aups-Sainte-Baume, France; Saint-Maximin-La-Sainte-Baume, France; Vézelay, France)

A tradition, which developed in the 13th century, holds that after the martyrdom of St James the Greater in Jerusalem many Christians were evicted from the city and placed upon a boat without a sail or a rudder. Miraculously this group, which included Mary Magdalene, Lazarus, and Martha, reached the southern shores of France. The group then began spreading the faith in the area. A legend holds that St Lazarus was able to convert a number of people in Marseille and then became its first bishop. Later during the persecution of Domitian he was beheaded. Martha is said to have eventually made it to the city of Tarascon. The local people of this city were terrorized by a ferocious beast; therefore, to test the power of Martha's Christian religion they challenged her to a duel with the beast. Miraculously with only a cross and some holy water Martha was able to calm the beast. As a result of this miracle the people in this town converted to Christianity. Mary Magdalene, however, chose a different path. She gave herself to a life of prayer and spent thirty years as a hermit in a cave above the present-day village of Plan-d'Aups-Sainte-Baume. A competing theory alleges that Mary Magdalene was buried in Ephesus close to the house of the Blessed Virgin Mary. From here her relics were transferred to Constantinople and then to Western Europe.

Cathédrale Sainte-Marie-Majeure / La Major
(Cathedral of Saint Mary Major / The Major)
Place de la Major
13002 Marseille, France
✝This impressive church was completed in 1896. It replaced an older cathedral that can trace its origins back to a 5th century monastery. This church has traditionally been in possession of some relics of St Lazarus including his skull.

Cathédrale Saint-Lazare
(Cathedral of Saint Lazarus)
Place du Terreau
71400 Autun, France
✝This church was built in the 12th century to hold the relics of St Lazarus. His tomb, however, was destroyed during the French Revolution.

Collégiale Royale Sainte-Marthe
(Royal Collegiate of Saint Martha)
Place de la Concorde
13150 Tarascon, France
✝For centuries the relics of St Martha resided in this church. However, during the French Revolution most of these relics were stolen and subsequently lost. Presently only small bone fragments remain. They rest within a reliquary bust in a chapel set behind an iron grate.

Grotte de Sainte-Marie-Madeleine
(Grotto of Saint Mary Magdalene)
83640 Plan-d'Aups-Sainte-Baume, France
✝The *Grotto of Saint Mary Magdalene* is carved into the side of a mountain located just to the east of Plan-d'Aups-Sainte-Baume.
✝Tradition claims that St Mary Magdalene spent the last 30 years of her life here. Some relics of St Mary Magdalene are located under the altar.

Basilique Sainte-Marie-Madeleine
(Basilica of Saint Mary Magdalene)
2 Route Asquins
89450 Vézelay, France
✝Tradition holds that St Mary Magdalene was originally buried in the *Church of St Maximin* in the present day French city of Saint-Maximin-La-Sainte-Baume. In the 8th century her remains were unearthed and transferred to Vézelay, France. Five centuries later the King of Naples, Charles II, claimed to have found her original tomb in *St Maximin*. In 1281 he was able to obtain official recognition of these relics. As a result, the shrine in Vézelay lost its prominence. Then in the 16th century the relics that remained in Vézelay were burned by French Huguenots. Presently only an empty tomb and a few small relics remain within this church. They are located in the Carolingian crypt.

Basilique Sainte-Marie-Madeleine
(Basilica of Saint Mary Magdalene)
Place de l'Hôtel de Ville
83470 Saint-Maximin-La-Sainte-Baume, France
✝In the 13th century this church was built over the recently found tomb of St Mary Magdalene. Five centuries later, however, it was severely damaged by supporters of the French Revolution. Despite this damage, both the tomb and a relic of St Mary Magdalene's skull were saved. These relics can be visited within the crypt of this church.

Louis Grignion de Montfort, priest (April 28th)

St Louis Grignion de Montfort (d. 1716, Saint-Laurent-sur-Sevre, France)
(Relics: Saint-Laurent-sur-Sevre, France)

Basilique Saint Louis-Marie Grignion de Montfort
(Basilica of Saint Louis Grignion de Montfort)
Rue Jean Paul II
85290 Saint-Laurent-sur-Sevre, France
✝The tomb of St Louis Grignion de Montfort rests within the crypt. The room where he died can be visited at an oratory located about one block from the basilica.

Margaret Mary Alacoque, virgin (October 16th) and Claude de la Colombiere

St Margaret Mary
Alacoque (d. 1690, Paray-
le-Monial, France)
(Relics: Paray-le-Monial,
France)

St Claude de la
Colombiere (d. 1682,
Paray-le-Monial, France)
(Relics: Paray-le-Monial,
France)

Chapelle des Apparitions
(Chapel of the Apparitions)
16 Rue de la Visitation
71600 Paray-le-Monial, France
✝The body of St Margaret Mary Alacoque is enshrined within this small church.
✝This is also the church where she received the visions of the Sacred Heart of Jesus.

La Chapelle de la Colombiere (The Chapel of Colombiere)
Rue Pasteur
71600 Paray-le-Monial, France
✝The remains of St Claude de la Colombiere are enshrined within this church.

Martin of Tours, bishop (November 11th)

St Martin of Tours (d. 397, Candes-Saint-Martin, France) (Relics: Tours, France)

Basilique Saint-Martin (Basilica of Saint Martin)
7 Rue Baleschoux
37000 Tours, France
✝This church was recently rebuilt in 1924 to replace the ancient church that was destroyed during the French Revolution. In the crypt of this church is a restored tomb of Saint Martin of Tours.

Perpetua, martyr (March 7th)

Saint Perpetua (d. 203, Carthage, Tunisia) (Relics: Carthage, Tunisia; Vierzon, France)

Paroisse Notre Dame (Parish of Notre Dame)
4 Rue du Presbytère
18100 Vierzon, France
✝Saints Perpetua and Felicity were originally buried in Tunisia. A tradition, however, maintains that at some point relics of St Perpetua were transferred to France. By 903 these relics were brought to the French city of Vierzon where they were first placed in *L'abbaye Saint-Pierre* and then later transferred to this church.
✝The chapel on the right side of the apse is dedicated to St Perpetua. Her relics are presented to the public once a year.

Peter Julian Eymard, priest (August 2nd)

St Peter Julian Eymard (d. 1868, La Mure, France) (Relics: Rome, Italy; Paris, France)

Chapelle du Corpus-Christi (Corpus Christi Chapel)
23 Avenue de Friedland
75008 Paris, France
✝The remains of St Peter Julian Eymard rest within a glass case in this chapel.

Simon Stock

St Simon Stock (d. 1265, Bordeaux, France) (Relics: Aylesford, United Kingdom; Bordeaux, France)

Cathédrale Saint-André (Saint Andrew's Cathedral)
Place Pey Berland
33000 Bordeaux, France
✝The body of St Simon Stock rests below an altar on the left side of the nave.

Therese of the Child Jesus, virgin and doctor (October 1ˢᵗ)

St Therese of the Child Jesus (d. 1897, Lisieux, France) (Relics: Lisieux, France)

Monastère du Carmel de Lisieux
(Carmelite Monastery of Lisieux)
37 Rue du Carmel
14100 Lisieux, France
✝St Therese lived and prayed in this convent with her Carmelite community from 1888 to 1897. Today the majority of her relics rest within a golden casket in the chapel at this convent below the statue of her likeness.

Basilique Sainte-Therese de Lisieux
(Basilica of Saint Therese of Lisieux)
Avenue Jean XXIII
14100 Lisieux, France
✝The right arm bones of St Therese are enshrined within an impressive reliquary in this basilica.

Thomas Aquinas, priest and doctor (January 28ᵗʰ)

St Thomas Aquinas (b. 1225, Roccasecca, Italy) (d. 1274, Fossanova, Italy)
(Relics: Toulouse, France; Aquino, Italy; Naples, Italy)

Couvent des Jacobins (Convent of the Jacobins)
Place des Jacobins
31000 Toulouse, France
†From 1274 to 1369 the remains of St Thomas Aquinas rested in Fossanova,
Italy. In 1369 they were transferred to the *Convent of the Jacobins* in Toulouse,
France. They remained here until the French Revolution. At this time they
were moved for their protection a few blocks away to the *Basilica of St Sernin*
in Toulouse. From 1789 to 1974 they remained within this church. Finally, in
1974 in honor of the 700ᵗʰ anniversary of the death of St Thomas Aquinas the
relics were returned to the *Convent of the Jacobins* in Toulouse. They now rest
within a bronze chest placed under an altar in this church.

Vincent, deacon and martyr (January 23ʳᵈ)*

St Vincent (d. 304, Valencia, Spain) (Relics: Lisbon, Portugal; Castres,
France)

Cathédrale Saint-Benoît (Cathedral of Saint Benedict)
9 Rue Barral
81100 Castres, France
†Tradition holds that some relics of St Vincent were brought to the *Abbey of
St Benedict* in Castres, France in 864 AD. Today all that remains of this abbey
is its Romanesque tower. In its place stands the *Cathedral of St Benedict*.

Vincent de Paul, priest (September 27th) and Catherine Laboure

St Vincent de Paul (d. 1660, Paris, France) (Relics: Paris, France)

St Catherine Laboure (d. 1876) (Relics: Paris, France)

Chapelle des Pères Lazaristes
(Chapel of the Vincentian Priests)
95 Rue de Sèvres
75006 Paris, France
✝This church is very near the Vaneau Metro Stop. The body of St Vincent de Paul rests above the main sanctuary and is accessed by means of a staircase.

La Chapelle Notre Dame de la Médaille Miraculeuse
(Chapel of Our Lady of the Miraculous Medal)
140 Rue du Bac
75006 Paris, France
✝The body of St Catherine Laboure is enshrined within this church. This is also the church where she had the visions of the Miraculous Medal.
✝Also the heart of St Vincent de Paul is preserved within a reliquary at this shrine.

Vincent Ferrer, priest (April 5th)

St Vincent Ferrer (d. 1419, Vannes, France) (Relics: Vannes, France)

Cathédrale Saint-Pierre de Vannes
(Cathedral of Saint Peter of Vannes)
22 Rue des Chanoines
56000 Vannes, France
✝The tomb of St Vincent Ferrer is on the left side of the nave within the Blessed Sacrament Chapel. Also located here is a reliquary bust of the saint. These relics have resided in the Blessed Sacrament Chapel since 1956.

First Class Relics Outside Of Italy

United Kingdom

** ** ** ** ** ** ** **

First Class Relics In The United Kingdom
(For The Saints On The Roman Catholic Liturgical Calendar)

Andrew, apostle	Patrick, bishop
Bede the Venerable, priest and doctor	Simon Stock*
John Fisher, bishop and martyr	Thomas Becket, bishop and martyr
Margaret of Scotland	Thomas More, martyr

Note: The Saints marked with an (*) are not on the Roman Catholic Liturgical Calendar.

Andrew, apostle (November 30th)

St Andrew (Relics: Patras, Greece; Amalfi, Italy; Florence, Italy; Edinburgh, Scotland; Cologne, Germany; Kiev, Ukraine)

The relics of St Andrew have played a pivotal role in the history of Scotland. Tradition claims that they first entered into the annals of Scottish history in the 4th century when they were brought to Scotland by the legendary Bishop of Patras, St Regulus. It is said that this bishop was warned in a dream by an angel that the safety of the relics were in jeopardy. He then set sail from Greece for the farthest western edges of the known world in order to protect the relics. Just off the coast of Scotland his voyage met with shipwreck and he was forced to come ashore at what is now the town of St Andrews. Despite this ancient tradition and the great historical influence that the relics of St Andrew have had upon the Scottish people the original relics met a tragic fate on June 14, 1559 when they were destroyed by supporters of the Scottish Reformation.

St Mary's Roman Catholic Cathedral
61 York Place
EH1 3JD, Edinburgh, United Kingdom (Scotland)
†In recent centuries the Scottish church has been blessed to receive several relics of St Andrew to replace the original relics that had been destroyed during the Scottish Reformation. In 1879 a large portion of the shoulder of St Andrew was taken from his remains in Amalfi, Italy and brought to Scotland. Also in 1969 Pope Paul VI gave additional relics of St Andrew to the Scottish church with the words, "Peter greets his brother Andrew." These relics of St Andrew now rest within this cathedral at an altar to the right of the main sanctuary.

Anselm, bishop and doctor (April 21st), Bartholomew, apostle (August 24th), and Thomas Becket, bishop and martyr (December 29th)

St Anselm (d. 1109, Canterbury, United Kingdom)

St Bartholomew (Relics: Rome, Italy; Benevento, Italy; Lipari, Sicily; Frankfurt, Germany)

St Thomas Becket (d. 1170, Canterbury, United Kingdom) (Relics: Canterbury, United Kingdom)

Canterbury Cathedral
CT1 2EH, Canterbury, United Kingdom
✝St Anselm was originally buried within this church; however, upon the closing of this monastery by the orders of King Henry VIII his relics were lost. Nevertheless, the memory of St Anselm continues within the chapel dedicated to him on the right side of the nave.
✝For centuries this church also housed the tomb St Thomas Becket. During the English Reformation, however, this tomb was destroyed. Some of his relics, nevertheless, still exist throughout the world.
✝In the 11th century an arm of St Bartholomew was gifted to this church. However, this relic is also lost.

Saint Thomas of Canterbury Roman Catholic Church
59 Burgate
CT1 2HJ, Canterbury, United Kingdom
✝A reliquary within the *Martyr's Chapel* of this church, located within the right transept, contains three relics of St Thomas Becket. The presence of these relics are partially explained by the following sequence of events. In 1220 AD several cardinals from Rome who were present for the translation of the body of St Thomas Becket from the crypt to the main floor of *Canterbury Cathedral* took several small relics of St Thomas Becket back to Italy. Upon the destruction of St Thomas Becket's shrine in 1538 these relics of the saint were preserved. In the past two centuries some of these relics and others from around Europe have been returned to Canterbury. In the 19th century the church received from Gubbio, Italy both a piece of his vestment and a bone from his body. Then in 1953 the Prior of Chevetogne, Father Thomas Becquet, presented to this church a piece of St Thomas Becket's finger. All three of these relics are now within the *Martyr's Chapel* as noted previously.

Bede the Venerable, priest and doctor (May 25th)

St Bede (d. 735, Jarrow, Northumbria, United Kingdom) (Relics: Durham, United Kingdom)

Durham Cathedral
The College
DH1 3EH, Durham, United Kingdom
✝The remains of St Bede rest within the _Galilee Chapel_. This is the large chapel located on the western end of the church.

John Fisher, bishop and martyr & Thomas More, martyr (June 22nd)

St John Fisher (d. 1535, London, United Kingdom) (Relics: London, United Kingdom)

St Thomas More (d. 1535, London, United Kingdom) (Relics: London, United Kingdom; Canterbury, United Kingdom)

Church of St Peter ad Vincula (Tower of London)
EC3N 4AB, London, United Kingdom
✝The headless bodies of St John Fisher and St Thomas More are said to rest in simple graves within the crypt of this church. Both of these saints were beheaded on Tower Hill in London.

St Dunstan's Church
80 London Road
CT2 8LS Canterbury, United Kingdom
✝The head of St Thomas More is said to rest in the Roper Vault of this church. His daughter, Margaret Roper, and his son-in-law, William Roper, are also believed to be buried in this church.

Margaret of Scotland (November 16th)

St Margaret of Scotland (d. 1093, Scotland) (Relics: Dunfermline, Scotland)

For centuries the remains of St Margaret rested within the _Dunfermline Abbey_ in Scotland. However, with the religious upheaval in the country in the 16th century her relics were dispersed to several other nations. Her head was taken to the _Scots College_ at Douay where it remained until its disappearance during the French Revolution. The remaining relics were taken to the _Royal Monastery of San Lorenzo de El Escorial_ in Spain where they also similarly disappeared. Nevertheless, in 1863 Bishop Gillis of Scotland came to Spain and was able to locate and authenticate one relic of St Margaret from the _Escorial_ source. He returned this relic to Scotland and placed it under the protection of the Ursuline sisters in Edinburgh where it remained for 145 years. In 2008 this relic was transferred to Dunfermline, Scotland. (Also of note: Since 1675 the _Scots College_ in Rome, Italy has been in possession of a small relic of St Margaret.)

St Margaret's National Memorial Church
East Port
KY12 7YN, Dunfermline, United Kingdom (Scotland)
†A shoulder bone of St Margaret of Scotland rests beneath the main altar of this church within a gothic reliquary. As noted above this relic was acquired in 2008.

Patrick, bishop (March 17th)

St Patrick (d. 461) (Relics: Downpatrick, United Kingdom)

Down Cathedral
English Street
BT30 6AB, Downpatrick, United Kingdom (Ireland)
✝The exact location of St Patrick's grave is uncertain. However, it is believed
that his remains rest under a large stone in the churchyard.

Simon Stock

St Simon Stock (d. 1265, Bordeaux, France) (Relics: Aylesford, United
Kingdom; Bordeaux, France)

Carmelite Friary
ME20 7BX, Aylesford, United Kingdom
✝Part of the skull of St Simon Stock rests within a reliquary located behind the
main altar of this church. It was transferred here in 1951.

First Class Relics Outside Of Italy

Austria, Belgium, Germany & Switzerland

** ** ** ** ** ** ** **

First Class Relics In Austria, Belgium, Germany, and Switzerland

(For The Saints On The Roman Catholic Liturgical Calendar)

Albert the Great, bishop and doctor
Andrew, apostle
Anne, mother of The Virgin Mary
Apollinaris, bishop and martyr
Bartholomew, apostle
Basil the Great, bishop and doctor
Boniface, bishop and martyr
Cornelius, pope and martyr
Cosmas and Damian, martyrs
Damien Joseph de Veuster, priest

Elizabeth of Hungary, religious
Fidelis of Sigmaringen
Francis Xavier, priest
Hedwig, religious
Henry
John the Baptist, martyr
Marcellinus and Peter, martyrs
Mark, evangelist
Matthias, apostle
Peter Canisius, priest and doctor

Albert the Great, bishop and doctor (November 15th) and Andrew, apostle (November 30th)

St Albert the Great (d. 1280, Cologne, Germany) (Relics: Cologne, Germany)

St Andrew (Relics: Amalfi, Italy; Florence, Italy; Patras, Greece; Edinburgh, Scotland; Cologne, Germany; Kiev, Ukraine)

Sankt Andreas
(Saint Andrew)
Komodienstraße 6-8
50667 Cologne, Germany
†The remains of St Albert the Great rest within a tomb in the crypt of this church. Also an arm of St Andrew rests within a reliquary located in the back of the choir in the main body of this church. It was placed here in 1997.
†The city of Cologne is also noted for a number of other prominent relics and traditions. The remains of the Three Kings are said to rest within a magnificent golden reliquary located in the apse of the *Cologne Cathedral*. Blessed John Duns Scotus is buried within a tomb in the church called the *Minoritenkirche*. Also it was in this city that St Thomas Aquinas studied theology under St Albert the Great and where St Bruno, the founder of the Carthusians, was born. Finally, it was here in 1933 that Edith Stein entered a Carmelite Convent and took the name Teresa Benedicta of the Cross.

Anne, mother of The Blessed Virgin Mary (July 26th)

(Relics: Apt, France; Bologna, Italy; Sainte-Anne d'Auray, France; Sainte-Anne de Beaupré, Quebec, Canada; Vienna, Austria)

Annakirche (Saint Anne's Church)
Annagasse 3b
1010 Vienna, Austria
†A relic of St Anne's hand is preserved within this church. Each year this relic is brought out on July 26th for public veneration.

Apollinaris, bishop and martyr (July 20ᵗʰ)

St Apollinaris (d. 1ˢᵗ century, Ravenna, Italy) (Relics: Ravenna, Italy; Remagen, Germany; Düsseldorf, Germany)

Apollinariskirche (Saint Apollinaris Church)
Apollinarisberg 4
53424 Remagen, Germany
✝Relics of St Apollinaris were brought to this city in the 12ᵗʰ century. In 1383 all of these relics, except the skull, were stolen by Duke Wilhelm I and brought to Düsseldorf, Germany. At a later date the skull was also taken and over the next few centuries transferred between several cities before its return to Remagen in 1857. It now rests within a magnificent reliquary bust placed within a large sarcophagus in the crypt of this church. Twice a year this bust is removed for the blessing of pilgrims.

Sankt Lambertus (Saint Lambertus)
Stiftsplatz 7
40213 Düsseldorf, Germany
✝The relics of St Apollinaris that were stolen by Duke Wilhelm I, as mentioned above, rest within the main sanctuary of this church.

Bartholomew, apostle (August 24ᵗʰ)

St Bartholomew (Relics: Rome, Italy; Benevento, Italy; Lipari, Sicily; Frankfurt, Germany)

Frankfurter Dom
(Frankfurt Cathedral)
Domplatz 1
60313 Frankfurt, Germany
✝The skull of St Bartholomew is venerated within this church. It rests within a Gothic reliquary located on the eastern wall of the right transept. Small wooden statues of Joachim, Cleopas, and Zebedee adorn the sides of this reliquary.

Basil the Great, bishop and doctor (January 2nd)

St Basil the Great (d. 379, Caesarea) (Relics: Mount Athos, Greece; Bruges, Belgium)

Basiliek van het Heilig Bloed (Basilica of the Holy Blood)
Burg 13
8000 Bruges, Belgium
✝For the last 750 years this church has preserved a precious relic of the Holy Blood of Jesus Christ. Veneration of this relic occurs every Friday in this basilica and culminates with a grand procession on the Solemnity of the Ascension.
✝The lower chapel of this church is dedicated to St Basil. Within this chapel to the left of the choir is an even smaller chapel dedicated to St Yves. It is within this chapel that a relic of St Basil rests. It was brought here during the first part of the 12th century.

Boniface, bishop and martyr (June 5th)

St Boniface (d. 754, Dokkum, Netherlands) (Relics: Fulda, Germany)

Fuldaer Dom
(Fulda Cathedral)
Eduard-Schick-Platz 3
36037 Fulda, Germany
✝Part of the skull of St Boniface rests upon an altar located within the museum of this church. A mitre is positioned upon this relic.
✝The tomb of St Boniface rests in the crypt chapel directly below the main sanctuary. The relief on the side of this tomb depicts St Boniface rising from his grave as he pushes the cover off of his coffin. The majority of his relics are presumed to be located within this tomb. However, some of his relics have been distributed as gifts over the centuries.
✝Other cities that hold St Boniface in great honor include the two Dutch cities of Dokkum and Groningen and the two German cities of Fritzlar and Mainz.

Cornelius, pope and martyr (September 16ᵗʰ)

St Cornelius (d. 253,
Civitavecchia, Italy)
(Relics: Rome, Italy;
Aachen, Germany)

**Pfarrkirche St.
Kornelius**
(Parish Church of Saint
Cornelius)
Benediktusplatz 11
52076 Aachen,
Germany

†This church was once
part of the historic *Kornelimünster Abbey* that was founded in the 9ᵗʰ century
by the Carolingian Emperor, Louis the Pious. However, in 1802 the abbey was
dissolved and this church was made into a parish. The abbey has since then
been reestablished and now exists in a new building just a short walk from this
church.

†A number of remarkable relics are preserved within this church. In 875,
through the efforts of Emperor Charles the Bald, this church received the relic
of St Cornelius' head from *L'abbaye Saint-Corneille* in Compiègne, France.
This relic is now enshrined within a magnificent reliquary bust positioned
within the center of an octagonal-shaped chapel located in the apse of this
church. Also preserved at this church are three separate cloths connected to the
life of Christ. One was used by Christ to wash the disciples' feet, a second to
wipe the brow of Christ, and the last in his burial. These relics are not often
available for public viewing.

Cosmas and Damian, martyrs (September 26th)

Saints Cosmas and Damian (d. 287, Syria) (Relics: Rome, Italy; Munich Germany)

Saints Cosmas and Damian suffered martyrdom during the beginning of the Diocletian persecutions around the year 287 AD. In life they were greatly respected as medical doctors who often offered their services free of charge. As a result many have adopted these two great saints as their patrons due to their connection to the medical field. In particular this was true for the powerful Medici family of Florence whose last name when translated to English means doctors. Thus Fra Angelico and other painters frequently depicted Saints Cosmas and Damian in the works commissioned by this family. (Due to the great popularity of these saints numerous shrines claim to have their relics. In addition to those listed in this work are *St Stephen's Cathedral* in Vienna, *San Giorgio Maggiore* in Venice, and a *Convent of Poor Clares* in Madrid)

Jesuitenkirche St. Michael (Jesuit Church of St Michael)
Neuhauser Straße 6
80333 Munich, Germany
†The skulls of Saints Cosmas and Damian purportedly rest within an ornate reliquary chest placed within a chapel on the right side of the nave of this church.

Damien Joseph de Veuster of Moloka'i, priest (May 10th)*

St Damien Joseph de Veuster of Moloka'i (d. 1889) (Relics: Leuven, Belgium; Kalawao, Hawaii, USA; Honolulu, Hawaii, USA)

Sint-Antoniuskapel (St Anthony's Chapel)
Pater Damiaanplein
3000 Leuven, Belgium
†St Damien Joseph de Veuster, who faithfully and heroically served the leper community in Moloka'i, Hawaii for over fifteen years before finally succumbing himself to the disease, is buried within the crypt of this church. He is a native of Belgium.

Elizabeth of Hungary, religious (November 17th)

St Elizabeth of Hungary (d.
1231, Marburg, Germany)
(Relics: Vienna, Austria)

Elisabethkirche
(Saint Elizabeth's Church)
Elisabethstraße 3
35037 Marburg, Germany
✝Today this church is only used
for Protestant worship services.
Nevertheless, the church still
promotes and maintains the
memory of St Elizabeth of
Hungary.
✝Prior to the Protestant
Reformation the remains of St
Elizabeth of Hungary rested
within two separate reliquaries
within this church. The one held

her bones and the other her skull. On special occasions these relics would be
placed upon the ornate mausoleum pedestal which can still be seen today
within the left transept of this church. However, all veneration of her relics
ceased in 1539 by decree of Philip of Hesse (d. 1567). He had the relics
removed and all Catholic services halted.

Kloster der Elisabethinen
(Convent of Saint Elizabeth)
Landstraßer Hauptstraße 4a
A-1030 Vienna, Austria
✝Resting within this convent are some bones and the skull of St Elizabeth of
Hungary. Her skull is crowned with the crown she wore during her life.

Fidelis of Sigmaringen, priest and martyr (April 24th)

St Fidelis of Sigmaringen (d. 1622, Grüsch, Switzerland) (Relics: Feldkirch, Austria; Chur, Switzerland)

Kapuzinerkloster Feldkirch
(Capuchin Monastery of Feldkirch)
Bahnhostraße 4
6800 Feldkirch, Austria
✝The skull of St Fidelis, a Capuchin friar of the Counter-Reformation, rests within this monastery. He was martyred in the nearby town of Grüsch, Switzerland.

Kathedrale Chur (Cathedral of Chur)
Hof 14
7000 Chur, Switzerland
✝Relics of St Fidelis rest within a reliquary in the crypt of this church.

Francis Xavier, priest (December 3rd)

St Francis Xavier (d. 1552, Shangchuan Island, China) (Relics: Rome, Italy; Goa, India; Antwerp, Belgium)

Sint-Carolus Borromeuskerk
(Saint Charles Borromeo Church) Hendrik Conscienceplein 12
2000 Antwerp, Belgium
✝A small relic of St Francis Xavier is preserved in this church in a chapel to the left of the main sanctuary.

Gertrude, virgin (November 16th)

St Gertrude the Great (d. 1301, Helfta, Germany)

The remains of St Gertrude the Great originally rested at the *Old Helfta Monastery* near Eisleben, Germany. Today, however, the location of her relics is unknown. (Note: This St Gertrude is not to be confused with St Gertrude of Nivelles or Gertrude of Hackeborn.)

Hedwig, religious (October 16th)

St Hedwig (d. 1243, Silesia, Poland) (Relics: Andechs, Germany; Berlin, Germany)

St Hedwig was both the Duchess of Silesia and a mother of seven children. Upon her husband's death she joined a Cistercian convent where she died in 1243. She should not be confused with St Hedwig, Queen of Poland (1371-1399), who was canonized in 1987 and is buried in the *Wawel Cathedral* in Kraków, Poland.

Kloster Andechs (Andechs' Abbey)
Bergstraße 2
82346 Andechs, Germany
✝In 1929 this abbey received a fragment of St Hedwig's skull from Cardinal Bertram of Breslau. This relic can be viewed in the *Holy Chapel*. Access, however, is only permitted for those who have reserved a tour.

St Hedwigs Kathedrale (Saint Hedwig's Cathedral)
Hinter der Katholischen Kirche 3
10117 Berlin, Germany
✝Some of St Hedwig's relics rest in the Treasury of this church within a small silver-gilded statue of her likeness. This statue depicts her holding both the Blessed Virgin Mary and a model of the church. It was completed in 1513 by Andreas Heidecker.

Henry (July 13th)

St Henry (d. 1024, Gottingen, Germany) (Relics: Bamberg, Germany)

Bamberger Dom (Bamberg Cathedral)
Domplatz 5
96049 Bamberg, Germany
✝St Henry was the Holy Roman Emperor from 1014-1024. Both he and his wife, St Cunegonde, are canonized saints. They are buried next to each other at the base of the east choir within this church.

John the Baptist, martyr (June 24th, August 29th)

St John the Baptist (Relics: Rome, Italy; Florence, Italy; Siena, Italy; Amiens, France; Munich, Germany; Damascus, Syria)

Residenzmuseum (Residenz Museum)
Residenzstraße 1
80333 Munich, Germany
✝A relic of the skull of St John Baptist rests within this museum. The authenticity is uncertain since this same relic is said to be located at a number of other places throughout the world including the _Cathedral of Amiens_ in France, _San Silvestro in Capite_ in Rome, Italy, and the _Umayyad Mosque_ in Damascus, Syria.

Marcellinus and Peter, martyrs (June 2ⁿᵈ)

St Marcellinus and Peter
(d. 304, Rome, Italy)
(Relics: Rome, Italy;
Seligenstadt, Germany)

**Basilika St Marcellinus
und Petrus /
Einhardbasilika**
(Basilica of Saints
Marcellinus and Peter /
Einhard Basilica)
63500 Seligenstadt,
Germany

✝Relics of Saints Marcellinus and Peter were transferred from Rome to this
church in the 9ᵗʰ century. Shortly thereafter the city took on its new name of
Seligenstadt which translated into English means 'Blessed City'. These relics
are now located within a golden chest under the main altar of this church.

Mark, evangelist (April 25ᵗʰ)

St Mark (d. Alexandria, Egypt) (Relics: Venice, Italy; Cairo, Egypt; Reichenau, Germany)

Münster St. Maria und Markus
(Cathedral of Saint Mary and Saint Mark)
78479 Reichenau, Germany

✝For many centuries the island of Reichenau served as a very important
monastic center in Medieval Europe. This island rests upon Lake Constance in
southern Germany near the Liechtenstein border. In 1803 the island was
secularized leading to the destruction of many of its churches and religious
buildings.

✝Relics of St Mark were brought to this island from Venice in the year 830
AD. This was just two years after Venetian merchants smuggled these relics
out of Egypt. Today these relics rest within this newly constructed church.

Matthias, apostle (May 14ᵗʰ)

St Matthias (Relics: Rome, Italy; Trier, Germany)

St Helena is said to have acquired the relics of St Matthias in the 4ᵗʰ century. These relics were then distributed to both Rome, Italy and Trier, Germany.

Benediktinerabtei St Matthias
(Saint Matthias Benedictine Abbey)
Matthiasstraße 85
54290 Trier, Germany
†The tomb of St Matthias lies within the nave of this church and is surrounded by candles. A sarcophagus within the crypt is said to contain some of his relics.

Peter Canisius, priest and doctor (December 21ˢᵗ)

St Peter Canisius (d. 1597, Fribourg, Switzerland) (Relics: Fribourg, Switzerland)

L'Eglise Saint-Michel
(The Church of Saint Michael)
Rue Saint-Pierre-Canisius 10
1700 Fribourg, Switzerland
†The relics of St Peter Canisius, a zealous preacher and defender of the faith during the Counter-Reformation, lie under the main altar of this church.
†In order to make his relics more accessible there is a possibility that his relics may be transferred in the near future. If this occurs his relics would be transferred just a few blocks away to the *Cathédrale Saint-Nicolas* in Fribourg.

First Class Relics Outside Of Italy

Other Countries To The North & East Of Italy

** ** ** ** ** ** ** **

First Class Relics
To The North & East of Italy
(For The Saints On The Roman Catholic Liturgical Calendar)

Adalbert, bishop and martyr
Andrew, apostle
Bridget, religious
Casimir
Faustina Kowalska*
John Chrysostom, bishop and doctor

John of Kanty, priest
Luke, evangelist
Norbert, bishop
Stanislaus, bishop and martyr
Stephen of Hungary
Wenceslaus, martyr

Includes the Following Countries: Czech Republic, Hungary, Lithuania, Poland, Russia, Sweden and Ukraine.

Note: The Saints marked with an (*) are not on the Roman Catholic Liturgical Calendar.

Adalbert, bishop and martyr (April 23rd), Luke, evangelist (October 18th), and Wenceslaus, martyr (September 28th)

St Adalbert [Wojciech in Polish] (d. 997) (Relics: Rome, Italy; Prague, Czech Republic; Gniezno, Poland)

St Luke (Relics: Rome, Italy; Padua, Italy; Prague, Czech Republic; Thebes, Greece)

St Wenceslaus (d. 935, Stará Boleslav, Czech Republic) (Relics: Prague, Czech Republic)

Cathedral of St Vitus
Hrad III. Nádvoří
119 00 Prague, Czech Republic
†In 1039 Bohemia achieved a key military victory in Gniezno, the capital city of Poland. According to Bohemian tradition among the spoils of victory returned to Bohemia following this victory were the relics of St Adalbert. In the spring of 2014 a special ceremony was held to honor these relics. During this ceremony some of the relics were placed within a new ornamental-house shaped reliquary. This reliquary was then placed within the *Old Archbishop's Chapel* in the cathedral. The skull of the saint, which is kept separate, was placed within the *Hilbert Treasury*. The remaining relics remain within *St Vitus Cathedral* and rest within an altar located to the left of the main sanctuary. A sign in Czech located below this altar reads 'Ostatky Svatého Vojtěcha Druhého Pražského Biskupa (982-997)'. (As noted on the following page this Bohemian tradition is disputed by the *Gniezno Cathedral* which continues to claim possession of St Adalbert's relics.)
†A relic of the head of St Luke is preserved in this church. It was brought here by Charles IV in 1354. A recent study on this relic was conducted at the request of Archbishop Antonio Mattiazzo of Padua in 1998. This study seems to suggest that the authentic relic of St Luke's head is the one located here and not the one found in the Treasury Museum of *St Peter's Basilica* in Rome, Italy.
†St Wenceslaus, a 10th century duke of Bohemia, is buried within a large chapel on the right side of the nave. Frescoes upon the wall of this chapel depict scenes from his life including his martyrdom. Each year on September 28th the relic of his skull is processed from *St Vitus Cathedral* to the church where he was martyred in Stará Boleslav. This twelve mile walk is well attended and includes the Castle Guards of the Prague Castle.

✝The remains of St John of Nepomuk (d. 1393) rest within a beautiful tomb just to the right of the main sanctuary. The tomb's odd placement creates a bottleneck for the pilgrims who are making their rounds through the church. His tomb is marked 'Stříbrný Náhrobek Svatého Jana Nepomuckého (1345-1393)'. Also outside of the cathedral upon *Charles Bridge* is a large statue of St John of Nepomuk. This statue marks the spot where St John was thrown to his death in 997 for refusing to betray the seal of Confession.

Gniezno Cathedral
Jana Łaskiego 9
62-200 Gniezno, Poland
✝This church continues to claim possession of the relics of St Adalbert despite the Bohemian tradition noted previously. These relics rest within the prominent silver tomb in the main sanctuary.

Andrew, apostle (November 30ᵗʰ)

St Andrew (Relics: Patras, Greece; Amalfi, Italy; Florence, Italy; Edinburgh, Scotland; Cologne, Germany; Kiev, Ukraine)

St Andrew's Church
Андріївський узвіз, 23
Kiev, Ukraine 02000
✝Legend holds that St Andrew's apostolic zeal led him as far north as Ukraine where he placed a cross in the very spot where this church now stands. The present church was erected in the 18th century and houses a small relic of St Andrew.

Bridget, religious (July 23ʳᵈ)

St Bridget (d. 1373, Rome, Italy) (Relics: Rome, Italy; Vadstena, Sweden)

Vadstena Klosterkyrka (Vadstena Abbey)
Lasarettsgatan
59230 Vadstena, Sweden
✝Relics of St Bridget were transferred here in 1374. They rest within the chapel in the right transept.

Casimir (March 4th)

St Casimir (d. 1484, Hrodna, Belarus) (Relics: Vilnius, Lithuania)

Vilnius Cathedral
Cathedral Square
01122 Vilnius, Lithuania
✝St Casimir was greatly beloved by the faithful in his country. If not for his early death at the age of twenty-five he would have become the King of Poland. He is remembered in particular for his exceptional piety and humility. His remains now rest in Vilnius, Lithuania and are placed within a silver sarcophagus in this church.

Faustina Kowalska

St Faustina Kowalska
(d. 1938, Kraków,
Poland) (Relics:
Kraków, Poland)

Sanktuarium Bożego Miłosierdzia (Shrine of
Divine Mercy)
Siostry Faustyny 3
30-420 Kraków, Poland
✝The remains of St
Faustina, to whom Jesus
revealed the
inexhaustible limits of His Divine Mercy, rest within the chapel at this convent. They are placed within a white urn located under an image of Divine Mercy just to the left of the main sanctuary. The original tomb of St Faustina can be visited in the cemetery adjacent to the new church.

John Chrysostom, bishop and doctor (September 13ᵗʰ)

St John Chrysostom (d. 407, NE Turkey) (Relics: Rome, Italy; Florence, Italy; Istanbul, Turkey; Moscow, Russia; Mount Athos, Greece)

Cathedral of Christ the Savior
ул. Волхонка, 15
119019 Moscow, Russia
✝The skull of St John Chrysostom is enshrined within this church. It was gifted to this church in the 17ᵗʰ century.

John of Kanty, priest (December 23ʳᵈ)

St John of Kanty (d. 1473, Kraków, Poland) (Relics: Kraków, Poland)

Church of St Anne
św. Anny 11
30-962 Kraków, Poland
✝St John of Kanty, a professor of theology and a parish priest, is buried in the right transept of this church. In Polish his tomb is marked as (św. Jan z Kęt).

Methodius, bishop (February 14ᵗʰ)

St Methodius (d. 885, Velehrad, Czech Republic)

Velehrad Monastery
Stojanovo nádvoří 206,
687 06 Velehrad, Czech Republic
✝After St Cyril's death St Methodius returned to Moravia where he zealously spread the Faith until his passing in 885 AD. A church was subsequently constructed over his tomb. However, both the church and his tomb were later destroyed. This monastery now stands in proximity to St Methodius' original resting place.

Norbert, bishop (June 6ᵗʰ)

St Norbert (d. 1134, Saxony-Anhalt, Germany) (Relics: Prague, Czech Republic)

Strahov Monastery
Strahovské Nádvoří 132/1
118 00 Prague, Czech Republic
✝The relics of St Norbert, who founded the Norbertine Order and later became the bishop of Magdeburg, Germany, were transferred from Magdeburg to this monastery in 1627. Since 1873 these relics have rested within a beautifully crafted gilded sarcophagus placed above the main altar of the large chapel located on the right side of the nave of this church.

Stanislaus, bishop and martyr (April 11ᵗʰ)

St Stanislaus (d. 1079, Kraków, Poland) (Relics: Kraków, Poland)

Wawel Cathedral
Wawel 3
31-001 Kraków, Poland
✝The remains of St Stanislaus rest within this church. They are placed within an exquisite silver-plated coffin located above the main altar in the center of this church. St Stanislaus was martyred by the King of Poland, Bolesław II, after he had placed the king under excommunication.
✝St John Paul II was ordained a priest in 1946 and celebrated his first Mass in the crypt of this church. It was also here where he was consecrated bishop.

Stephen of Hungary (August 16ᵗʰ)

St Stephen of Hungary (d. 1038, Hungary) (Relics: Budapest, Hungary)

St Stephen's Cathedral
Szent István tér 1
1051 Budapest, Hungary
✝The right hand of St Stephen of Hungary rests within an ornate reliquary in a chapel to the left of the main sanctuary.

First Class Relics Outside Of Italy

Other Countries To The South & East Of Italy

** ** ** ** ** ** ** **

First Class Relics
To The South & East Of Italy
(For The Saints On The Roman Catholic Liturgical Calendar)

Andrew, apostle	John Damascene, priest
Anthony, abbot	John the Baptist, martyr
Athanasius, bishop and doctor	John of Capistrano, priest
Augustine, bishop and doctor	Korean martyrs
Barnabas, apostle	Lazarus*
Basil the Great, bishop and doctor	Luke, evangelist
Blaise, bishop and martyr	Mark, evangelist
Catherine of Alexandria, virgin and martyr	Paul, apostle
Charles Lwanga and Companions	Paul Miki and Companions
Francis Xavier, priest	Perpetua and Felicity, martyrs
George, martyr	Sharbel Makhluf, priest
Gregory Nazianzen, bishop and doctor	Thomas, apostle
James the Greater, apostle	Titus, bishop
James the Less, apostle	Vietnamese martyrs
John Chrysostom, bishop and doctor	

Includes the Following Countries: Algeria, Croatia, Cyprus, Egypt, Greece, India, Israel, Japan, Lebanon, Malaysia, Malta, South Korea, Syria, Tunisia, Turkey, and Uganda

Note: The Saints marked with an (*) are not on the Roman Catholic Liturgical Calendar.

Andrew, apostle (November 30th)

St Andrew (Relics:
Amalfi, Italy; Florence,
Italy; Patras, Greece;
Edinburgh, Scotland;
Cologne, Germany;
Kiev, Ukraine)

**Basilica of Saint
Andrew**
Αγίου Ανδρέου
Patras, Greece
✝Tradition holds that St
Andrew was martyred
upon an X shaped cross in Patras, Greece. Remnants of this cross are preserved
within this church to the left of the main sanctuary.
✝In 1964 the skull of St Andrew was returned to this church from *St Peter's
Basilica* in Rome, Italy. This relic now rests within a beautiful shrine to the
right of the main sanctuary.
✝Also venerated here are several additional relics of St Andrew including his
finger.

Anthony, abbot (January 17th)

St Anthony (d. 356, Mt. Colzim, Egypt) (Relics: Zaafarana, Egypt; Saint-
Antoine l'Abbaye, France; Arles, France)

Saint Anthony's Monastery
Zaafarana, Egypt
✝A tradition holds that this monastery was built directly over the tomb of St
Anthony. However, since he had requested to be buried secretly in an
unmarked grave this claim is uncertain.

Athanasius, bishop and doctor (May 2ⁿᵈ) and Mark, evangelist (April 25ᵗʰ)

St Athanasius (d. 373, Alexandria, Egypt) (Relics: Venice, Italy; Cairo, Egypt)

St Mark (d. Alexandria, Egypt) (Relics: Venice, Italy; Cairo, Egypt; Reichenau, Germany)

St Mark's Coptic Orthodox Cathedral
Al Abbasiya, Cairo, Egypt
✝In 1968 Pope Paul VI gave some of the Venetian relics of St Mark to the Coptic Orthodox Patriarch of Alexandria. They are now kept at this church in Cairo. A similar situation happened in 1973 when some relics of St Athanasius were likewise returned to the Coptic Orthodox Patriarch of Alexandria. These relics are also kept at this same church.

Augustine, bishop and doctor (August 28ᵗʰ)

St Augustine (d. 430, Annaba, Algeria) (Relics: Pavia, Italy; Annaba, Algeria)

Basilique Saint-Augustin (Basilica of Saint Augustine)
Annaba, Algeria
✝This magnificent basilica was completed in 1881 and rests upon a hill overlooking the ruins of the ancient city of Hippo. In 1842 several arm bones of St Augustine, the former bishop of Hippo, were returned to this city. These bones now rest within a glass tube inserted into the arm of a life-size marble statue of the saint.

Barnabas, apostle (June 11ᵗʰ)

St Barnabas (d. Cyprus) (Relics: Famagusta, Cyprus)

Monastery of St Barnabas
Famagusta, Cyprus
✝Tradition claims that the remains of St Barnabas rest within a tomb in this monastery. His relics, according to legend, were discovered in 488 AD by the Archbishop of Constantia. According to this legend St Barnabas appeared to the Archbishop in a dream and revealed to him the location of his tomb. Upon opening the tomb a manuscript of St Matthew's Gospel was found resting upon St Barnabas' breast.

Basil the Great, bishop and doctor (January 2ⁿᵈ)

St Basil the Great (d. 379, Caesarea) (Relics: Mount Athos, Greece; Bruges, Belgium)

Monastery of Great Lavra
Mount Athos, Greece
✝This monastery is located at the southeastern foot of Mount Athos.
✝The skull of St Basil the Great rests in this monastery.

Blaise, bishop and martyr (February 3ʳᵈ)

St Blaise (d. 316, Armenia) (Relics: Rome, Italy; Maratea, Italy; Dubrovnik, Croatia)

Dubrovnik Cathedral
20000 Općina Dubrovnik, Croatia
✝Relics of St Blaise are kept within precious reliquaries in this church. On February 2ⁿᵈ and 3ʳᵈ they are removed from the church and joyfully processed throughout the city during the Festival of St Blaise.

Catherine of Alexandria, virgin and martyr (November 25ᵗʰ)

St Catherine of Alexandria (d. 305, Alexandria, Egypt) (Relics: Mount Catherine, Egypt)

Saint Catherine's Monastery
Mount Catherine, Egypt
✝This is the oldest continually inhabited Christian monastery in the world. It has never been destroyed and can trace its history back seventeen centuries. Tradition claims that this monastery rests upon the land where God spoke to Moses in the burning bush and at the foot of the mountain where Moses received the Ten Commandments.
✝As for the relics of St Catherine a tradition claims that a monk at this monastery saw in a vision angels carrying the body of St Catherine to the top of the highest mountain in Sinai. The monks then miraculously found her body as the vision indicated and subsequently buried her body in this monastery. Today these relics rest within a marble reliquary at an altar to the right of the main sanctuary.

✝In the early 11ᵗʰ century the monk, Symeon Pentaglosses, brought one finger of St Catherine of Alexandria to Rouen, France. A church was built to house this relic. Since that time, however, this French church has been destroyed and the relic lost.

Charles Lwanga and Companions, martyrs (June 3ʳᵈ)

Honored on this day are 22 martyrs who died in Uganda from the years 1885-1887. (Relics: Namugongo, Uganda)

Uganda Martyrs Shrine
Namugongo, Uganda
✝This shrine is built upon the spot where St Charles Lwanga suffered martyrdom. Also preserved here are additional relics from other Ugandan martyrs who lost their lives during this same persecution.

Cyril of Jerusalem, bishop and doctor (March 18ᵗʰ)

St Cyril of Jerusalem (d. 386, Israel)

Eleona / Église du Pater Noster
(Church of the Our Father)
Mount of Olives
91190 Jerusalem, Israel
✝St Cyril of Jerusalem and many other early patriarchs of Jerusalem were buried in a church called the *Apostoleion* located upon the Mount of Olives. At some point this church was destroyed and the relics lost. Today a French Carmelite Monastery called *Eleona* rests upon this land. Even though St Cyril's remains are lost this church is notable for its proximity to his ancient burial site.

Francis Xavier, priest (December 3rd)

St Francis Xavier (d. 1552, Shangchuan Island, China) (Relics: Rome, Italy; Goa, India; Antwerp, Belgium)

Basilica of Bom Jesus
Near Gandhi Circle
403402 Old Goa, Goa, India
✝The body of St Francis Xavier rests within a casket in the right transept of this church.

George, martyr (April 23rd)

St George (d. 303, Lydda, Palestine) (Relics: Lod, Israel; Rome, Italy)

Church of St George
Lod (Lydda), Israel
✝St George was an early Christian martyr who died in this city. Many shrines throughout the world now claim possession of his relics. Preserved within the crypt of this church are St George's original tomb and a few relics accredited to him.

Gregory Nazianzen, bishop and doctor (January 2nd) and John Chrysostom, bishop and doctor (September 13th)

St Gregory Nazianzen (d. 389, Cappadocia) (Relics: Rome, Italy; Istanbul, Turkey; Mount Athos, Greece; Lisbon, Portugal)

St John Chrysostom (d. 407, NE Turkey) (Relics: Rome, Italy; Florence, Italy; Istanbul, Turkey; Moscow, Russia; Mount Athos, Greece)

Cathedral of St George (Ecumenical Patriarchate)
Yavuz Sultan Selim Mh.
34083 Fatih/Istanbul Province, Turkey
✝On November 27, 2004 a major part of the relics of St Gregory Nazianzen and of St John Chrysostom were returned to the Ecumenical Patriarch of Constantinople by St John Paul II and placed within this church.

Vatopedi Monastery
Mount Athos, Greece
†The skulls of both St Gregory Nazianzen and St John Chrysostom are said to rest within this monastery. They are preserved within ornate reliquaries.

James the Greater, apostle (July 25th) and James the Less, apostle (May 3rd)

St James the Greater – The brother of St John the Evangelist (d. 44) (Relics: Santiago de Compostela, Spain; Jerusalem, Israel)

St James the Less – The cousin of the Lord and the son of Alphaeus. (d. 62) (Relics: Rome, Italy; Jerusalem, Israel)

St James Cathedral
Armenian Quarter
91190 Jerusalem, Israel
†St James the Less is purportedly buried next to his reputed throne on the left side of the main sanctuary. This is the large chair below the onion-shaped baldacchino.
†The head of St James the Greater is said to rest under a small circular piece of red marble located within the third chapel on the left side of the nave. This chapel is also said to mark the location of his martyrdom.
†Access to this church is limited. It is generally open for only forty minutes during the Vigil service at the 3pm hour.

Tomb of the Sons of Hezir
Kidron Valley
Jerusalem, Israel
†This tomb was traditionally attributed to St James the Less. However, recent scholarship concludes that is was constructed to honor a Jewish priestly family from the 2nd century BC.

Joachim and Anne, parents of The Blessed Virgin Mary - July 26th

St Anne (Relics: Apt, France; Bologna, Italy; Sainte-Anne d'Auray, France; Sainte-Anne de Beaupré, Quebec, Canada; Vienna, Austria)

Church of St Anne
91190 Jerusalem, Israel
✝Formerly this church was called *St Mary in Probatica.*

✝Tradition claims that this church rests over the house of Saints Joachim and Anne. Thus it is presumed that the Blessed Virgin Mary was born here. The crypt below this church honors this tradition. Also located just outside of this church is the Pool of Bethesda where Jesus healed a man who had been ill for thirty-eight years.
✝Historically the tombs of Saints Joachim and Anne have also been thought to rest below this church. However, at present this tradition is not noted in the church.

John Damascene, priest and doctor - December 4th

St John Damascene (d. 750, Jerusalem) (Relics: Mar Saba Monastery)

Mar Saba Monastery
✝Located in a remote area eighteen miles south-east of Jerusalem.
✝St John Damascene, like his father before him, held a high position as a civil-servant in Damascus. However, at some point in the early 8th century he left this to become a monk at *Mar Saba Monastery.* Upon his death he was buried in this monastery where his remains are said to still be located.

John of Capistrano, priest – October 23rd

St John of Capistrano (d. 1456, Ilok, Croatia) (Relics: Ilok, Croatia)

The Friary of St John of Capistrano
Ilok, Croatia
✝St John of Capistrano played an important role in organizing a crusade against the Ottoman Turks at the Battle of Belgrade in 1456. Shortly thereafter he succumbed to a plague and died in this friary. His relics remain here today.

John the Baptist, martyr (June 24th, August 29th)

St John the Baptist (Relics: Rome, Italy; Florence, Italy; Amiens, France; Munich, Germany; Damascus, Syria)

Umayyad Mosque
Souq Al Hamidya Street
Damascus, Syria
✝Relics of St John the Baptist, including his skull, rest within a shrine in this mosque. The authenticity of these relics are uncertain since the skull of St John the Baptist is also said to be located at a number of other places throughout the world including the *Cathedral of Amiens* in France, *San Silvestro in Capite* in Rome, Italy, and the *Residenz Museum* in Munich, Germany.

Cathedral of St John the Baptist
✝This cathedral, which is in ruins, is located in the ancient Samarian city of Sebastia. A tradition going back to the 4th century places the tomb of St John the Baptist in a crypt below this church. This crypt can still be visited.

Joseph, husband of Mary (March 19th)

Tradition and Scripture are silent with regard to the death of St Joseph. However, a possible location of his burial is a 1st century tomb located in Nazareth beneath the *Sisters of Nazareth Convent* next door to the Franciscan *Casa Nova*.

Korean martyrs (September 20th)

Honored on this day are 103 martyrs who died in Korea from the years 1839-1867. (Relics: Mirinaeseongji-ro, South Korea; Seoul, South Korea)

Mirinae Shrine
420 Mirinaeseongji-ro, Yangseong-myeon,
Anseong-si, Gyeonggi-do, South Korea
✝The remains of St Andrew Kim Taegon rest in a cemetery near this shrine. Within this same cemetery are the remains of Bishop Ferréol who ordained St Andrew Kim Taegon as Korea's first native-born priest.

Songsin Theological Campus (The Catholic University of Korea)
296-12 Changgyeonggung-ro,
Jongno-gu, Seoul, South Korea
✝Some small relics of St Andrew Kim Taegon are preserved here.
✝Note: Within Seoul the following shrines also honor the Korean martyrs: Myeongdong Cathedral, Seosomun Martyrs' Shrine, Danggogae Martyrs' Shrine, Saenamteo Martyrs' Shrine, and Jeoldusan Martyrs' Shrine.

Lazarus

St Lazarus (Relics: Marseille, France; Larnaca, Cyprus)

As noted previously a 13th century legend claims that Lazarus reached the shores of France and became the first bishop of Marseille. A separate tradition claims that he settled in Cyprus where he became the bishop of modern day Larnaca.

Church of Saint Lazarus
Larnaca, Cyprus
✝Tradition claims that the tomb of St Lazarus was discovered in this city in the 9th century. Records depict that his remains were later transferred to Constantinople; however, this church in Larnaca continues to claim the possession of his relics.

Tomb of Lazarus

†Jesus raised Lazarus from the dead in the small city of Bethany just east of Jerusalem. During the time of Jesus this city was within walking distance of Jerusalem. However, today because of the large wall separating Israel from the West Bank this walk is impossible. The tomb, nevertheless, can still be visited. It is located in the modern day city of Bethany which has been renamed Eizariya. In Arabic this means Lazarus.

Luke, evangelist (October 18th)

St Luke (Relics: Rome, Italy; Padua, Italy; Prague, Czech Republic; Thebes, Greece)

St Luke is believed to have died in Thebes, Greece during the latter part of the first century. Records then indicate the transfer of his remains to Constantinople in the fourth century. From here one theory suggests that his remains were transferred to Padua during the Iconoclastic persecutions in the 8th century. Documented proof of their presence in Padua surfaces by the year 1177 when a tomb is unearthed next to *Santa Giustina* bearing the symbols of St Luke. Papal recognition of these relics followed soon after.

Church of St Luke
Thebes, Greece
†This church is located near an old cemetery southeast of the ancient citadel called the Cadmea.
†The original tomb of St Luke rests here.
†Recently a rib bone was taken from the body of St Luke in Padua, Italy and given to this church.

Paul, apostle (January 25th)

(Relics: Rome, Italy; Valletta, Malta)

St Paul's Shipwreck Church
74 St Paul's Street
1212 Valletta, Malta
†A wrist bone of St Paul rests within a reliquary in the right transept of this church. Also to the right of the main sanctuary is part of the pillar to which St Paul was tied when he was martyred.

Paul Miki and Companions, martyrs (February 6th)

Honored on this day are 26 martyrs who died by crucifixion in Nagasaki, Japan in 1597. (Relics: Nagasaki, Japan)

Twenty-Six Martyrs Church
Nagasaki, Japan
✝Nearly all of the remains of the 26 martyrs honored on this day were destroyed after their martyrdom. However, one remaining relic of a bone has survived and rests within this shrine. This bone belongs to Jacob Kisai, a Jesuit lay brother.
✝The museum of this church also holds additional items that are connected to the 26 martyrs.

Perpetua and Felicity, martyrs (March 7th)

Saint Perpetua (d. 203, Carthage, Tunisia) (Relics: Carthage, Tunisia; Vierzon, France)

Saint Felicity (d. 203, Carthage, Tunisia) (Relics: Carthage, Tunisia)

Basilica Maiorum
Carthage, Tunisia
✝This ancient church was erected over the original tombs of Saints Perpetua and Felicity.

Philip, apostle (May 3rd)

St Philip – (Relics: Rome, Italy; Florence, Italy)

In July of 2011 it was reported that archaeologists had discovered the original tomb of Saint Philip in Hierapolis, Denizli, Turkey.

Sharbel Makhluf, priest (July 24th)

St Sharbel Makhluf (d. 1898, Annaya, Jbeil District, Lebanon) (Relics: Annaya, Lebanon)

Monastery of St Maron
Annaya, Jbeil District, Lebanon
✝St Sharbel Makhluf was a Maronite monk who lived the last 23 years of his life in a hermitage near this monastery. His remains now rest within this monastery.

Stephen, first martyr (December 26th)

St Stephen
(Relics: Rome, Italy)

St Stephen was martyred in Jerusalem shortly after the death and resurrection of Christ. The earliest tradition places the location of his martyrdom on the northern edge of the Old City where the present Damascus Gate is located. At the time of St Stephen's death this location would have been just outside of the city walls. The Byzantines later expanded Jerusalem and named the present Damascus Gate after St Stephen to honor the location of his martyrdom. In the 16th century the Ottoman Turks rebuilt the walls and gave this gate its current name. A later tradition places the martyrdom near the Lion's Gate on the eastern edge of the city. This tradition is commemorated by a small chapel built over a small outcropping of stone at *St Stephen's Orthodox Church*. This chapel is accessed by a side entrance along the church's northern edge. One then descends a flight of stairs to the chapel. Opening hours for this chapel are irregular. The relics of St Stephen, like the location of his martyrdom, have also been tied to various traditions. The tomb of St Stephen is said to have been miraculously discovered in Jerusalem in 415 AD through a special revelation given to a priest named Lucian. St Stephen's relics were then placed within the now-destroyed

Church of Holy Zion which was located in the south-west corner of the city. Then in 439 AD they were translated to a newly constructed Byzantine church just north of Jerusalem's walls near the Damascus Gate. This Byzantine church was destroyed by the Persians in 614 AD and the relics lost. A new church built over the ruins of this ancient church, called the *Basilique de Saint-Étienne*, was dedicated in 1900. It honors the memory of Stephen. At some point relics of St Stephen were purportedly transferred westward to Europe. They are now found in many different cities. Among these is Rome where a long-standing tradition holds that a large portion of his remains rest in *San Lorenzo fuori le Mura.*

Basilique de Saint-Étienne (Basilica of St Stephen)
6 Nablus Road
91190 Jerusalem, Israel
✝As noted above this church honors the memory of St Stephen.

Greek Orthodox Church of St Stephen
Kidron Valley
91190 Jerusalem, Israel
✝As noted above a chapel just below this church marks a possible location of St Stephen's martyrdom.

Thomas, apostle (July 3ʳᵈ)

St Thomas (Relics: Rome, Italy; Ortona, Italy; Mylapore, India)

A tradition holds that in the 3rd century the bones of St Thomas the Apostle were taken from India and brought to Edessa, Turkey. In 1258 they were transferred to Ortona, Italy.

San Thome Basilica
19/38, Santhome High Road
600004 Mylapore, Chennai, Tamil Nadu, India
✝Tradition holds that St Thomas the Apostle preached in this region and was martyred on St Thomas Mount.
✝This church is built over the tomb of St Thomas. The tomb is empty; however, a few small relics of St Thomas rest within the church.

Titus, bishop (January 26ᵗʰ)

St Titus (Relics: Heraklion, Crete, Greece)

The Church of St Titus
Αγίου Τίτου
Heraklion, Crete, Greece
✝St Titus is revered as the first bishop of Crete. He is said to have been buried on this island in Cortyna. Later his remains were transferred to Constantinople and his skull to Venice. In 1966 his skull was returned to Crete and placed within this church in Heraklion.

Vietnamese Martyrs (November 24ᵗʰ)

More than 100,000 Vietnamese Catholics died for their faith during the seventeenth, eighteenth, and nineteenth centuries. One hundred seventeen of these martyrs were canonized in 1988 and are honored on this day. A further martyr, Blessed Andrew Phú Yên, was beatified in the year 2000. (Relics: Paris, France; Penang, Malaysia)

College General Major Seminary
Jalan Cengai
11200 Tanjung Bungah, Penang, Malaysia
✝Preserved here are relics from the Vietnamese martyrs including some who were alumni from this college.

First Class Relics Outside Of Italy

The Americas

** ** ** ** ** ** ** **

First Class Relics In The Americas
(For The Saints On The Roman Catholic Liturgical Calendar)

Andre Bessette, religious
Anne, mother of The Virgin Mary
Christopher Magallanes and Companions
Damien Joseph de Veuster
Elizabeth Ann Seton, religious
Frances Xavier Cabrini, virgin
Francis Xavier Seelos, priest (Blessed)
John Neumann, bishop
Jude, apostle
Junipero Serra, priest (Blessed)
Kateri Tekakwitha

Katharine Drexel, virgin
Marianne Cope, virgin
Marie Rose Durocher, virgin (Blessed)
Martin de Porres, religious
Miguel Agustin Pro, priest and
   martyr (Blessed)
North American Martyrs
Peter Claver, priest
Rose of Lima, virgin
Rose Philippine Duchesne, virgin
Turibius de Mongrovejo, bishop

André Bessette, religious (January 6th)*

St André Bessette (d. 1937, Montreal, Quebec, Canada) (Relics: Montreal, Quebec, Canada)

L'Oratoire Saint-Joseph Du Mont-Royal
(St Joseph's Oratory of Mount Royal)
3800 Chemin Queen Mary
Montreal, Quebec, H3V 1H6, Canada
†A relic of St André Bessette's heart is kept within the museum of this church. His body rests within a large black marble tomb in the votive chapel within the lower church.

Anne, mother of The Blessed Virgin Mary (July 26th)

(Relics: Apt, France; Bologna, Italy; Sainte-Anne d'Auray, France; Sainte-Anne de Beaupré, Quebec, Canada; Vienna, Austria)

Sanctuaire Sainte-Anne de Beaupré
(Sanctuary of Saint Anne of Beaupré)
10018 Avenue Royale
Sainte-Anne de Beaupré, Quebec, G0A C30, Canada
†During the last four centuries this shrine has obtained three relics of St Anne. In 1670 it obtained a portion of a bone from her finger. Then in 1892 and again in 1960 the shrine received two separate forearm bones. One of these forearm bones is currently enshrined in the left transept of the upper church.

Christopher Magallanes, priest and martyr, and Companions, martyrs (May 21st)

Honored on this day are 25 martyrs who died in Mexico from the years 1915-1937. (Relics: Totatiche, Mexico)

Parroquia de Nuestra Señora del Rosario
(Parish of Our Lady of the Rosary)
Totatiche, Mexico
†Relics of St Christopher Magallanes rest within a golden urn in this church. In 1927 he was arrested by Mexican officials while he was on his way to celebrate Mass. A few days later he was shot without a trial.

Damien Joseph de Veuster of Moloka'i, priest (May 10th)*

St Damien Joseph de Veuster of Moloka'i (d. 1889) (Relics: Leuven, Belgium; Kalawao, Hawaii, USA; Honolulu, Hawaii, USA)

St Philomena Church
Kalawao, Hawaii, USA
✝St Damien Joseph de Veuster faithfully and heroically served the leper community in Moloka'i, Hawaii for over fifteen years before finally succumbing himself to the disease. In 1995 the right hand of St Damien Joseph was returned to Hawaii and placed within his original tomb located in the cemetery at this church.

Cathedral of Our Lady of Peace
1184 Bishop Street
Honolulu, Hawaii, 96813, USA
✝During the canonization of St Damien Joseph in 2009 a bone fragment from his heel was given to the Hawaiian Catholic Church. Today this relic is enshrined in this cathedral. It is located within a glass case to the right of the main sanctuary.

Elizabeth Ann Seton, religious (January 4th)*

St Elizabeth Ann Seton (d. 1821, Emmitsburg, Maryland, USA) (Relics: Emmitsburg, Maryland, USA)

National Shrine of St Elizabeth Ann Seton
339 S. Seton Avenue
Emmitsburg, Maryland, 21727, USA
✝The remains of St Elizabeth Ann Seton rest within this shrine. It was here that she established the *Sisters of Charity of St Joseph* which was the first religious order of women founded in America. This community adopted the rules written by St Vincent de Paul in the 17th century for the *Daughters of Charity* in France. In 1850 the Emmitsburg community officially united with this French community and are now known as the *Daughters of Charity*.

Frances Xavier Cabrini, virgin* (November 13th)

St Frances Xavier Cabrini (d. 1917, Chicago, Illinois, USA) (Relics: New York City, New York, USA; Chicago, Illinois, USA; Rome, Italy; Codogno, Italy; Sant'Angelo Lodigiano, Italy)

St Frances Xavier Cabrini Shrine
701 Fort Washington Avenue
New York City, New York, 10040, USA
✝A life-size representation of St Frances Xavier Cabrini rests below the main altar of the church at this shrine. Within this simulation is a large portion of the extant remains of St Frances.

The National Shrine of St Frances Xavier Cabrini
2520 N. Lakeview Avenue
Chicago, Illinois, 60614, USA
✝An arm bone of St Frances Xavier Cabrini is enshrined beneath the main altar of the church at this shrine.

Francis Xavier Seelos, priest* (October 5th)

Blessed Francis Xavier Seelos (d. 1867, New Orleans, Louisiana, USA) (Relics: New Orleans, Louisiana, USA)

National Shrine of Blessed Francis Xavier Seelos
919 Josephine Street
New Orleans, Louisiana, USA 70130
*The remains of Blessed Francis Xavier Seelos rest within an ornate house-like reliquary within this shrine.

John de Brebeuf and Isaac Jogues, priests and martyrs, and Companions, martyrs (October 19th)*

Honored on this day are eight Jesuit martyrs who died in North America from the years 1642-1649. (Relics: Midland, Ontario, Canada)

The Martyr's Shrine
16163 Highway 12 West
Midland, Ontario, L4R 4K6, Canada
†The skull of St John de Brebeuf and some small bone fragments from St Gabriel Lalemant and St Charles Garnier rest within two reliquaries in the left transept. These are the only extant relics of the eight Jesuit martyrs honored on this day.

John Neumann, bishop (January 5th)*

St John Neumann (d. 1860, Philadelphia, Pennsylvania, USA) (Relics: Philadelphia, Pennsylvania, USA)

National Shrine of St John Neumann
1019 N. 5th Street
Philadelphia, Pennsylvania, 19123, USA
†The body of St John Neumann is enshrined under the main altar.

Jude, apostle (October 28th)

St Jude (Relics: Rome, Italy; Chicago, Illinois, USA)

National Shrine of St Jude
3200 East 91st Street
Chicago, Illinois, 60617, USA
†Two bone fragments of St Jude rest within this church. They are located at the *Altar of St Jude* on the right side of the main sanctuary. The larger fragment is placed within a reliquary above the altar. The smaller piece is positioned on the kneeler directly in front of the altar.

Junipero Serra, priest (July 1ˢᵗ)*

Blessed Junipero Serra (d. 1784, Carmel, California, USA) (Relics: Carmel, California, USA)

Mission San Carlos Borromeo
3080 Rio Road
Carmel, California, 93923, USA
✝ At the age of thirty-six Blessed Junipero Serra left Spain to enter the mission fields of the New World. After spending many years in Mexico he was transferred to California where he established a total of nine missions and evangelized many of the natives. It was at this mission in Carmel, which he had established in 1770, that he eventually died. His body is now buried beneath the sanctuary floor of this church.

Kateri Tekakwitha - (July 14ᵗʰ)*

St Kateri Tekakwitha (d. 1680, Kahnawake, Quebec, Canada) (Relics: Kahnawake, Quebec, Canada)

St Francis Xavier Mission
1 Church Street
Kahnawake, Quebec, J0L 1B0, Canada
✝ The remains of St Kateri Tekakwitha rest within this church.

Katharine Drexel, virgin (March 3ʳᵈ)*

St Katharine Drexel (d. 1955, Philadelphia, Pennsylvania, USA) (Relics: Bensalem, Pennsylvania, USA)

National Shrine of Katharine Drexel
1663 Bristol Pike
Bensalem, Pennsylvania, 19020, USA
✝ The body of St Katharine Drexel rests at this shrine under the main altar of the *Saint Elizabeth Chapel*.

Marianne Cope, virgin* (January 23rd)

St Marianne Cope (d. 1918, Kalaupapa, Hawaii, USA) (Relics: Syracuse, New York, USA)

Shrine & Museum of Saint Marianne Cope
St Anthony Convent
1024 Court Street
Syracuse, New York, 13208, USA
†The remains of St Marianne Cope rest at this shrine within a large reliquary in the convent chapel. It was here in Syracuse in 1862 that she joined the _Sisters of St Francis_. Fifteen years later she became the mother general of this community. Despite her many responsibilities, in 1883 she embraced a call to take charge of several hospitals and schools in Hawaii including those at a leper colony in Moloka'i. It was here that she helped assist St Damien Joseph de Veuster in caring for the lepers.

Marie Rose Durocher, virgin* (October 6th)

Blessed Marie Rose Durocher (d. 1849, Longueuil, Quebec, Canada) (Relics: Longueuil, Quebec, Canada)

Co-Cathédrale Saint-Antoine de Padoue
(St Anthony of Padua Co-Cathedral)
55 Sainte Elizabeth Rue
Longueuil, Quebec, 74H 1J3, Canada
†The remains of Blessed Marie Rose Durocher rest within the right transept in the _Marie Rose Chapel_. It was in this city that she founded the _Sisters of the Holy Names of Jesus and Mary_ with the charism of providing a Christian education to the poor and the needy.

Martin de Porres, religious (November 3rd) and Rose of Lima, virgin (August 23rd)

St Martin de Porres (d. 1639, Lima, Peru) (Relics: Lima, Peru)

St Rose of Lima (d. 1617, Lima, Peru) (Relics: Lima, Peru)

Convento de Santo Domingo (Convent of Saint Dominic)
Jr. Camaná 170
Lima, Peru
✝The remains of three prominent Peruvian saints rest within this convent. The tomb of St Martin de Porres is located within a chapel in the convent's second cloister. St Rose of Lima is buried in the crypt below the Chapter House. Also located at this convent are the remains of St John Macías (d. 1645).

Miguel Agustin Pro, priest and martyr* (November 23rd)

Blessed Miguel Agustin Pro (d. 1927, Mexico City, Mexico) (Relics: Mexico City, Mexico)

Parroquia de la Sagrada Familia
(Parish of the Holy Family)
Calle Puebla 144
Colonia Roma, Mexico City, 06700, Mexico
✝The remains of Blessed Miguel Agustin Pro rest within a silver reliquary to the right of the main sanctuary.

Peter Claver, priest (September 9ᵗʰ)*

St Peter Claver (d. 1654, Cartagena, Colombia) (Relics: Cartagena, Colombia)

Iglesia de San Pedro Claver (Church of St Peter Claver)
Carrera 4
Cartagena, Colombia
†The remains of St Peter Claver rest under the main altar of this church. For forty years he attended to the many slaves who arrived in the city upon slave ships. Through his ministry he would offer at least a glimmer of hope and love before they were carted off to the auction blocks. It is estimated that during his life he baptized over 300,000 of these individuals.

Rose Philippine Duchesne, virgin (November 18ᵗʰ)*

St Rose Philippine Duchesne (d. 1852, St Charles, Missouri, USA) (Relics: St Charles, Missouri, USA)

Shrine of Saint Rose Philippine Duchesne
619 North Second Street
St Charles, Missouri, 63301, USA
†The remains of St Rose Philippine Duchesne rest at this church within a marble sarcophagus on the right side of the nave. In 1818 she left her native France and came to America where she began establishing schools in Missouri and Louisiana. In 1852 at the age of 83 she passed away in St Charles, Missouri.

Turibius of Mogrovejo, bishop (March 23rd)

St Turibius (d. 1606, Sana, Peru) (Relics: Lima, Peru)

Capilla del Palacio Arzobispal de Lima
(Chapel of the Archbishop's Palace of Lima)
Plaza de Armas de Lima
Lima, Peru
✝Some bones of St Turibius are preserved within a reliquary in this chapel. On his feast day these relics are often presented for public veneration within the *Lima Cathedral*. St Turibius was known for his evangelical activity as the Archbishop of Lima. During his time in Peru he is said to have baptized over 500,000 individuals including St Rose of Lima and St Martin de Porres.

PART III

Devotional Guide to the City of Rome Throughout The Liturgical Year

** ** ** ** ** ** ** **

Roman Forum

Note to the Reader

The following section is intended for pilgrims visiting Rome. It follows the liturgical calendar and locates places of veneration for each saint throughout the year.

All of the churches listed are located in Rome. Most do not preserve relics of the saints but are noteworthy for having side chapels or paintings honoring the saints.

This section is not meant to be read in one sitting but to be used throughout the liturgical year as a daily guide. For those with the book form a small holy card can be inserted into the pages and moved from day-to-day as one progresses throughout the year.

The following text repeats a fair amount of what has already been presented in this book. Nevertheless, plenty of new material is also included which should assist in day-to-day devotion.

January

January 1st
Solemnity of The Blessed Virgin Mary, Mother of God

Basilica of St Mary Major
Piazza di Santa Maria Maggiore 42

†This basilica is dedicated to Mary the Mother of God and was built by Pope Sixtus III shortly after Mary was given this title at the Council of Ephesus. It replaced an earlier church that had been built by Pope Liberius in the 4th century.

†Within the porphyry base of the Papal Altar in the main body of this church are some relics of St Matthias. Also prominently placed within the confessio below this altar are five pieces of wood believed to be from the crib of Jesus Christ.

†The remains of St Jerome (d. 420) were brought to this basilica in the 12th century. There is some doubt as to their exact location. They either rest under the Papal Altar within the main body of the church or within the confessio in the right transept.

FOR ADDITIONAL MARIAN CHURCHES TO VISIT PLEASE SEE THE LIST AT THE END OF THIS BOOK.

January 2nd
Memorial of Basil the Great and Gregory Nazianzen, bishops and doctors

St Basil the Great (d. 379, Caesarea) (Relics: Mount Athos, Greece; Bruges, Belgium)

St Gregory Nazianzen (d. 389, Cappadocia) (Relics: Rome, Italy; Istanbul, Turkey; Mount Athos, Greece; Lisbon, Portugal)

The body of St Gregory Nazianzen was first buried near his hometown in Cappadocia and then later transferred to Constantinople. In the 8th century his remains were removed from Constantinople and brought to Rome by a group of Basilian nuns who were escaping the Iconoclastic persecutions in the East. These nuns were given residence in the Campo Marzio district just north of the Pantheon in Rome. They then placed the remains of St Gregory Nazianzen within their church.

St Peter's Basilica
†Some relics of St Gregory Nazianzen rest within this basilica beneath the *Altar of Our Lady of Succour*. This altar is located near the entrance to the confessional area on the right side of the nave. In 2004 a major part of these relics were returned to the Ecumenical Patriarch of Constantinople.

†At the nearby *Altar of St Basil*, located on the back side of the first column, is a mosaic depicting St Basil celebrating Holy Mass. The original painting that this mosaic replaced hangs within the Roman church *Santa Maria degli Angeli*.

Santa Maria della Concezione in Campo Marzio (Our Lady of the Conception in Campo Marzio)
Piazza Campo Marzio 45

†This church is north of the Pantheon.

†As noted previously Basilian nuns brought the relics of St Gregory Nazianzen to Rome in the 8th century. They were kept in Rome at Campo Marzio and eventually placed within this church.

✝With the exception of one arm the remains of St Gregory Nazianzen were transferred to *St Peter's Basilica* in 1580. This arm remained at *Santa Maria della Concezione* as compensation and was eventually placed in the nearby church of *San Gregorio*. This relic, however, is not accessible to the general public since *San Gregorio* is the church used by the Deputies of the Italian Parliament.

San Basilio agli Orti Sallustiani
(Saint Basil at the Sullstian Gardens)
Via di San Basilio 51/A
✝This church is northeast of the Barberini metro stop. It is dedicated to St Basil.

January 3rd
Optional Memorial of The Most Holy Name of Jesus

Il Gesu (The Jesus)
Via degli Astalli 16
✝This church is located along the Corso Vittorio Emanuele. It is dedicated to the Holy Name of Jesus.
✝St Ignatius of Loyola (d. 1556) is buried under the altar in the left transept.
✝An arm of St Francis Xavier (d. 1552) rests within a reliquary above the altar in the right transept.

Gesu e Maria (Jesus and Mary)
Via del Corso 45
✝This church is near Piazza del Popolo. It is dedicated to the Holy Names of Jesus and Mary.

January 4th
Memorial of Elizabeth Ann Seton, religious*

St Elizabeth Ann Seton (d. 1821, Emmitsburg, Maryland, USA) (Relics: Emmitsburg, Maryland, USA)

January 5th
Memorial of John Neumann, bishop*

St John Neumann (d. 1860, Philadelphia, Pennsylvania, USA) (Relics: Philadelphia, Pennsylvania, USA)

January 6th
Optional Memorial of André Bessette, religious*

St André Bessette (d. 1937, Montreal, Quebec, Canada) (Relics: Montreal, Quebec, Canada)

January 7th
Optional memorial of Raymond of Penyafort, priest

St Raymond of Penyafort (d. 1275, Barcelona, Spain) (Relics: Barcelona, Spain)

Santa Maria sopra Minerva
(Our Lady Above Minerva)
Piazza della Minerva 42
✝This church is near the Pantheon.
✝The seventh chapel on the right side of the nave is dedicated to St Raymond of Penyafort.
✝Also the body of St Catherine of Siena (d. 1380) rests under the main altar.

January 13th
Optional memorial of Hilary, bishop and doctor

St Hilary (d. 368, Poitiers, France) (Relics: Poitiers, France)

Basilica of St John Lateran
Piazza San Giovanni in Laterano 4
✝The fifth chapel on the left side of the nave is dedicated to St Hilary. The painting within this chapel depicts him contemplating the Holy Trinity.

January 17th
Memorial of Anthony, abbot

St Anthony (d. 356, Mt. Colzim, Egypt)
(Relics: Zaafarana, Egypt; Saint-Antoine l'Abbaye, France; Arles, France)

Sant'Antonio Abate all'Esquilino
(Saint Anthony the Abbot on the Esquiline Hill)
Via Carlo Alberto 2
✝This church is near the *Basilica of St Mary Major*. It is dedicated to St Anthony of Egypt.

Sant'Antonio dei Portoghesi
(Saint Anthony of the Portuguese)
Via dei Portoghesi 2
✝This church is northeast of Piazza Navona. It is dedicated to St Anthony of Padua. The first chapel on the left side of the nave, however, is dedicated to St Anthony of Egypt.

San Giovanni Battista dei Fiorentini
(Saint John the Baptist of the Florentines)
Via Acciaioli 2
✝This church is just east of the Vatican. It is next to the Tiber River and the Corso Vittorio Emanuele.
✝The fourth chapel on the left side of the nave is dedicated to St Anthony of Egypt.
✝A relic of St Mary Magdalene's foot also rests in a shrine to the left of the main sanctuary.

January 20th
Optional memorial of Fabian, pope and martyr

St Fabian (d. 250, Rome, Italy) (Relics: Rome, Italy)

San Sebastiano Fuori Le Mura
(Saint Sebastian Outside the Walls)
Via Appia Antica 136
✝This church is south of the Aurelian Walls.
✝The last chapel on the right side of the nave is dedicated to the pope, St Fabian. Also a reliquary chapel near the center of the church on the right side of the nave contains relics of the saint. St Fabian was originally buried in the *Catacombs of San Callisto* but later his remains were moved to this church. Also within this same chapel are the column to which St Sebastian was tied, an arrow that pierced his flesh, and some small relics from a number of other saints including St Peter, St Paul, and St Andrew.
✝Directly across from this chapel and on the left side of the nave is a chapel dedicated to St Sebastian (d. 288). St Sebastian was originally buried in the catacombs located under this church. At some point, however, his remains were removed. Some of these remains are now located within an urn in this chapel below the very impressive statue of St Sebastian created by Giuseppe Giorgetti.
✝This church has an ancient tradition connecting it to St Peter and to St Paul. The *Depositio Martyrum* shows that in the year 258 pilgrims came to *San Sebastiano Fuori Le Mura* on June 29th, the Feast Day of Saints Peter and Paul, to honor these two great saints. Therefore, it is presumed that at one time this church housed the remains of both St Peter and St Paul.
✝Tradition also claims that within the catacombs located under this church St Philip Neri (d. 1595) experienced such an enlargement of his heart due to a supernatural infusion of God's love that two of his ribs cracked.

Catacombs of San Callisto
Via Appia Antica 110/126
†These catacombs are located south of the Aurelian Walls.
†St Fabian, St Pontian (d. 235), St Cornelius (d. 253), St Sixtus II (d. 258), and a number of other early popes were originally buried here. The remains of St Fabian were later moved to *San Sebastiano Fuori Le Mura*, the remains of St Cornelius to *Santa Maria in Trastevere*, and the remains of St Sixtus II to *San Sisto Vecchio*.
†St Cecilia was also buried in these catacombs. In 821 her remains were removed and taken to *Santa Cecilia in Trastevere*.
†Finally, it was at this location in the year 258 that Roman soldiers burst into a chapel and arrested St Sixtus II and four other deacons while they were celebrating the liturgy. St Lawrence (d. 258) was not present for this arrest; however, a legend holds that St Lawrence was able to speak to St Sixtus just before the pope was martyred. In this conversation St Sixtus prophetically stated, "You shall follow me in three days." St Lawrence then in three days went on to suffer his own martyrdom by being burnt alive on a gridiron.

January 20th
Optional memorial of Sebastian, martyr

St Sebastian (d. 288, Rome, Italy)
(Relics: Rome, Italy)

A major part of the relics of St Gregory the Great and the body of St Sebastian are said to have been taken to Soissons, France in 826 AD. Alban Butler in *The Lives of the Fathers, Martyrs, and Other Principal Saints* claims that in 1564 these relics were stolen and thrown into a ditch by Calvinists. This tradition then maintains that some of these desecrated relics were recovered and subsequently placed into surrounding churches in that area. Despite this tradition the veneration of their relics in Rome has been maintained for centuries.

San Sebastiano Fuori Le Mura
(Saint Sebastian Outside the Walls)
Via Appia Antica 136
†This church is south of the Aurelian Walls.
†Please see the entry under St Fabian on the previous page for details on this church.

St Peter's Basilica
Treasury Museum
†The skull of St Sebastian is placed within a glass-sided reliquary in this museum.
†Also the second chapel on the right side of the nave is dedicated to St Sebastian. A mosaic within this chapel depicts his martyrdom. The original painting that this mosaic replaced hangs within the Roman church *Santa Maria degli Angeli*.

Santi Quattro Coronati
(Four Holy Crowned Ones)
Piazza dei Santi Quattro Coronati 20
†This church is east of the Colosseum.
†For centuries the skull of St Sebastian was venerated within the crypt of this church. Signage at an altar on the left side of the nave continues to indicate its presence. However, at some point in the last century the skull was removed. It can now be found within a reliquary in the Treasury Museum of *St Peter's Basilica* as previously noted.

Sant'Andrea della Valle
(Saint Andrew of the Valley)
Piazza Sant'Andrea della Valle / Piazza Vidoni 6

✝This church is located along the Corso Vittorio Emanuele. Prior to the construction of this church in the 17ᵗʰ century a small church dedicated to St Sebastian was located here. Tradition claims that this ancient church rested upon a sewer from which the body of St Sebastian was recovered following his martyrdom. Today a remnant of this ancient church is partially preserved within a niche found in the first chapel on the left side of the nave.

✝Also the third chapel on the left side of the nave is dedicated to St Sebastian. The altarpiece within this chapel was painted by Giovanni de' Vecchi in 1614.

San Sebastiano al Palatino
(Saint Sebastian at the Palatine)
Via San Bonaventura 1

✝This church is located in the Roman Forum. It is not open often.

✝St Sebastian had been a member of the Roman Emperor's Praetorian Guard and therefore lived and worked in the Roman Forum. This church honors the memory of St Sebastian's presence here and his attempts to evangelize the Roman people. A small relic of St Sebastian rests in the sacristy of this church.

January 21ˢᵗ
Memorial of Agnes, virgin and martyr

St Agnes (d. 304, Rome, Italy) (Relics: Rome, Italy)

Sant'Agnese Fuori le Mura
(Saint Agnes Outside the Walls)
Via S Agnese 315

✝This church is northeast of the Aurelian Walls and is located on Via Nomentana.

✝The bones of St Agnes rest in the crypt under the main sanctuary.

Sant'Agnese in Agone
(Saint Agnes in Agone)
Piazza Navona

✝According to tradition St Agnes was martyred at this location in 304 AD. A relic of her skull is present in a chapel located to the left of the main sanctuary.

✝A large statue of St Agnes is prominently placed above an altar on the right side of this church. It was completed by Ercole Ferrata in the 17ᵗʰ century.

Santissima Trinità dei Spagnoli
(The Most Holy Trinity of the Spanish)
Via dei Condotti 41

✝This church is near the Spanish Steps.

✝The first chapel on the left side of the nave is dedicated to St Agnes. Three paintings within this chapel depict scenes from her life.

January 23ʳᵈ
*Optional memorial of Vincent, deacon and martyr**

St Vincent (d. 304, Valencia, Spain) (Relics: Lisbon, Portugal; Castres, France)

Tre Fontane
(The Three Fountains)
Via Acque Salvie 1

✝Located south of the Aurelian Walls.

✝There are three churches located at this shrine, one of which is *Santi Anastasio e Vincenzo*. This is the large church on the left as one enters. It is dedicated to St Vincent and to St Anastasius.

January 23rd
Optional memorial of Marianne Cope,
virgin*

St Marianne Cope (d. 1918, Kalaupapa, Hawaii, USA) (Relics: Syracuse, New York, USA)

January 24th
Memorial of Francis de Sales, bishop
and doctor

St Francis de Sales (d. 1622, Lyon, France) (Relics: Treviso, Italy; Annecy, France)

Sacro Cuore di Gesu a Castro Pretorio (Sacred Heart of Jesus at Castro Pretorio)
Via Marsala 42
✝This church is near the Termini Train Station. It was built by St John Bosco and finished in 1887. The church continues to be served by the Salesians.
✝A chapel on the right side of the nave is dedicated to St Francis de Sales.

January 25th
Feast of The Conversion of Paul,
apostle

St Paul (Relics: Rome, Italy; Valletta, Malta)

Basilica of St Paul Outside the Walls
Via Ostiense 186
✝St Paul is buried in the confessio of this church. Above his tomb are the chains that had been used to imprison him prior to his martyrdom. These chains were placed in this prominent location in 2008.
✝Also the main altar in the left transept is dedicated to the *Conversion of St Paul*. The painting above this altar, completed by Vincenzo Camuccini, depicts this event.

Tre Fontane
(The Three Fountains)
Via Acque Salvie 1
✝Located south of the Aurelian Walls.
✝There are three churches located at this shrine. The one located on the backside of the property, called *San Paolo alle Tre Fontane*, is believed to mark the spot of St Paul's martyrdom. Legend says that after St Paul was decapitated his head bounced three times and with each bounce a fountain of water sprang up. Three grated areas along the eastern wall of this church cover up the locations of these three fountains. Also within this church is the column to which St Paul was bound and the table upon which he died.
✝Another church on this property, *Santa Maria Scala Coeli*, is believed to mark the spot of St Paul's imprisonment prior to his martyrdom. This is the first church on the right as one enters. A crypt below the main sanctuary of this church marks the spot where St Paul was imprisoned.

Basilica of St John Lateran
Piazza San Giovanni in Laterano 4
✝Positioned above the Papal Altar of this church are two busts of St Peter and St Paul. According to tradition the skulls or parts of the skulls of St Peter and St Paul are within these busts. Also located within the Papal Altar is a wooden table that St Peter and many of the earliest popes are said to have celebrated the Eucharist upon.
✝Located to the left of the Papal Altar is another very ancient table. This table rests above the altar where the Blessed Sacrament is reserved. It is placed directly behind a bronze relief of the Last Supper. Tradition claims that it was upon this table that Jesus and the apostles celebrated the Last Supper.

San Paolo alla Regola
(Saint Paul at the Regola)
Via di San Paolo alla Regola 6
✝This church is near the Jewish quarter.
✝This church claims to be built over the spot where St Paul lived for two years while he was under house arrest in Rome. A chapel to the right of the main sanctuary marks the location of his rooms.
✝Also within the main sanctuary are three frescoes depicting scenes from St Paul's life.

Santa Maria in Via Lata
(Our Lady on Via Lata)
Via del Corso 306
✝This church is near Piazza Venezia.
✝It is believed that this church is also built over a location where St Paul resided while he was under house arrest in Rome.

Santa Maria del Popolo
(Our Lady of the People)
Piazza del Popolo 12
✝This church is at Piazza del Popolo.
✝In the *Cerasi Chapel*, to the left of the main altar, are two exceptional works by Caravaggio. The one to the right is entitled the *Conversion of St Paul*.

San Pietro in Montorio
(Saint Peter in Montorio)
Piazza San Pietro in Montorio 2
✝This church is located on the Janiculum hill.
✝A painting within the right transept by Giorgio Vasari depicts the *Conversion of St Paul*.

Santa Maria in Campitelli
(Our Lady in Campitelli)
Piazza di Campitelli 9
✝This church is near the Jewish quarter.

✝A painting within the third chapel on the left side of the nave, entitled the *Conversion of St Paul*, depicts St Paul falling off of his horse. It was completed by Ludovico Geminiani in the 17th century.
✝The body of St John Leonardi (d. 1609) is enshrined in the second chapel on the left side of the nave.

January 26th
Memorial of Timothy and Titus, bishops

St Timothy (Relics: Termoli, Italy)
St Titus (Relics: Heraklion, Crete, Greece)

January 27th
Optional memorial of Angela Merici, virgin

St Angela Merici (d. 1540, Brescia, Italy) (Relics: Brescia, Italy)

January 28th
Memorial of Thomas Aquinas, priest and doctor

St Thomas Aquinas (b. 1225, Roccasecca, Italy) (d. 1274, Fossanova, Italy) (Relics: Toulouse, France; Aquino, Italy; Naples, Italy)

Santa Sabina
(Saint Sabina)
Piazza Pietro d'Illiria 1
✝This church is located on the Aventine Hill just south of Circo Massimo.
✝St Thomas Aquinas lived here when he opened a house of studies at *Santa Sabina* to teach theology to Dominican students in 1265. It was also around this time that he began to write the *Summa Theologica*.

✝One of the oldest depictions of the crucifixion in Christian art is located on the uppermost left panel of the left entrance door. This wooden door dates back to the year 430 AD. (Note: This is not the entrance off of the street but the entrance from the narthex.)

January 31st
Memorial of John Bosco, priest

St John Bosco (d. 1888, Turin, Italy)
(Relics: Turin, Italy)

Sacro Cuore di Gesu a Castro Pretorio (Sacred Heart of Jesus at Castro Pretorio)
Via Marsala 42
✝This church was built by St John Bosco and finished in 1887. It is located near the Termini Train Station.
✝St John Bosco celebrated Mass at the altar in the left transept. It was at this altar that he profoundly realized that his life had fulfilled the vision of his youth.
✝In the museum to the right of the main sanctuary are various relics. One reliquary contains a bone fragment of St John Bosco. Also upon request one can visit the rooms of St John Bosco.

February

February 2nd
Feast of The Presentation of the Lord

San Pietro in Montorio
(Saint Peter in Montorio)
Piazza San Pietro in Montorio 2
✝This church is located on the Janiculum hill.
✝Within the third chapel on the right side of the nave is a painting of the Presentation of Jesus. To the sides of this painting are two works completed by Michelangelo Cerruti depicting the Annunciation and the Immaculate Conception.

February 3rd
Optional memorial of Blaise, bishop and martyr

St Blaise (d. 316, Armenia) (Relics: Rome, Italy; Maratea, Italy; Dubrovnik, Croatia)

San Carlo ai Catinari
(Saint Charles at the Catinari)
Piazza Benedetto Cairoli 117
✝This church is near the Largo di Torre Argentina. It is dedicated to St Blaise as its full name *Santi Biagio e Carlo ai Catinari* indicates.
✝On February 3rd several relics of St Blaise are presented within this church for veneration. Of special note is a reliquary which contains a bone from the throat of St Blaise. This relic is used to bless the throats of the faithful.
✝The second chapel on the right side of the nave is also dedicated to St Blaise.

San Biagio degli Armeni
(Saint Blaise of the Armenians)
Via Giulia 63
✝This church is on the north end of Via Giulia. It is dedicated to St Blaise.

February 3rd
Optional memorial of Ansgar, bishop

St Ansgar (d. 865, Bremen, Germany)

February 5th
Memorial of Agatha, virgin and martyr

St Agatha (d. 251, Catania, Sicily)
(Relics: Catania, Sicily)

Sant'Agata dei Goti
(Saint Agatha of the Goths)
Via Mazzarino 16 / Via Panisperna
✝This church is west of the *Basilica of St Mary Major*. It was originally an Arian church. However, in 593 after the Imperial forces defeated the Arian Goths the church was reconsecrated to St Agatha.

Sant'Agata in Trastevere
(Saint Agatha in Trastevere)
Largo San Giovanni de Matha 9
✝This church is located in Trastevere. It is not open often.
✝A painting in the sanctuary depicts the martyrdom of St Agatha.

February 6th
Memorial of Paul Miki and Companions, martyrs

Honored on this day are 26 martyrs who died in Japan in 1597 by crucifixion. (Relics: Nagasaki, Japan)

February 8th
Optional memorial of Jerome Emiliani, priest

St Jerome Emiliani (d. 1537, Somasca di Vercurago, Italy) (Relics: Somasca di Vercurago, Italy)

Santa Maria in Aquiro
(Our Lady in Aquiro)
Via della Guglia 69/B
†This church is near the Pantheon.
†The fourth chapel on the left side of the nave is dedicated to St Jerome Emiliani. The community that he founded, the Somascan Fathers, administer the parish.

February 8th
Optional memorial of Josephine Bakhita, virgin

St Josephine Bakhita (d. 1947, Schio, Italy) (Relics: Schio, Italy)

February 10th
Memorial of Scholastica, virgin

St Scholastica (b. 480, Norcia, Italy) (d. 547, Monte Cassino, Italy) (Relics: Monte Cassino, Italy; Juvigny-sur-Loison, France)

It is uncertain if the relics of Saint Benedict and Saint Scholastica are still at Monte Cassino or if they were moved in the seventh century to Saint-Benoît-sur-Loire, France.

Santi Benedetto e Scolastica
(Saints Benedict and Scholastica)
Vicolo Sinibaldi 1
†This church is just south of the Pantheon. Its postal address is on Vicolo Sinibaldi; however, its front door is just around the corner on Via Torre Argentina.

†The church is very small and is set into the surrounding buildings. It is dedicated to both St Benedict and St Scholastica. It is not open often.

February 11th
Optional memorial of Our Lady of Lourdes

Santa Rita da Cascia alle Vergini
(Saint Rita of Cascia at the Vergini)
Via del Umiltà 83B
†This church is just south of the Trevi Fountain.
†A grotto honoring Our Lady of Lourdes is found within a small room immediately on the left after entering.

Santi Marcellino e Pietro
(Saints Marcellinus and Peter)
Via Merulana 162
†This church is near the *Basilica of St John Lateran.*
†The side chapel to the right of the main sanctuary contains a grotto that is dedicated to Our Lady of Lourdes.
†Also remnants from a statue of the Blessed Virgin Mary, which was smashed by protesters who broke into the church in 2011, are preserved in a shrine located near the sacristy.
†Some relics of Saints Marcellinus and Peter rest within the altar in the main sanctuary.

Santa Maria in Aquiro
(Our Lady in Aquiro)
Via della Guglia 69/B
†This church is near the Pantheon.
†The third chapel on the left side of the nave is dedicated to Our Lady of Lourdes.

San Rocco (Saint Roch)
Largo San Rocco 1
✝This church is near the Tiber River just west of the Spanish Steps.
✝The first chapel on the left side of the nave contains a grotto that is dedicated to Our Lady of Lourdes.

FOR ADDITIONAL MARIAN CHURCHES TO VISIT PLEASE SEE THE LIST AT THE END OF THIS BOOK.

February 14th
Memorial of Cyril, monk; and Methodius, bishop

St Cyril (d. 869, Rome, Italy) (Relics: Rome, Italy)
St Methodius (d. 885, Velehrad, Czech Republic)

St Cyril is believed to have discovered both the anchor and the relics of St Clement I in Crimea in 861 AD. St Cyril then brought these relics to Rome during his visit in 868 AD. He died in Rome a year later. His brother, St Methodius, wished to return the body of St Cyril to his homeland in Thessalonica; however, Pope Adrian II would not allow this. As a result the body of St Cyril was kept in Rome and buried in the *Basilica of San Clemente*, the same church where he had deposited the relics of St Clement I a year prior. The remains of St Cyril remained in this church until their removal and disappearance during the French establishment of the Roman Republic in the late 18th century. In the 1960's, a fortunate discovery by an Irish Dominican led to the retrieval of a small relic of St Cyril. This relic is now within this church as noted below.

Basilica di San Clemente
(Basilica of Saint Clement)
Via Labicana 95 / Piazza San Clemente
✝This church is east of the Colosseum.
✝A chapel on the right side of the nave is dedicated to Saints Cyril and Methodius. The relic of St Cyril found in the 1960's rests within the altar of this chapel.
✝Also the remains of St Ignatius of Antioch (d. 107) and of St Clement I (d. 97) rest below the main altar.

San Girolamo dei Croati
(Saint Jerome of the Croatians)
Via Tomacelli 132
✝This church is near the Tiber River just west of the Spanish Steps.
✝The first chapel on the left side of the nave contains a painting that depicts Saints Cyril and Methodius giving the relics of St Clement I to Pope Adrian II.

February 17th
Optional memorial of The Seven Holy Founders of the Servite Order

Santa Maria in Via
(Our Lady of the Way)
Via del Mortaro 24
✝This church is near the Spanish Steps. It is run by the Servite friars.
✝The third chapel on the left side of the nave is dedicated to the Seven Holy Founders of the Servite Order.
✝On September 26, 1256 a miraculous icon of the Blessed Virgin Mary appeared at this location. It was found painted on a stone and floating upon the water of an overflowing well. The first chapel on the right side of the nave preserves this miraculous well and icon. Cups are normally provided so that pilgrims can drink some of the water from this well.

San Marcello al Corso
(Saint Marcellus on the Corso)
Piazza di San Marcello 5
†This church is located north of Piazza Venezia.
†A chapel on the left side of the nave near the entrance is dedicated to the Seven Holy Founders of the Servites.
†This church is served by the Servite friars and the Order's Generalate is adjacent to the church.
†A fire on the night of May 22, 1519 destroyed most of this church. Only the outer walls and a 15th century wooden crucifix survived. This miraculous crucifix can now be found in the fourth chapel on the right side of the nave. A relic of the true cross is also preserved within this chapel in a reliquary.

February 21st
Optional memorial of Peter Damian, bishop and doctor

St Peter Damian (d. 1072, Faenza, Italy)
(Relics: Faenza, Italy)

February 22nd
Feast of the Chair of St Peter, apostle

St Peter (Relics: Rome, Italy)

St Peter's Basilica
†Tradition holds that St Peter was crucified upside down in the middle of Nero's Circus. The *Altar of The Crucifixion*, located in the left transept of *St Peter's Basilica*, is very close to the actual site where this crucifixion took place.
†The bones of St Peter are in the confessio below the Papal Altar and his jawbone can be seen on the Scavi tour.

†Tradition also holds that within the large bronze chair located above the *Altar of the Chair* in the apse of the church is a second smaller chair made out of wood. This second chair is said to consist of fragments from the original Episcopal chair that St Peter once sat in.

Basilica of St John Lateran
Piazza San Giovanni in Laterano 4
†Positioned above the Papal Altar of this church are two busts of St Peter and St Paul. According to tradition the skulls or parts of the skulls of St Peter and St Paul are within these busts. Also located within the Papal Altar is a wooden table that St Peter and many of the earliest popes are said to have celebrated the Eucharist upon.
†Located to the left of the Papal Altar is another very ancient table. This table rests above the altar where the Blessed Sacrament is reserved. It is placed directly behind a bronze relief of the Last Supper. Tradition claims that it was upon this table that Jesus and the apostles celebrated the Last Supper.

Domine Quo Vadis
(Lord, Where Are You Going?)
Via Appia Antica
†This church is southeast of the Aurelian Walls.
†This is the location where Christ allegedly appeared to St Peter as he was fleeing Rome. Upon seeing the Lord St Peter asked, "Domine, Quo Vadis?" (Lord, where are you going?) to which Jesus replied, "I am going to Rome to be crucified again." Spurred on by this encounter St Peter returned to Rome where he became a martyr.

San Giuseppe dei Falegnami / Carcere Mamertino

(Saint Joseph of the Carpenters / Mamertine Prison)

Clivo Argentario 1

†This church is located in the Roman Forum above the Mamertine Prison. It was in this prison that the Romans incarcerated individuals of great importance. As a result a long standing tradition has placed St Peter's imprisonment here. Such a high profile imprisonment would seem likely from today's perspective, however, at the time of St Peter's death his role as the leader of a little-known Jewish sect would have almost certainly been regarded as insignificant. As a result his imprisonment at this location is doubted. Nevertheless, this prison continues to actively promote tours. Within St Peter's alleged cell is a raised ring that is believed to be the spot where a spring of water arose allowing St Peter to baptize two guards.

San Pietro in Vincoli

(Saint Peter in Chains)

Piazza San Pietro in Vincoli 4/a

†This church is near the Cavour metro stop.

†A tradition claims that St Peter was condemned and imprisoned near this site. This tradition is probably more credible than the one held at the Mamertine Prison.

†Venerated within the confessio of this church are the chains of St Peter. A tradition holds that these chains are a result of the chains from St Peter's imprisonment in Jerusalem coming into contact with the chains from St Peter's imprisonment in Rome. Miraculously these two chains were fused into the one inseparable chain that is now found in the confessio.

Santa Pudenziana

(Saint Pudentiana)

Via Urbana 160

†This church is near the *Basilica of St Mary Major*.

†It is believed that St Peter lodged here while he was in Rome. The house in which he stayed was owned and provided for by St Pudens, a Roman Senator. Since early Christians did not have public places for worship it is also presumed that St Peter celebrated Mass here. Remnants from the ancient wooden altar used for these Masses are said to be preserved in the chapel dedicated to him on the left side of the main sanctuary.

San Pietro in Montorio

(Saint Peter in Montorio)

Piazza San Pietro in Montorio 2

†This church is located on the Janiculum hill.

†Within the main sanctuary of this church is a painting by Vincenzo Camuccini entitled the *Crucifixion of St Peter*. This is a copy of the original that was done by Guido Reni. This painting recalls a mistaken medieval tradition which placed the martyrdom of St Peter at the location of this church and not at *St Peter's Basilica*. This tradition, which has in modern times been disproved, led to the construction of a small circular chapel within the cloister adjacent to this church. This chapel, called the *Tempietto*, is considered one of the best examples of Italian Renaissance architecture in Rome. It was designed by Bramante in the early part of the 16th century. Special permission is needed to access this chapel.

Santa Maria del Popolo

(Our Lady of the People)

Piazza del Popolo 12

✝This church is at Piazza del Popolo.
✝In the *Cerasi Chapel*, to the left of the main altar, are two exceptional works by Caravaggio. The one to the left is entitled the *Crucifixion of St Peter*.

February 23rd
Memorial of Polycarp, bishop and martyr

St Polycarp (d. 155, Smyrna) (Relics: Rome, Italy)

Sant'Ambrogio della Massima
(Saint Ambrose)
Via San Ambrogio 3
✝This church is located west of Piazza Venezia near the Fontana delle Tartarughe. It is set behind some buildings and is not easy to notice from the street. It is not open often.
✝The relics of St Polycarp are set in a marble memorial stone under the main altar.
✝Tradition also holds that this church rests on land that was formerly the location of a house owned by St Ambrose's father and occupied by his older sister.

March

March 3rd
Optional memorial of Katharine Drexel, virgin*

St Katharine Drexel (d. 1955, Philadelphia, Pennsylvania, USA) (Relics: Bensalem, Pennsylvania, USA)

March 4th
Optional memorial of Casimir

St Casimir (d. 1484, Hrodna, Belarus) (Relics: Vilnius, Lithuania)

March 7th
Memorial of Perpetua and Felicity, martyrs

Saint Perpetua (d. 203, Carthage, Tunisia) (Relics: Carthage, Tunisia; Vierzon, France)

Saint Felicity (d. 203, Carthage, Tunisia) (Relics: Carthage, Tunisia)

March 8th
Optional memorial of John of God, religious

St John of God (d. 1550, Granada, Spain) (Relics: Granada, Spain)

San Giovanni Calibita
(Saint John Calibytes)
Isola Tiberina 39
✝This church is located on Tiber Island just across from *San Bartolomeo all' Isola*.
✝St John of God was the patron saint of the community that founded this church and the hospital adjacent to it. Several works within this church depict various events from his life. Also placed upon a small obelisk in the piazza just outside of this church is a small statue of the saint.

March 9th
Optional memorial of Frances of Rome, religious

St Frances of Rome (d. 1440, Rome, Italy) (Relics: Rome, Italy)

Santa Francesca Romana
(Saint Frances of Rome)
Piazza di Santa Francesca Romana 4
✝This church is next to the Roman Forum.
✝The remains of St Frances of Rome are in the crypt below the main sanctuary. Her skeleton is vested in the habit of the Oblate Sisters.
✝To the right of the sanctuary is the tomb of Pope Gregory XI (d. 1378). He returned the papal seat to Rome after the exile in Avignon. St Catherine of Siena (d. 1380) was instrumental in persuading him to return. A relief depicting her involvement can be seen on the tomb.
✝Two flagstones within the right transept of the church are said to bear the imprints of the knees of St Peter. According to a legend the magician, Simon Magus, levitated in the Roman Forum to demonstrate that his powers were superior to those of Peter. In response, Peter fell to the ground in prayer causing the knee imprints on the stone. Simon Magus then immediately fell to his death.

Sant'Agnese in Agone
(Saint Agnes in Agone)
Piazza Navona
✝St Frances of Rome received the sacraments of Baptism and Confirmation in this church.
✝According to tradition St Agnes was martyred at this location in 304 AD. A

relic of her skull is present in a chapel located to the left of the main sanctuary.

Casa di Santa Francesca Romana
(House of St Frances of Rome)
Via dei Vascellari 61
✝Located in Trastevere at the Ponte Rotto Hotel.
✝Ask within the hotel for access to St Frances' house. Generally access is only available during weekday mornings.

Santa Maria Annunziata a Tor de' Specchi
(Annunciation of Mary at the Tower of Mirrors)
Via del Teatro di Marcello 32
✝This church is west of Piazza Venezia.
✝St Frances of Rome lived here with her oblate community after the death of her husband. This church is only open to the public on March 9th the feast day of St Frances of Rome.

Santa Maria in Trastevere
(Our Lady in Trastevere)
Via della Paglia 14 / Piazza Santa Maria in Trastevere
✝This church is located in Trastevere.
✝Within the first chapel on the right side of the nave is a painting by Giacomo Zoboli that depicts St Frances of Rome receiving the Eucharist.
✝Relics of the two popes, St Callistus I (d. 222) and St Cornelius (d. 253), rest under the main altar of this church. These relics are joined by others in particular those of the priest and martyr St Calepodius (d. 232).

March 17ᵗʰ
Optional memorial of Patrick, bishop

St Patrick (d. 461) (Relics: Downpatrick, United Kingdom)

San Patrizio a Villa Ludovisi
(Saint Patrick at Villa Ludovisi)
Via Boncompagni 31
✝This church is east of the Spanish Steps. It is dedicated to St Patrick.

March 18ᵗʰ
Optional memorial of Cyril of Jerusalem, bishop and doctor

St Cyril of Jerusalem (d. 386, Israel)

March 19ᵗʰ
Solemnity of Joseph, husband of Mary

Tradition and Scripture are silent with regard to the death of St Joseph. However, a possible location of his burial is a 1ˢᵗ century tomb located in Nazareth beneath the *Sisters of Nazareth Convent* next door to the Franciscan *Casa Nova*.

St Peter's Basilica
St Joseph's Altar
✝This is the main altar in the left transept. The Blessed Sacrament is reserved here. It is dedicated to St Joseph.
✝Relics of St Simon and St Jude rest under this altar.

San Giuseppe al Trionfale
(Saint Joseph at the Trionfale)
Via Bernardino Telesio 4/B
✝This church is located in the Trionfale district just north of the Vatican.
✝St Luigi Guanella was instrumental in the founding of this church. It is a major center of devotion to St Joseph for the people of Rome.

San Giuseppe alla Lungara
(Saint Joseph at the Lungara)
Via della Lungàra 45

✝This church is along the Tiber River just north of Trastevere. The community located here focuses on catechizing rural areas.

✝The church is dedicated to St Joseph. The altarpiece in the main sanctuary by Mariano Rossi depicts an angel appearing to St Joseph in a dream.

San Giuseppe dei Falegnami / Carcere Mamertino

(Saint Joseph of the Carpenters / Mamertine Prison)

Clivo Argentario 1

✝This church is located in the Roman Forum above the Mamertine Prison. It is dedicated to St Joseph.

San Giuseppe a Capo le Case

(Saint Joseph at the Head of the Houses)

Via Francesco Crispi

✝This church is near the Spanish Steps. It is dedicated to St Joseph.

Santi Giovanni e Paolo

(Saints John and Paul)

Piazza dei Santi Giovanni e Paolo 13

✝This church is south of the Colosseum.

✝The third chapel on the left side of the nave is dedicated to St Joseph.

✝Located beneath this church is a complex of well preserved ancient Roman houses. Among these is an ancient house church. These ruins can be visited.

✝St Paul of the Cross (d. 1775) is buried under the altar in the large side chapel on the right side of the nave. Upon request one can visit the room in which he died in the monastery adjacent to the church.

Sant'Ignazio (Saint Ignatius)

Via del Caravita 8/a

✝This church is east of the Pantheon.

✝A painting within the second chapel on the right side of the nave depicts the death of St Joseph. It was completed by Francesco Trevisani.

✝The remains of St Aloysius Gonzaga (d. 1591) rest under the altar in the right transept. His rooms are next to the church and can be visited by appointment.

✝The body of St Robert Bellarmine (d. 1621) rests under the altar in the third chapel on the right side of the nave.

✝The remains of St John Berchmans (d. 1621), the patron saint of altar servers, rest under the altar in the left transept.

Santissimo Nome di Maria al Foro Traiano

(The Most Holy Name of Mary at Trajan's Forum)

Piazza Foro Traiano 89

✝This church is near Trajan's column just east of Piazza Venezia.

✝A painting within the third chapel on the right side of the nave depicts the death of St Joseph.

Sant'Andrea della Valle

(Saint Andrew of the Valley)

Piazza Sant'Andrea della Valle / Piazza Vidoni 6

✝This church is located along the Corso Vittorio Emanuele.

✝A marble relief in the first chapel on the right side of the nave depicts the dream of St Joseph that prompted the Holy Family to flee to Egypt.

Santa Maria in Campitelli

(Our Lady in Campitelli)

Piazza di Campitelli 9

✝This church is near the Jewish quarter.

✝The first chapel on the left side of the nave is dedicated to St Joseph.

✝The body of St John Leonardi (d. 1609) is enshrined in the second chapel on the left side of the nave.

Sant'Andrea delle Fratte
(Saint Andrew of the Bushes)
Via Sant'Andrea delle Fratte 1
✝This church is near the Spanish Steps.
✝A painting within the fourth chapel on the left side of the nave depicts St Joseph and the infant Jesus. It was completed by Francesco Gozza in 1732.
✝The third altar on the left side of the nave is where the Blessed Virgin Mary appeared to Ratisbonne, an agnostic Jew, in 1842. Ratisbonne converted on the spot. In 1918 St Maximilian Mary Kolbe (d. 1941) offered his first Mass in this very same chapel.

March 23rd
Optional memorial of Turibius of Mogrovejo, bishop

St Turibius (d. 1606, Sana, Peru) (Relics: Lima, Peru)

Sant'Anastasia (Saint Anastasius)
Piazza di Sant'Anastasia
✝This church is near Circo Massimo.
✝To the right of the main sanctuary is an altar dedicated to St Turibius.

March 25th
Solemnity of The Annunciation

Santa Maria sopra Minerva
(Our Lady Above Minerva)
Piazza della Minerva 42
✝This church is near the Pantheon.
✝A 15th century painting of the Annunciation by Antoniazzo Romano is placed within the fifth chapel on the right side of the nave. Also the chapel in the right transept is dedicated to the Annunciation.

✝The body of St Catherine of Siena (d. 1380) rests under the main altar.

Sant'Onofrio (Saint Onuphrius)
Piazza di Sant'Onofrio 2
✝This church is on the Janiculum Hill.
✝Within the first chapel on the right side of the nave are a pair of frescoes by Antoniazzo Romano. They are uniquely placed upon the upper pinnacles of the vault above the altar. Together they depict the miraculous exchange of the Archangel Gabriel and the Blessed Virgin Mary at the Annunciation.

San Carlo ai Catinari
(Saint Charles at the Catinari)
Piazza Benedetto Cairoli 117
✝This church is near the Largo di Torre Argentina.
✝Within the first chapel on the right side of the nave is a beautiful painting of the Annunciation by Giovanni Lanfranco.
✝Also a chapel in the right transept preserves a copy of the miraculous image of the Blessed Virgin Mary entitled *Mother of Divine Providence*. The original is located in a Barnabite church in Trastevere.

Santa Maria in Aquiro
(Our Lady in Aquiro)
Via della Guglia 69/B
✝This church is near the Pantheon.
✝The third chapel on the right side of the nave is dedicated to the Annunciation.

San Marcello al Corso
(Saint Marcellus on the Corso)
Piazza di San Marcello 5
✝This church is north of Piazza Venezia.
✝The first chapel on the right side of the nave is dedicated to the Annunciation.
✝A fire on the night of May 22, 1519 destroyed most of this church. Only the outer walls and a 15th century wooden

crucifix survived. This miraculous crucifix can now be found in the fourth
chapel on the right side of the nave. A
relic of the true cross is also preserved
within this chapel in a reliquary.

San Lorenzo in Lucina
(Saint Lawrence in Lucina)
Via in Lucina 16/a
†This church is north of the Pantheon.
†The fourth chapel on the right side of
the nave is dedicated to the Annunc-
iation.
†The grill used to burn St Lawrence (d.
258) is preserved under the altar in the
first chapel on the right side of the nave.

Santissima Trinità dei Monti
(Most Holy Trinity of the Mounts)
Piazza della Trinità dei Monti
†This church is at the top of the Spanish
Steps.
†Within the third chapel on the left side
of the nave is a fresco of the Annunc-
iation by Joseph Ernst Tunner.

San Salvatore in Onda
(The Holy Savior in the Deluge)
Via dei Pettinari 51
†This church is near Tiber Island.
†A chapel on the right side of the nave
honors the Annunciation.
†The remains of St Vincent Pallotti (d.
1850) rest below the main altar.

FOR ADDITIONAL MARIAN
CHURCHES TO VISIT PLEASE SEE
THE LIST AT THE END OF THIS
BOOK.

April

April 2nd
Optional memorial of Francis of Paola, hermit

St Francis of Paola (d. 1507, Plessis, France) (Relics: Paola, Italy)

In the 15th century St Francis of Paola founded a new religious community of friars called the Minims. This community, whose name expresses the great humility that they strive for, has a long history in Rome.

San Francesco di Paola ai Monti
(Saint Francis of Paola at the Hills)
Piazza di San Francesco a Paola 10
✝ This church is near the Cavour metro stop. It is dedicated to St Francis of Paola and has served in the past as the Generalate for the Order of Minims. Recently, however, the church has suffered structural damage and is currently not open.

Santissima Trinità dei Monti
(Most Holy Trinity of the Mounts)
Piazza della Trinità dei Monti
✝ This church is at the top of the Spanish Steps. St Francis of Paola established this church with the help of King Charles VIII to provide a place for the Order of Minims in Rome. It remained in possession of the Minims until it was suppressed in 1797 by Napoleon Bonaparte.
✝ The second chapel on the right side of the nave is dedicated to St Francis of Paola.

Sant'Andrea delle Fratte
(Saint Andrew of the Bushes)
Via Sant'Andrea delle Fratte 1
✝ This church is near the Spanish Steps. It is administered by the Order of Minims.
✝ The chapel in the right transept is dedicated to St Francis of Paola.
✝ The third altar on the left side of the nave is where the Blessed Virgin Mary appeared to Ratisbonne, an agnostic Jew, in 1842. Ratisbonne converted on the spot. In 1918 St Maximilian Mary Kolbe (d. 1941) offered his first Mass in this very same chapel.

San Rocco (Saint Roch)
Largo San Rocco 1
✝ This church is near the Tiber River just west of the Spanish Steps.
✝ The first chapel on the right side of the nave is dedicated to St Francis of Paola.

Nostra Signora del Sacro Cuore
(Our Lady of the Sacred Heart)
Corso del Rinascimento 27
✝ This church is at Piazza Navona.
✝ The third chapel on the right side of the nave is dedicated to St Francis of Paola.

La Maddalena (The Magdalene)
Piazza della Maddalena 53
✝ This church is just north of the Pantheon.
✝ The first chapel on the right side of the nave is dedicated to St Francis of Paola.
✝ In the chapel in the right transept is a miraculous crucifix that is said to have spoken to St Camillus de Lellis.
✝ In the third chapel on the right side of the nave are the remains of St Camillus de Lellis. He lived in the adjacent monastery and died here in 1614. His rooms can be visited by asking the sacristan. One of these rooms has been transformed into a chapel and contains the relic of his heart.

April 4th
Optional memorial of Isidore, bishop and doctor

St Isidore Bishop (d. 636, Seville, Spain) (Relics: Leon, Spain; Murcia, Spain)

April 5th
Optional memorial of Vincent Ferrer, priest

St Vincent Ferrer (d. 1419, Vannes, France) (Relics: Vannes, France)

Santa Maria sopra Minerva
(Our Lady Above Minerva)
Piazza della Minerva 42
✝This church is near the Pantheon.
✝Within the fourth chapel on the left side of the nave is a painting depicting St Vincent Ferrer at the Council of Constance.
✝The body of St Catherine of Siena (d. 1380) rests under the main altar.

San Giovanni Battista dei Fiorentini
(Saint John the Baptist of the Florentines)
Via Acciaioli 2
✝This church is just east of the Vatican. It is next to the Tiber River and the Corso Vittorio Emanuele.
✝The first chapel on the right side of the nave is dedicated to St Vincent Ferrer.
✝A relic of St Mary Magdalene's foot rests in a shrine to the left of the main sanctuary.

Santi Quirico e Giulitta
(Saints Quiricus and Julitta)
Via Tor dei Conti 31/A
✝This church is east of Piazza Venezia.
✝The first chapel on the left side of the nave is dedicated to St Vincent Ferrer. The painting above the altar depicts St Vincent Ferrer and St Nicholas of Bari adoring the Christ child.

April 7th
Memorial of John Baptist de la Salle, priest

St John Baptist de la Salle (d. 1719, Rouen, France) (Relics: Rome, Italy)

Casa Generalizia dei Fratelli delle Scuole Cristiane
(Generalate of the Brothers of Christian Schools)
Via Aurelia 476
✝Located west of the Vatican.
✝The remains of St John Baptist de la Salle were transferred here in 1937. They now rest in the sanctuary of the church.

April 11th
Memorial of Stanislaus, bishop and martyr

St Stanislaus (d. 1079, Kraków, Poland) (Relics: Kraków, Poland)

San Stanislao alle Botteghe Oscure
(Saint Stanislaus at the Hidden Shops)
Via delle Botteghe Oscure 15
✝This church is near Piazza Venezia. It is dedicated to St Stanislaus. It is not open often.
✝All liturgies are in Polish

April 13th
Optional memorial of Martin I, pope and martyr

St Martin I (d. 655, Chersonesus Taurica or 'Cherson/Kherson', Ukraine) (Relics: Rome, Italy)

Pope Martin I ardently opposed the heresy of Monothelitism and the attempts by Emperor Constans II to halt debates over it. As a result, he was exiled to Crimea in 654 AD. A year later he died in exile.

San Martino ai Monti
(Saint Martin at the Hills)
Viale Monte Oppio 28

✝This church is south of the *Basilica of St Mary Major.*

✝The greater part of the remains of St Martin I were transferred from Crimea to this church in Rome. They now rest in the confessio below the main altar. This confessio also houses the relics of many other saints taken from the *Catacombs of Priscilla.*

✝A tradition claims that the pope, St Sylvester I (d. 335), and many other bishops met here to prepare for the Council of Nicaea. They then reconvened at this same church after the Council to announce the newly formulated Nicene Creed. Constantine was in attendance for this. The large painting on the left side of the nave created in 1640 recalls one of these meetings. However, this tradition is often tied to the 'Symmachian Forgeries' thus throwing some doubt on its credibility. Nevertheless, it does seem probable that some agreement was achieved between Constantine and St Sylvester I that allowed for the success of the Council of Nicaea.

April 21ˢᵗ
Optional memorial of Anselm, bishop and doctor

St Anselm (d. 1109, Canterbury, United Kingdom)

Sant'Anselmo all'Aventino
(Saint Anselm on the Aventine)
Piazza dei Cavalieri di Malta 5

✝This church is located on the Aventine Hill just south of Circo Massimo. It is dedicated to St Anselm.

April 23ʳᵈ
Optional memorial of George, martyr

St George (d. 303, Lydda, Palestine)
(Relics: Lod, Israel; Rome, Italy)

San Giorgio in Velabro
(Saint George in Velabro)
Via del Velabro 19

✝This church is just east of Tiber Island.

✝Part of the skull of St George rests beneath the main altar. (Other shrines throughout the world also claim to have the relic of his skull.)

April 23ʳᵈ
Optional Memorial of Adalbert, bishop and martyr

St Adalbert [Wojciech in Polish] (d. 997)
(Relics: Rome, Italy; Prague, Czech Republic; Gniezno, Poland)

San Bartolomeo all'Isola
(Saint Bartholomew on the Island)
Piazza San Bartolomeo, Tiber Island

✝The Holy Roman Emperor, Otto III, began building *San Bartolomeo all'Isola* in 998 to honor his friend St Adalbert who had been recently martyred. An arm of St Adalbert is currently enshrined in the chapel to the left of the main sanctuary. It rests within a little metal box placed under the altar of this chapel.

✝Relics of the apostle, St Bartholomew, rest within the red porphyry basin that supports the main altar.

✝Enshrined in each of the side altars are relics of recent martyrs from around the world.

✝This church also housed the relics of St Paulinus of Nola (d. 431) for about 1000 years until they were transferred to the Italian city of Nola in 1909.

April 24th
Optional memorial of Fidelis of Sigmaringen, priest and martyr

St Fidelis of Sigmaringen (d. 1622, Grüsch, Switzerland) (Relics: Feldkirch, Austria; Chur, Switzerland)

Santa Maria della Concezione
(Our Lady of the Immaculate Conception)
Via Veneto 27
† This church is just north of the Barberini metro stop.
† The fifth chapel on the right side of the nave contains a painting of St Fidelis of Sigmaringen. It is placed upon the right side-wall of this chapel.

April 25th
Feast of Mark, evangelist

St Mark (d. Alexandria, Egypt) (Relics: Venice, Italy; Cairo, Egypt; Reichenau, Germany)

San Marco (Saint Mark)
Piazza San Marco 48
† This church is on the west side of Piazza Venezia. It is dedicated to St Mark the Evangelist.
† The church was founded in 336 by a pope who took the name of Mark. The remains of this pope and not the evangelist rest beneath the main altar.

April 28th
Optional Memorial of Peter Chanel, priest and martyr

St Peter Chanel (d. 1841, Futuna Island, Pacific Ocean) (Relics: Futuna Island)

April 28th
Optional Memorial of Louis Grignion de Montfort, priest

St Louis Grignion de Montfort (d. 1716, Saint-Laurent-sur-Sevre, France) (Relics: Saint-Laurent-sur-Sevre, France)

April 29th
Memorial of Catherine of Siena, virgin and doctor

St Catherine of Siena (d. 1380, Rome, Italy) (Relics: Rome, Italy; Siena, Italy; Venice, Italy)

Santa Maria sopra Minerva
(Our Lady Above Minerva)
Piazza della Minerva 42
† This church is near the Pantheon.
† The body of St Catherine of Siena rests under the main altar. She spent the last two years of her life in Rome before her passing in 1380. A devotional chapel made out of the room where she died can be visited by entering the sacristy. Originally this room was located a few blocks away at Via Santa Chiara, 14. However, in the 1630s it was reconstructed and brought here.
† Along the walls of the *Capranica Chapel*, located just to the right of the main sanctuary, are a number of frescoes by Giovanni de' Vecchi that depict scenes from the life of St Catherine of Siena. Her remains rested in this chapel from 1430 to 1855.

Monastero della Madonna del Rosario a Monte Mario
(Monastery of Our Lady of the Rosary at Monte Mario)
Via Alberto Cadlolo 51

†This monastery is on Monte Mario northwest of the Aurelian Walls.

†The left hand of St Catherine of Siena rests within the church at this monastery.

Cappella del Transito di Santa Caterina da Siena

(Chapel of the Transit of St Catherine of Siena)

Palazzo Santa Chiara

Via Santa Chiara, 14

†This small chapel is located within the *Palazzo Santa Chiara* just a few blocks from the church of *Santa Maria sopra Minerva*. It marks the very spot where St Catherine of Siena died. The original walls and floor have been moved to *Santa Maria sopra Minerva* as noted previously. However, in 1638 the room was renovated and made into the chapel as seen today. Ask at the front desk for access.

Santa Sabina (Saint Sabina)

Piazza Pietro d'Illiria 1

†This church is located on the Aventine Hill just south of Circo Massimo.

†The large chapel on the left side of the nave is dedicated to St Catherine of Siena. The painting above the altar in this chapel, entitled *Madonna of the Rosary*, was completed by Giovanni Battista Salvi in 1643.

Santa Francesca Romana

(Saint Frances of Rome)

Piazza di Santa Francesca Romana 4

†This church is next to the Roman Forum.

†To the right of the sanctuary is the tomb of Pope Gregory XI (d. 1378). He returned the papal seat to Rome after the exile in Avignon. St Catherine of Siena (d. 1380) was instrumental in persuading him to return. A relief depicting her involvement can be seen on the tomb.

†The remains of St Frances of Rome (d. 1440) are in the crypt below the main sanctuary. Her skeleton is vested in the habit of the Oblate Sisters.

†Two flagstones within the right transept of the church are said to bear the imprints of the knees of St Peter. According to a legend the magician, Simon Magus, levitated in the Roman Forum to demonstrate that his powers were superior to those of Peter. In response, Peter fell to the ground in prayer causing the knee imprints on the stone. Simon Magus then immediately fell to his death.

Santa Caterina da Siena in Via Giulia

(Saint Catherine of Siena on Via Giulia)

Via Giulia 162/A

†This church is located on Via Giulia between the Corso Vittorio Emanuele and the Tiber River. It is not open often.

†The painting in the main sanctuary depicts the mystical marriage of St Catherine of Siena.

Santa Caterina a Magnanapoli

(Saint Catherine at Magnanapoli)

Salita del Grillo 37

†This church is east of Piazza Venezia and it is dedicated to St Catherine of Siena. It serves the Italian military.

April 30th
Optional memorial of Pius V, pope

St Pius V (d. 1572, Rome, Italy) (Relics: Rome, Italy)

Basilica of St Mary Major

Piazza di Santa Maria Maggiore 42

✝This basilica has two large transept chapels. The chapel in the right transept contains the remains of St Pius V. His body is enshrined on the left side of this chapel.

✝Within the porphyry base of the Papal Altar in the main body of this church are some relics of St Matthias. Also prominently placed within the confessio below this altar are five pieces of wood believed to be from the crib of Jesus Christ.

✝The remains of St Jerome (d. 420) were brought to this basilica in the 12th century. There is some doubt as to their exact location. They either rest under the Papal Altar within the main body of the church or within the confessio in the right transept.

Santa Maria sopra Minerva

(Our Lady Above Minerva)

Piazza della Minerva 42

✝This church is near the Pantheon.

✝The sixth chapel on the left side of the nave is dedicated to St Pius V.

✝The body of St Catherine of Siena (d. 1380) rests under the main altar.

May

May 1st
Optional Memorial of Saint Joseph the Worker

SEE THE 'FEAST OF ST JOSEPH' ON MARCH 19TH FOR CHURCHES IN HIS HONOR.

May 2nd
Memorial of Athanasius, bishop and doctor

St Athanasius (d. 373, Alexandria, Egypt) (Relics: Venice, Italy; Cairo, Egypt)

Sant'Atanasio (Saint Athanasius)
Via del Babuino 149
✝This church is near Piazza del Popolo and it is dedicated to St Athanasius. It is not open often.

May 3rd
Feast of Philip and James, apostles

St James the Less – The cousin of the Lord and the son of Alphaeus. (d. 62) (Relics: Rome, Italy; Jerusalem, Israel)

St Philip (Relics: Rome, Italy; Florence, Italy)

Santi Apostoli (Holy Apostles)
Piazza dei Santi Apostoli 51
✝This church is just east of Piazza Venezia.
✝Relics of St Philip and St James the Less rest within the confessio of this church. During the 6th century they were transferred from Constantinople to Rome by Pope Pelagius I (d. 561). In 1873, as excavations commenced below the central altar, their relics were unearthed. They were then carefully examined and repositioned within the confessio where they rest today.
✝Also the painting above the main altar depicts the martyrdom of St Philip and St James the Less. It was completed by Domenico Maria Muratori in the early 18th century.

May 10th
Optional memorial of Damien Joseph de Veuster of Moloka'i, priest*

St Damien Joseph de Veuster of Moloka'i (d. 1889) (Relics: Leuven, Belgium; Kalawao, Hawaii, USA; Honolulu, Hawaii, USA)

May 12th
Optional memorial of Nereus and Achilleus, martyrs

Saints Nereus and Achilleus (d. 4th century) (Relics: Rome, Italy)

Chiesa Nuova (The New Church)
Via del Governo Vecchio 134
✝This church is located along the Corso Vittorio Emanuele.
✝In 1597 this church received the skulls of Saints Nereus and Achilleus. They rest within reliquaries in the sacristy and are sometimes brought out for public veneration on May 12th.
✝The additional remains of Saints Nereus and Achilleus are said to rest within a porphyry urn under the main altar of this church. In 1870 they were stolen from the church of *Santi Nereo e Achilleo*; however, they were later recovered and are now said to rest here.
✝The body of St Philip Neri is enshrined in the left transept of this church. His private rooms can be visited on certain days of the week. They are located in the right wall of the left transept.

Santi Nereo e Achilleo
(Saints Nereus and Achilleus)
Via delle Terme di Caracalla 28
✝This church is south of the Colosseum. It is not open often.
✝In 1597 this church received relics of Saints Nereus and Achilleus through the efforts of Cardinal Cesare Baronio. They now rest in *Chiesa Nuova* as previously noted.

Basilica dei Santi Nereo ed Achilleo / Catacombe di Domitilla
(Basilica of Saints Nereus and Achilleus / Catacombs of Domitilla)
Via delle Sette Chiese 282
✝This ancient church is located south of the Aurelian Walls. It is not open often. Saints Nereus and Achilleus were originally buried in the catacombs located here.

May 12th
Optional memorial of Pancras, martyr

St Pancras (d. 4th century) (Relics: Rome, Italy)

San Pancrazio (Saint Pancras)
Piazza San Pancrazio 5/D
✝This church is west of Trastevere and was built on the site of St Pancras' tomb.
✝In 1798 a general under Napoleon Bonaparte invaded Rome and established the Roman Republic. During this time intruders entered the church of *San Pancrazio* and severely damaged the remains of St Pancras. His head, which was kept in the *Basilica of St John Lateran* from 850 to 1966, fortunately was left untouched. In 1966 Pope Paul VI returned this relic to *San Pancrazio*. It now rests within a reliquary bust on the right side of the nave.
✝Additionally, a few relics of St Pancras and other early church martyrs are said

to rest within the porphyry urn that makes up the base of the altar in the main sanctuary.

May 13th
Optional memorial of Our Lady of Fatima

Nostra Signora di Fatima a San Vittorino
(Our Lady of Fatima at San Vittorino)
Via Ponte Terra, San Vittorino
00132 Rome, Italy
✝This church is east of the city of Rome. It is the Italian shrine to Our Lady of Fatima.

FOR ADDITIONAL MARIAN CHURCHES TO VISIT PLEASE SEE THE LIST AT THE END OF THIS BOOK.

May 14th
Feast of Matthias, apostle

St Matthias (Relics: Rome, Italy; Trier, Germany)

St Helena is said to have acquired the relics of St Matthias in the 4th century. These relics were then distributed to both Rome, Italy and Trier, Germany.

Basilica of St Mary Major
Piazza di Santa Maria Maggiore 42
✝Some relics of St Matthias rest within the porphyry urn that makes up the base of the Papal Altar. Also in the confessio below this altar are five pieces of wood believed to be from the crib of Jesus Christ.
✝The remains of St Jerome (d. 420) were brought to this basilica in the 12th century. There is some doubt as to their exact location. They either rest under the Papal Altar within the main body of the

church or within the confessio in the right transept.

May 15th
Optional memorial of Isidore*

St Isidore the Farmer (d. 1130, Madrid, Spain) (Relics: Madrid, Spain)

Sant'Isidoro a Capo le Case
(St Isidore at the Head of the Houses)
Via degli Artisti 41
✝This church is north of the Barberini metro stop. It is not open often. However, if one rings at the gate the sacristan may grant access.

May 18th
Optional memorial of John I, pope and martyr

St John I (d. 526, Ravenna, Italy) (Relics: Rome, Italy)

St Peter's Basilica
✝St John I reigned as pope for less than three years. During his brief papacy he ardently supported orthodoxy despite intense pressures exerted by the Arian ruler of Italy, King Theodoric. Eventually the king had him arrested. Due to the poor treatment that he received while imprisoned he passed away in 526 AD. His body now rests in the crypt of this basilica.

May 20th
Optional memorial of Bernardine of Siena, priest

St Bernardine of Siena (d. 1444, d. L'Aquila, Italy) (Relics: L'Aquila, Italy)

San Bernardino da Siena ai Monti
(Saint Bernardine of Siena at the Hills)

Via Panisperna 256
✝This church is west of the *Basilica of St Mary Major*. It is dedicated to St Bernardine of Siena. At present it serves the Chinese community.

Santa Maria in Aracoeli
(Our Lady in Aracoeli)
Piazza del Campidoglio 4
✝This church is on top of the Capitoline Hill.
✝The first chapel on the right side of the nave depicts scenes from the life of St Bernardine of Siena.

May 21st
Optional memorial of Christopher Magallanes, priest and martyr, and Companions, martyrs

Honored on this day are 25 martyrs who died in Mexico from the years 1915-1937. (Relics: Totatiche, Mexico)

May 22nd
Optional memorial of Rita of Cascia, religious

St Rita of Cascia (d. 1457, Cascia, Italy) (Relics: Cascia, Italy)

Santa Rita da Cascia alle Vergini
(Saint Rita of Cascia at the Vergini)
Via del Umiltà 83B
✝This church is south of the Trevi Fountain. It is dedicated to St Rita of Cascia.

Sant'Agostino (Saint Augustine)
Piazza Sant'Agostino
✝This church is near Piazza Navona.
✝The third chapel on the right side of the nave is dedicated to St Rita of Cascia.
✝Relics of St Monica (d. 387) rest in the chapel to the left of the main altar.

Santa Maria del Popolo
(Our Lady of the People)
Piazza del Popolo 12
✝This church is at Piazza del Popolo.
✝A chapel to the right of the main sanctuary is dedicated to St Rita of Cascia.

May 25th
Optional memorial of Bede the Venerable, priest and doctor

St Bede (d. 735, Jarrow, Northumbria, United Kingdom) (Relics: Durham, United Kingdom)

May 25th
Optional memorial of Gregory VII, pope

St Gregory VII (d. 1085, Salerno, Italy) (Relics: Salerno, Italy)

San Gregorio Settimo
(Saint Gregory the Seventh)
Via del Cottolengo 4
✝This is a modern church located near the Vatican. It is dedicated to St Gregory VII.

May 25th
Optional memorial of Mary Magdalene de Pazzi, virgin

St Mary Magdalene de Pazzi (d. 1607, Florence, Italy) (Relics: Florence, Italy)

Santa Maria in Traspontina
(Our Lady in Traspontina)
Via della Conciliazione 14
✝This church is near the Vatican.
✝The chapel in the right transept is dedicated to St Mary Magdalene de Pazzi.
✝Also the third chapel on the right side of the nave contains a beautiful statue of

Our Lady of Mt Carmel. A memorial at this chapel recalls that this church provided a new scapular for St John Paul II after the assassination attempt upon his life in 1981.

San Martino ai Monti
(Saint Martin at the Hills)
Viale Monte Oppio 28
✝This church is south of the *Basilica of St Mary Major*.
✝The first chapel on the right side of the nave is dedicated to St Mary Magdalene de Pazzi.
✝The greater part of the remains of St Martin I (d. 655) were transferred from Crimea to this church in Rome. They now rest in the confessio below the main altar. This confessio also houses the relics of many other saints taken from the *Catacombs of Priscilla*.

San Giovanni Battista dei Fiorentini
(Saint John the Baptist of the Florentines)
Via Acciaioli 2
✝This church is just east of the Vatican. It is next to the Tiber River and the Corso Vittorio Emanuele.
✝The second chapel on the left side of the nave is dedicated to St Mary Magdalene de Pazzi.
✝A relic of St Mary Magdalene's foot also rests in a shrine to the left of the main sanctuary.

May 26th
Memorial of Philip Neri, priest

St Philip Neri (d. 1595, Rome, Italy) (Relics: Rome, Italy)

Chiesa Nuova (The New Church)
Via del Governo Vecchio 134
✝This church is located along the Corso Vittorio Emanuele.

✝The body of St Philip Neri is enshrined in the left transept of this church. His private rooms can be visited on certain days of the week. They are located in the right wall of the left transept. St Philip Neri spent the last 12 years of his life at *Chiesa Nuova*.

✝In 1597 this church received the skulls of Saints Nereus and Achilleus. They rest within reliquaries in the sacristy and are sometimes brought out for public veneration on May 12th.

✝The additional remains of Saints Nereus and Achilleus are said to rest within a porphyry urn under the main altar of this church. In 1870 they were stolen from the church of *Santi Nereo e Achilleo*; however, they were later recovered and are now said to rest here.

San Sebastiano Fuori Le Mura
(Saint Sebastian Outside the Walls)
Via Appia Antica 136

✝This church is south of the Aurelian Walls.

✝Tradition claims that within the catacombs located under this church St Philip Neri experienced such an enlargement of his heart due to a supernatural infusion of God's love that two of his ribs cracked.

✝These same catacombs also at one time housed the remains of St Sebastian (d. 288). At some point, however, his remains were removed. Some of these remains are now located within an urn in a chapel on the left side of the nave. This is the chapel with the very impressive statue of St Sebastian created by Giuseppe Giorgetti.

✝Directly across from this chapel on the right side of the nave is a reliquary chapel that contains the column to which St Sebastian was tied and an arrow that pierced his flesh. Also within this same reliquary chapel are some small relics said to be from St Peter, St Paul, St Andrew, and a number of other saints including the pope, St Fabian (d. 250). St Fabian was originally buried in the *Catacombs of San Callisto* but later his remains were moved to this church.

✝This church also has an ancient tradition connecting it to St Peter and to St Paul. The *Depositio Martyrum* shows that in the year 258 pilgrims came to *San Sebastiano Fuori Le Mura* on June 29th, the Feast Day of Saints Peter and Paul, to honor these two great saints. Therefore, it is presumed that at one time this church housed the remains of both St Peter and St Paul.

San Giovanni Battista dei Fiorentini
(Saint John the Baptist of the Florentines)
Via Acciaioli 2

✝This church is just east of the Vatican. It is next to the Tiber River and the Corso Vittorio Emanuele.

✝St Philip Neri became rector of this church in 1564. He also founded the Congregation of the Oratory at this church.

✝A relic of St Mary Magdalene's foot rests in a shrine to the left of the main sanctuary.

San Girolamo della Carità
(Saint Jerome of Charity)
Via di Monserrato 62/a

✝This church is near Piazza Farnese.

✝St Philip Neri lived here from 1551 to 1583.

✝In the left transept is a spectacular chapel honoring St Philip Neri. A marble statue of the saint is surrounded by a gilded frame. The ceiling opens up revealing a small domed space filled with further statues of angels.

✝This church was built on the site of the house of St Paula. Tradition claims that St Jerome (d. 420) lived in this house when he was secretary to Pope St Damasus I (d. 384).

Sant'Agostino (Saint Augustine)
Piazza Sant'Agostino
✝This church is near Piazza Navona.
✝Prior to his ordination, St Philip Neri prayed at this church in front of the crucifix located within the fifth chapel on the right side of the nave. Through these prayers he was inspired to sell all that he had and to give his life completely to the Lord.
✝Relics of St Monica (d. 387) rest in the chapel to the left of the main altar.

May 27th
Optional memorial of Augustine of Canterbury, bishop

St Augustine of Canterbury (d. 605, Canterbury, United Kingdom) (Relics: St Augustine of Canterbury's shrine was destroyed and his relics were lost during the English Reformation.)

May 31st
Feast of The Visitation of The Blessed Virgin Mary

Chiesa Nuova (The New Church)
Via del Governo Vecchio 134
✝This church is along the Corso Vittorio Emanuele.
✝The fourth chapel on the left side of the nave is dedicated to the Visitation.
✝The body of St Philip Neri (d. 1595) is enshrined in the left transept. His private rooms can be visited on certain days of the week. They are located in the right wall of the left transept.

Santa Maria del Popolo
(Our Lady of the People)
Piazza del Popolo 12
✝This church is at Piazza del Popolo.
✝A painting of the Visitation completed by Giovanni Maria Morandi in 1659 rests above the altar in the right transept.

Santissima Trinità dei Monti
(Most Holy Trinity of the Mounts)
Piazza della Trinità dei Monti
✝This church is at the top of the Spanish Steps.
✝Within the third chapel on the left side of the nave is a fresco of the Visitation by Joseph Ernst Tunner.

FOR ADDITIONAL MARIAN CHURCHES TO VISIT PLEASE SEE THE LIST AT THE END OF THIS BOOK.

June

June 1st
Memorial of Justin, martyr

St Justin (d. 165, Rome, Italy) (Relics: Rome, Italy; Sacrofano, Italy)

Santa Maria della Concezione
(Our Lady of the Immaculate Conception)
Via Veneto 27
✝This church is just north of the Barberini metro stop.
✝Relics of St Justin the Martyr rest under the altar within the choir chapel. Kindly ask the sacristan for access. The remains of St Justin the Martyr were temporarily transferred in 1992 to the parish church of *San Giustino a Centocelle* in Rome; however, they have now been returned to this church.
✝The bones of nearly 4,000 Capuchin friars are located in the crypt.

San Lorenzo fuori le Mura
(Saint Lawrence Outside the Walls)
Piazzale del Verano 3
✝This church is east of the Aurelian Walls.
✝The remains of St Lawrence (d. 258), St Stephen, and St Justin lie in the confessio below the main altar. (Note: The relics are labeled as St Justin the Presbyter. Therefore, it is likely that this is not St Justin the Martyr.)
✝A marble stone slab beneath the choir floor is said to be the stone on which St Lawrence was placed after his execution. Also enshrined in this lower area is the body of Blessed Pius IX (d. 1878).

June 2nd
Optional memorial of Marcellinus and Peter, martyrs

Saints Marcellinus and Peter (d. 304, Rome, Italy) (Relics: Rome, Italy; Seligenstadt, Germany)

Santi Marcellino e Pietro
(Saints Marcellinus and Peter)
Via Merulana 162
✝This church is near the *Basilica of St John Lateran*.
✝Relics of Saints Marcellinus and Peter are preserved within the main altar of this church. Typically on their feast day they are brought out and exposed for public veneration. A large painting depicting their martyrdom is also placed above the main altar.

Catacombs of Marcellinus and Peter
Via Casilina 641
✝These catacombs are located east of the Aurelian Walls.
✝The bodies of Saints Marcellinus and Peter were buried in these catacombs prior to their transfer to *Santi Marcellino e Pietro*.

June 3rd
Memorial of Charles Lwanga and Companions, martyrs (Uganda martyrs)

Honored on this day are 22 martyrs who died in Uganda from the years 1885-1887. (Relics: Namugongo, Uganda)

June 5th
Memorial of Boniface, bishop and martyr

St Boniface (d. 754, Dokkum, Netherlands) (Relics: Fulda, Germany)

June 6th
Optional memorial of Norbert, bishop

St Norbert (d. 1134, Saxony-Anhalt, Germany) (Relics: Prague, Czech Republic)

June 9th
Optional memorial of Ephrem, deacon and doctor

St Ephrem (d. 373, Edessa, Turkey)

June 11th
Memorial of Barnabas, apostle

St Barnabas (d. Cyprus) (Relics: Famagusta, Cyprus)

San Carlo al Corso
(Saint Charles on the Corso)
Via del Corso 437
✝This church is near the Spanish Steps.
✝The first chapel on the left side of the nave is dedicated to St Barnabas. An early legend claimed that he was the first bishop of Milan.
✝The heart of St Charles Borromeo (d. 1584) rests within a reliquary in an altar located behind the main sanctuary.

June 13th
Memorial of Anthony of Padua, priest and doctor

St Anthony of Padua (d. 1231, Padua, Italy) (Relics: Padua, Italy)

Sant'Antonio dei Portoghesi
(Saint Anthony of the Portuguese)
Via dei Portoghesi 2
✝This church is northeast of Piazza Navona. It is dedicated to St Anthony of Padua.

✝The altarpiece within the main sanctuary depicts St Anthony with the Blessed Virgin Mary and the Christ Child.

Sant'Antonio da Padova
(Saint Anthony of Padua)
Via Merulana 124
✝This church is near the *Basilica of St John Lateran*. It is dedicated to St Anthony of Padua.

Santi Apostoli (Holy Apostles)
Piazza dei Santi Apostoli 51
✝This church is just east of Piazza Venezia.
✝The third chapel on the right side of the nave is dedicated to St Anthony of Padua.
✝Relics of St Philip and St James the Less also rest within the confessio.

Santa Maria in Aracoeli
(Our Lady in Aracoeli)
Piazza del Campidoglio 4
✝This church is on top of the Capitoline Hill.
✝The third chapel on the left side of the nave is dedicated to St Anthony of Padua. The fresco in this chapel was completed by Benozzo Gozzoli in the 15th century.

Santa Maria della Concezione
(Our Lady of the Immaculate Conception)
Via Veneto 27
✝This church is just north of the Barberini metro stop.
✝The fifth chapel on the right side of the nave is dedicated to St Anthony of Padua. The altarpiece, completed by Andrea Sacchi, depicts St Anthony raising a dead man.

June 19th
Optional memorial of Romuald, abbot

St Romuald (d. 1027, Val di Castro, Italy) (Relics: Fabriano, Italy)

June 21st
Memorial of Aloysius Gonzaga, religious

St Aloysius Gonzaga (d. 1591, Rome, Italy) (Relics: Rome, Italy; Castiglione delle Stiviere, Italy)

Sant'Ignazio (Saint Ignatius)
Via del Caravita 8/a
†This church is east of the Pantheon.
†The remains of St Aloysius Gonzaga rest under the altar in the right transept. His rooms are next to the church and can be visited by appointment.
†The body of St Robert Bellarmine (d. 1621) rests under the altar in the third chapel on the right side of the nave.
†The remains of St John Berchmans (d. 1621), the patron saint of altar servers, rest under the altar in the left transept.

Santa Maria della Consolazione
(Our Lady of Consolation)
Piazza della Consolazione 94
†This church is east of Tiber Island.
†In 1506 a hospital was founded adjacent to this church. It was at this hospital that St Aloysius Gonzaga contracted the plague while caring for the sick. He eventually died from this disease at the age of twenty-three.

Santissimo Nome di Maria al Foro Traiano (The Most Holy Name of Mary at Trajan's Forum)
Piazza Foro Traiano 89

†This church is near Trajan's column just east of Piazza Venezia.
†The first chapel on the right side of the nave is dedicated to St Aloysius Gonzaga.

Santo Spirito in Sassia
(Holy Spirit in Sassia)
Via dei Penitenzieri 12
†This church is near the Vatican.
†A statue of St Aloysius Gonzaga is placed within the first chapel on the left side of the nave.

San Carlo al Corso
(Saint Charles on the Corso)
Via del Corso 437
†This church is near the Spanish Steps.
†A painting depicting St Aloysius Gonzaga among the plague stricken is within the second chapel on the left side of the nave.
†The heart of St Charles Borromeo (d. 1584) rests within a reliquary in an altar located behind the main sanctuary.

June 22nd
Optional memorial of Paulinus of Nola, bishop

St Paulinus of Nola (d. 431, Sicily) (Relics: Nola, Italy; Sutera, Sicily)

San Bartolomeo all'Isola
(Saint Bartholomew on the Island)
Piazza San Bartolomeo, Tiber Island
†This church housed the relics of St Paulinus of Nola for about 1000 years until they were transferred to the Italian city of Nola in 1909.
†Relics of the apostle, St Bartholomew, rest within the red porphyry basin that supports the main altar.

✝The Holy Roman Emperor, Otto III, began building *San Bartolomeo all'Isola* in 998 to honor his friend St Adalbert (d. 997) who had been recently martyred. An arm of St Adalbert is currently enshrined in the chapel to the left of the main sanctuary. It rests within a little metal box placed under the altar of this chapel.

June 22nd
Optional memorial of John Fisher, bishop and martyr; Thomas More, martyr

St John Fisher (d. 1535, London, United Kingdom) (Relics: London, United Kingdom)

St Thomas More (d. 1535, London, United Kingdom) (Relics: London, United Kingdom; Canterbury, United Kingdom)

San Tommaso Moro
(Saint Thomas More)
Via dei Marrucini 1
✝This church is outside of the Aurelian Walls just east of Termini. It is dedicated to St Thomas More.

June 24th
Solemnity of the Birth of John the Baptist

St John the Baptist (Relics: Rome, Italy; Florence, Italy; Siena, Italy; Amiens, France; Munich, Germany; Damascus, Syria)

San Silvestro in Capite
(Saint Sylvester in Capite)
Piazza San Silvestro
✝This church is near the Spanish Steps.
✝A relic of the skull of St John the Baptist rests within the chapel to the left

of the main entrance. The authenticity is uncertain since this same relic is said to be located at a number of other places throughout the world including the *Cathedral of Amiens* in France, the *Residenz Museum* in Munich, Germany, and the *Umayyad Mosque* in Damascus, Syria.
✝The remains of St Sylvester I (d. 335) rest in the confessio below the main altar. Also a work from 1688 depicting the legend of St Sylvester I baptizing Constantine can be seen in the apse vault.

Basilica of St John Lateran
Piazza San Giovanni in Laterano 4
✝This basilica is dedicated to both St John the Baptist and St John the Evangelist.
✝Within the *Colonna Chapel* to the left of the main sanctuary is a painting completed by Giuseppe Cesari of St John the Baptist and St John the Evangelist pointing to Christ. Another painting of these two saints is on the left wall of the *Lancellotti Chapel*. Also within the confessio below the Papal Altar is a statue of St John the Baptist.
✝The baptistry next to the basilica also has a chapel dedicated to St John the Baptist.

San Giovanni Battista dei Fiorentini
(Saint John the Baptist of the Florentines)
Via Acciaioli 2
✝This church is just east of the Vatican. It is next to the Tiber River and the Corso Vittorio Emanuele. It is dedicated to St John the Baptist.
✝In the sanctuary is a large sculpture of the Baptism of Christ.
✝Also a relic of St Mary Magdalene's foot rests in a shrine to the left of the main sanctuary.

Santissima Trinità dei Monti
(Most Holy Trinity of the Mounts)
Piazza della Trinità dei Monti
†This church is at the top of the Spanish Steps.
†The first chapel on the right side of the nave is dedicated to St John the Baptist.

Sant'Antonio dei Portoghesi
(Saint Anthony of the Portuguese)
Via dei Portoghesi 2
†This church is northeast of Piazza Navona.
†The second chapel on the right side of the nave is dedicated to St John the Baptist.

Santa Maria sopra Minerva
(Our Lady Above Minerva)
Piazza della Minerva 42
†This church is near the Pantheon.
†Within the second chapel on the left side of the nave is a painting of St John the Baptist completed by Francesco Nappi.
†Also the body of St Catherine of Siena (d. 1380) rests under the main altar.

June 27th
Optional memorial of Cyril of Alexandria, bishop and doctor

St Cyril of Alexandria (d. 444)

June 28th
Memorial of Irenaeus, bishop and martyr

St Irenaeus of Lyon (d. 203, Lyon, France) (Relics: St Irenaeus was buried in Lyon; however, his tomb and remains were totally destroyed by Huguenots in 1562.)

June 29th
Solemnity of Peter and Paul, apostles

St Peter (Relics: Rome, Italy)
St Paul (Relics: Rome, Italy; Valletta, Malta)

St Peter's Basilica
†Tradition holds that St Peter was crucified upside down in the middle of Nero's Circus. The *Altar of The Crucifixion*, located in the left transept of *St Peter's Basilica*, is very close to the actual site where this crucifixion took place.
†The bones of St Peter are in the confessio below the Papal Altar and his jawbone can be seen on the Scavi tour.
†Tradition also holds that within the large bronze chair located above the *Altar of the Chair* in the apse of the church is a second smaller chair made out of wood. This second chair is said to consist of fragments from the original Episcopal chair that St Peter once sat in.

Basilica of St Paul Outside the Walls
Via Ostiense 186
†St Paul is buried in the confessio of this church. Above his tomb are the chains that had been used to imprison him prior to his martyrdom. These chains were placed in this prominent location in 2008.
†Also a crucifix that is said to have spoken to St Bridget in 1370 is in the Blessed Sacrament Chapel.

Basilica of St John Lateran
Piazza San Giovanni in Laterano 4
†Positioned above the Papal Altar of this church are two busts of St Peter and St Paul. According to tradition the skulls or

parts of the skulls of St Peter and St Paul are within these busts. Also located within the Papal Altar is a wooden table that St Peter and many of the earliest popes are said to have celebrated the Eucharist upon.

✝Located to the left of the Papal Altar is another very ancient table. This table rests above the altar where the Blessed Sacrament is reserved. It is placed directly behind a bronze relief of the Last Supper. Tradition claims that it was upon this table that Jesus and the apostles celebrated the Last Supper.

San Sebastiano Fuori Le Mura
(Saint Sebastian Outside the Walls)
Via Appia Antica 136

✝This church is south of the Aurelian Walls.

✝This church has an ancient tradition connecting it to St Peter and St Paul. The *Depositio Martyrum* shows that in the year 258 pilgrims came to *San Sebastiano Fuori Le Mura* on June 29th, the Feast Day of Saints Peter and Paul, to honor these two great saints. Therefore, it is presumed that at one time this church housed the remains of both St Peter and St Paul.

✝St Sebastian (d. 288) was originally buried in the catacombs located under this church. At some point, however, his remains were removed. Some of these remains are now located within an urn in a chapel on the left side of the nave. This is the chapel with the very impressive statue of St Sebastian created by Giuseppe Giorgetti.

✝Directly across from this chapel on the right side of the nave is a reliquary chapel that contains the column to which St Sebastian was tied and an arrow that pierced his flesh. Also within this same reliquary chapel are some small relics said to be from St Peter, St Paul, St Andrew, and a number of other saints including the pope, St Fabian (d. 250). St Fabian was originally buried in the *Catacombs of San Callisto* but later his remains were moved to this church.

✝Tradition also claims that within the catacombs located under this church St Philip Neri (d. 1595) experienced such an enlargement of his heart due to a supernatural infusion of God's love that two of his ribs cracked.

SEE 'THE CHAIR OF ST PETER' ON FEBRUARY 22ND FOR ADDITIONAL CHURCHES IN ST PETER'S HONOR.

SEE 'THE CONVERSION OF ST PAUL' ON JANUARY 25TH FOR ADDITIONAL CHURCHES IN ST PAUL'S HONOR.

June 30th
Optional memorial of The First Martyrs of the Church of Rome

Pantheon / Santa Maria dei Martiri
(Our Lady of the Martyrs)
Piazza della Rotonda

✝This ancient temple was converted into a Christian church in the year 609. It now honors the Blessed Virgin Mary and the Christian martyrs.

July

July 1st
Optional memorial of Blessed Junipero Serra, priest*

Blessed Junipero Serra (d. 1784, Carmel, California, USA) (Relics: Carmel, California, USA)

July 3rd
Feast of Thomas, apostle

St Thomas (Relics: Rome, Italy; Ortona, Italy; Mylapore, India)

Santa Croce in Gerusalemme
(Holy Cross In Jerusalem)
Piazza di Santa Croce in Gerusalemme 12
✝This church is east of the the *Basilica of St John Lateran.*
✝A bone from the index finger of St Thomas the Apostle is located here. It is said that this is the same finger that he inserted into the side of the Risen Christ. Also the first chapel on the left side of the nave is dedicated to St Thomas.
✝Also found here are relics of the True Cross brought to Rome by St Helena in 325. These relics include: the Titulus Crucis (This is the sign that hung over the head of Christ and that declared him to be the King of the Jews), a Crucifixion nail, a fragment of the True Cross, two thorns from the Crown of Thorns, the greater part of the sponge used to give Christ vinegar, and a piece of the cross from the good thief (St Dismas).
✝This chapel can be accessed by the staircase on the left side of the sanctuary.

San Tommaso in Parione
(Saint Thomas in Parione)
Via Parione 33
✝This church is near Piazza Navona. It is not open often.
✝This is the national church of Ethiopia and it is dedicated to St Thomas the Apostle.

July 5th
Optional memorial of Elizabeth of Portugal*

St Elizabeth of Portugal (d. 1336, Coimbra, Portugal) (Relics: Coimbra, Portugal)

Sant'Antonio dei Portoghesi
(Saint Anthony of the Portuguese)
Via dei Portoghesi 2
✝This church is northeast of Piazza Navona. It is the national church of Portugal.
✝The chapel in the right transept is dedicated to St Elizabeth of Portugal. The altarpiece is entitled *St Elizabeth Reconciling Her Husband and Son.*

July 5th
Optional memorial of Anthony Zaccaria, priest

St Anthony Zaccaria (d. 1539, Cremona, Italy) (Relics: Milan, Italy)

San Carlo ai Catinari
(Saint Charles at the Catinari)
Piazza Benedetto Cairoli 117
✝This church is near the Largo di Torre Argentina. For many centuries it was run by the Barnabites. The third chapel on the left side of the nave is dedicated to their founder, St Anthony Zaccaria.

July 6th
Optional memorial of Maria Goretti, virgin and martyr

St Maria Goretti (d. 1902, Le Ferriere / Ferriere di Conca, Italy) (Relics: Nettuno, Italy)

July 9th
Optional Memorial of Augustine Zhao Rong, priest and martyr, and Companions, martyrs (Chinese martyrs)

Honored on this day are 120 martyrs who died in China from the years 1648-1930. (Relics: Paris, France)

July 11th
Memorial of Benedict, abbot

St Benedict (b. 480, Norcia, Italy) (d. 547, Monte Cassino, Italy) (Relics: Monte Cassino, Italy; Saint-Benoît-sur-Loire, France; Brescia, Italy)

San Benedetto a Piscinula
(Saint Benedict at Piscinula)
Piazza in Piscinula 40
†This church is located in Trastevere near the Ponte Sisto Bridge.
†Tradition claims that St Benedict stayed at the location of this church during a visit to Rome.

Basilica of St Paul Outside the Walls
Via Ostiense 186
†This basilica is south of the Aurelian Walls.
†In the right transept is a small chapel dedicated to St Benedict.
†St Paul is buried in the confessio. Above his tomb are the chains that had been used to imprison him prior to his martyrdom. These chains were placed in this prominent location in 2008.

†Also a crucifix that is said to have spoken to St Bridget in 1370 is in the Blessed Sacrament Chapel.

Santi Benedetto e Scolastica
(Saint Benedict and Scholastica)
Vicolo Sinibaldi 1
†This church is just south of the Pantheon. Its postal address is on Vicolo Sinibaldi; however, its front door is just around the corner on Via Torre Argentina.
†The church is very small and it is set into the surrounding buildings. It is dedicated to both St Benedict and St Scholastica. It is not open often.

July 13th
Optional memorial of Henry

St Henry (d. 1024, Gottingen, Germany) (Relics: Bamberg, Germany)

July 14th
Memorial of Kateri Tekakwitha, virgin*

St Kateri Tekakwitha (d. 1680, Kahnawake, Quebec, Canada) (Relics: Kahnawake, Quebec, Canada)

July 15th
Memorial of Bonaventure, bishop and doctor

St Bonaventure (d. 1274, Lyon, France) (Relics: Bagnoregio, Italy)

San Bonaventura al Palatino
(Saint Bonaventure at the Palatine)
Via San Bonaventura 7
†This church is in the Roman Forum. It is not open often.
†Within this small church are a number of paintings by Giovanni Battista Benaschi from the 17th century.

Santi Apostoli (Holy Apostles)
Piazza dei Santi Apostoli 51
✝This church is just east of Piazza Venezia.
✝The first chapel on the right side of the nave is dedicated to St Bonaventure.
✝Relics of St Philip and St James the Less rest within the confessio.

Santa Maria della Concezione
(Our Lady of the Immaculate Conception)
Via Veneto 27
✝This church is just north of the Barberini metro stop.
✝The fifth chapel on the left side of the nave is dedicated to St Bonaventure. The altarpiece within this chapel was completed by Andrea Sacchi.

Santa Croce e San Bonaventura dei Lucchesi
(Holy Cross and Saint Bonaventure of the Lucchesi)
Via dei Lucchesi 3
✝This church is near the Trevi Fountain. It is not open often.
✝The first chapel on the left side of the nave is dedicated to St Bonaventure.

July 16th
Optional memorial of Our Lady of Mt Carmel

Santa Maria in Traspontina
(Our Lady in Traspontina)
Via della Conciliazione 14
✝This church is near the Vatican.
✝The third chapel on the right side of the nave contains a beautiful statue of Our Lady of Mt Carmel. A memorial at this chapel recalls the new scapular that this church gifted to St John Paul II after the assassination attempt upon his life in 1981.

Santa Maria della Vittoria
(Our Lady of the Victory)
Via XX Settembre 17
✝This church is north of Piazza della Repubblica.
✝A marble statue within the third chapel on the right side of the nave depicts St Simon Stock receiving the scapular from the Blessed Virgin Mary.
✝Also located in this church is Gian Lorenzo Bernini's famous sculpture entitled *The Ecstasy of St Teresa*.

San Martino ai Monti
(Saint Martin at the Hills)
Viale Monte Oppio 28
✝This church is south of the *Basilica of St Mary Major*. The chapel to the left of the main sanctuary honors Our Lady of Mt Carmel.
✝The greater part of the remains of St Martin I (d. 655) were transferred from Crimea to this church in Rome. They now rest in the confessio below the main altar. This confessio also houses the relics of many other saints taken from the *Catacombs of Priscilla*.

Santa Maria della Scala
(Our Lady at the Steps)
Piazza della Scala 23
✝This church is located in Trastevere.
✝The first chapel on the left side of the nave is dedicated to Our Lady of Mount Carmel.
✝The right foot of St Teresa of Avila (d. 1582) rests within a beautiful chapel to the left of the main sanctuary. It was gifted to this church in 1617. (This chapel is not visible from the nave of the church and it is rarely open to the public. However, if one kindly asks the sacristan access may be granted. If the sacristan is not present he or she can be called at the neighboring convent door.)

FOR ADDITIONAL MARIAN CHURCHES TO VISIT PLEASE SEE THE LIST AT THE END OF THIS BOOK.

July 18th
Optional memorial of Camillus de Lellis, priest*

St Camillus de Lellis (d. 1614, Rome, Italy) (Relics: Rome, Italy)

La Maddalena (The Magdalene)
Piazza della Maddalena 53
†This church is just north of the Pantheon.
†In the chapel in the right transept is a miraculous crucifix that is said to have spoken to St Camillus de Lellis.
†In the third chapel on the right side of the nave are the remains of St Camillus de Lellis. He lived in the adjacent monastery and died here in 1614. His rooms can be visited by asking the sacristan. One of these rooms has been transformed into a chapel and contains the relic of his heart.

San Camillo de Lellis
(Saint Camillus de Lellis)
Via Sallustiana 24
†This church is north of Piazza della Repubblica.
†A small relic of St Camillus de Lellis is venerated on the left side of the nave.

San Giacomo in Augusta /
San Giacomo degli Incurabili
(Saint James in Augusta / Saint James of the Incurables)
Via del Corso 499
†This church is near Piazza del Popolo.
†This was traditionally a hospital church. St Camillus de Lellis used to live and work at the hospital next to this church.

July 20th
Optional Memorial of Apollinaris, bishop and martyr

St Apollinaris (d. 1st century, Ravenna, Italy) (Relics: Ravenna, Italy; Remagen, Germany; Düsseldorf, Germany)

Basilica di Sant'Apollinare alle Terme
(Basilica of Saint Apollinaris at the Baths)
Piazza Sant'Apollinare 49
†This church is located just north of Piazza Navona. It is dedicated to St Apollinaris.
†This is the church at the *Santa Croce University.*

July 21st
Optional memorial of Lawrence of Brindisi, priest and doctor

St Lawrence of Brindisi (d. 1619, Lisbon, Portugal) (Relics: Villafranca del Bierzo, Spain)

Santa Maria in Aracoeli
(Our Lady in Aracoeli)
Piazza del Campidoglio 4
†This church is on top of the Capitoline Hill.
†The eighth chapel on the right side of the nave, located just after the side entrance, is dedicated to St Lawrence of Brindisi. A small fresco above the altar depicts him writing about the Blessed Virgin Mary.

July 22nd
Memorial of Mary Magdalene

St Mary Magdalene (Relics: Rome, Italy; Plan-d'Aups-Sainte-Baume, France; Saint-Maximin-La-Sainte-Baume, France; Vézelay, France)

San Giovanni Battista dei Fiorentini

(Saint John the Baptist of the Florentines)
Via Acciaioli 2

✝This church is just east of the Vatican. It is next to the Tiber River and the Corso Vittorio Emanuele.

✝A relic of St Mary Magdalene's foot rests in a shrine to the left of the main sanctuary. Also the chapel in the left transept is dedicated to her.

La Maddalena (The Magdalene)

Piazza della Maddalena 53

✝This church is just north of the Pantheon. It is dedicated to St Mary Magdalene.

✝Within the passageway to the left of the main sanctuary is a 15th century statue of St Mary Magdalene. She is also depicted in the large painting in the main sanctuary.

Santa Maria sopra Minerva

(Our Lady Above Minerva)
Piazza della Minerva 42

✝This church is near the Pantheon.

✝Within the small baptismal chapel on the right side of the nave is a 16th century painting of Mary Magdalene by Marcello Venusti entitled *Noli me tangere*.

Santissima Trinità dei Monti

(Most Holy Trinity of the Mounts)
Piazza della Trinità dei Monti

✝This church is at the top of the Spanish Steps.

✝Within the fifth chapel on the left side of the nave is another 16th century masterpiece entitled *Noli me tangere*.

July 23rd
Optional memorial of Bridget, religious

St Bridget (d. 1373, Rome, Italy)
(Relics: Rome, Italy; Vadstena, Sweden)

Santa Brigida a Campo de' Fiori

(Saint Bridget at the Field of Flowers)
Piazza Farnese 96

✝This church is at Piazza Farnese.

✝Following the death of her husband, St Bridget of Sweden devoted herself completely to a life of prayer and service. After founding the Bridgettine Sisters in Sweden she felt compelled to visit Rome in order to seek official approval for her community. Her visit resulted in her permanently remaining in the city for the next twenty-four years until her passing in 1373. Today a few of her relics rest within this Bridgettine convent which still to this day is occupied by members of her community. Her body was returned to Sweden shortly after her death.

San Lorenzo in Panisperna

(Saint Lawrence in Panisperna)
Via Panisperna 90

✝This church is west of the *Basilica of St Mary Major*. It is often closed during the week. However, it is always open for the faithful during Sunday liturgies.

✝The second chapel on the left side of the nave is dedicated to St Bridget. Her body was originally buried in this chapel before being moved to Sweden. She used to beg for alms for the poor outside of this church and prayed before the crucifix by the main altar.

✝This church also rests over the spot of St Lawrence's martyrdom (d. 258). A chapel built under the porch marks where it occurred.

Basilica of St Paul Outside the Walls
Via Ostiense 186
✝This basilica is south of the Aurelian Walls. In the Blessed Sacrament Chapel is a crucifix that is said to have spoken to St Bridget in 1370.
✝St Paul is buried in the confessio. Above his tomb are the chains that had been used to imprison him prior to his martyrdom. These chains were placed in this prominent location in 2008.

July 24th
Optional Memorial of Sharbel Makhluf, priest

St Sharbel Makhluf (d. 1898, Annaya, Jbeil District, Lebanon) (Relics: Annaya, Jbeil District, Lebanon)

July 25th
Feast of James, apostle

St James the Greater – The brother of St John the Evangelist (d. 44) (Relics: Santiago de Compostela, Spain; Jerusalem, Israel)

San Giacomo in Augusta /
San Giacomo degli Incurabili
(Saint James in Augusta / Saint James of the Incurables)
Via del Corso 499
✝This church is near Piazza del Popolo. It is dedicated to St James the Greater.
✝Within the second chapel on the left side of the nave is a large statue of St James the Greater sculpted by Ippolito Buzio.

Santa Maria in Monserrato
(Our Lady of Montserrat)
Via di Monserrato
✝This church is near the Piazza Farnese.
✝The third chapel on the left side of the nave is dedicated to St James the Great.

Within this chapel is a large statue of St James completed by Jacopo Sansovino in the 16th century. Prior to the French occupation of Rome this statue had been located at *San Giacomo dei Spagnoli* near Piazza Navona. The damage that this church suffered during the French occupation prompted the Spanish to abandon this church in the 19th century. Much of its art was then transferred to *Santa Maria in Monserrato* or returned to Spain.

Santa Maria sopra Minerva
(Our Lady Above Minerva)
Piazza della Minerva 42
✝This church is near the Pantheon.
✝Within the fifth chapel on the left side of the nave is a painting of St James the Greater completed by Marcello Venusti in the 16th century.
✝Also the body of St Catherine of Siena (d. 1380) rests under the main altar.

Nostra Signora del Sacro Cuore
(Our Lady of the Sacred Heart)
Corso del Rinascimento 27
✝This church is at Piazza Navona. Prior to the French occupation of Rome it was the national church of Spain and was called *San Giacomo dei Spagnoli*.
✝The second chapel on the left side of the nave is dedicated to St James the Greater. Prominently placed within this chapel is a copy of Jacopo Sansovino's 16th century statue of St James the Greater. Upon the sidewalls are several frescoes by Pellegrino Munari depicting alleged events from St James' life.

San Giacomo alla Lungara
(Saint James at the Lungara)
Via della Lungara 12
✝This church is just north of Trastevere and it is dedicated to St James the Greater. It is not open often.

July 26th
Memorial of Joachim and Anne, parents of The Blessed Virgin Mary

St Anne (Relics: Apt, France; Bologna, Italy; Sainte-Anne d'Auray, France; Sainte-Anne de Beaupré, Quebec, Canada; Vienna, Austria)

San Gioacchino ai Prati di Castello
(Saint Joachim at the Meadows of the Castle)
Piazza dei Quiriti 17
✝This church is located north of *Castel Sant'Angelo* and it is dedicated to St Joachim.

Sant'Andrea delle Fratte
(Saint Andrew of the Bushes)
Via Sant'Andrea delle Fratte 1
✝This church is near the Spanish Steps.
✝The chapel in the left transept is dedicated to St Anne. A sculpture under the altar of this chapel, completed by Giovanni Battista Maini, is entitled *The Dying of St Anne.*
✝The third altar on the left side of the nave is where the Blessed Virgin Mary appeared to Ratisbonne, an agnostic Jew, in 1842. Ratisbonne converted on the spot. In 1918 St Maximilian Mary Kolbe (d. 1941) offered his first Mass in this very same chapel.

San Carlo ai Catinari
(Saint Charles at the Catinari)
Piazza Benedetto Cairoli 117
✝This church is near the Largo di Torre Argentina. The second chapel on the left side of the nave is dedicated to St Anne.

Sant'Ignazio (Saint Ignatius)
Via del Caravita 8/a
✝This church is east of the Pantheon.
✝The third chapel on the right side of the

nave is dedicated to St Joachim. The large painting within this chapel, completed by Stefano Pozzi, is entitled *The Virgin Presented by Joachim to God the Father.* Also under the altar of this chapel is the body of St Robert Bellarmine.

Santa Maria in Campitelli
(Our Lady in Campitelli)
Piazza di Campitelli 9
✝This church is near the Jewish quarter.
✝The second chapel on the right side of the nave is dedicated to St Anne.
✝The body of St John Leonardi (d. 1609) is enshrined in the second chapel on the left side of the nave.

Santi Gioacchino e Anna ai Monti
(Saints Joachim and Anne at the Hills)
Via Monte Polacco 5
✝This church is near the Cavour metro stop. It is dedicated to both St Joachim and St Anne. It is not open often.

Sant'Anna dei Palafrenieri
(Saint Anne of the Palafrenieri)
Via di Porta Angelica
✝This is the parish church of the Vatican. It is dedicated to St Anne.

San Pietro in Montorio
(Saint Peter in Montorio)
Piazza San Pietro in Montorio 2
✝This church is located on the Janiculum hill.
✝The third chapel on the left side of the nave is dedicated to St Anne.

Santissimo Nome di Maria al Foro Traiano (The Most Holy Name of Mary at Trajan's Forum)
Piazza Foro Traiano 89
✝This church is near Trajan's column just east of Piazza Venezia.

†A painting within the second chapel on the right side of the nave depicts St Anne teaching Mary how to read.

Gesu e Maria
(Jesus and Mary)
Via del Corso 45
†This church is near Piazza del Popolo. It is dedicated to the Holy Names of Jesus and Mary.
†The third chapel on the right side of the nave is dedicated to St Anne.

Santa Maria in Aracoeli
(Our Lady in Aracoeli)
Piazza del Campidoglio 4
†This church is on top of the Capitoline Hill.
†The fourth chapel on the left side of the nave is dedicated to St Anne.
†Relics of St Helena, the mother of Constantine, rest in the left transept.

July 29th
Memorial of Martha

St Martha (Relics: Tarascon, France)

July 30th
Optional memorial of Peter Chrysologus, bishop and doctor

St Peter Chrysologus (d. 450, Imola, Italy) (Relics: Imola, Italy)

July 31st
Memorial of Ignatius of Loyola, priest

St Ignatius of Loyola (d. 1556, Rome, Italy) (Relics: Rome, Italy)

Il Gesu (The Jesus)
Via degli Astalli 16
†This church is located along the Corso Vittorio Emanuele. It honors a number of Jesuit saints.

†St Ignatius of Loyola, the founder of the Jesuits, is buried under the altar in the left transept. His rooms are located in the Generalate next to the church and may be visited.
†An arm of St Francis Xavier (d. 1552) rests within a reliquary above the altar in the right transept. With this arm he baptized thousands of individuals in India and the Far East.
†The remains of St Peter Faber (d. 1546), an early companion of St Ignatius, are also located here. They are said to rest below the main entrance to this church having been placed here when the church was built in the 16th century. During the placement of these relics it was impossible to separate the bones of St Peter Faber from the bones of other individuals; therefore, his bones are buried together with theirs.

Sant'Ignazio (Saint Ignatius)
Via del Caravita 8/a
†This church is east of the Pantheon. It is dedicated to St Ignatius of Loyola.
†The remains of St Aloysius Gonzaga (d. 1591) rest under the altar in the right transept. His rooms are next to the church and can be visited by appointment.
†The body of St Robert Bellarmine (d. 1621) rests under the altar in the third chapel on the right side of the nave.
†The remains of St John Berchmans (d. 1621), the patron saint of altar servers, rest under the altar in the left transept.

Basilica of St Mary Major
Piazza di Santa Maria Maggiore 42
†On Christmas night in 1538 St Ignatius of Loyola celebrated his first Mass in this church within the *Chapel of the Nativity*. At the time of St Ignatius this chapel was located within the confessio in the right transept and housed the five highly ven-

erated pieces of wood from the manger of the Lord. Today this chapel, whose relics have been relocated to the confessio below the Papal Altar, has lost its association to the Nativity.

Basilica of St Paul Outside the Walls
Via Ostiense 186
✝This basilica is south of the Aurelian Walls.
✝On April 22, 1541 St Ignatius of Loyola and five companions made their profession of solemn vows in front of a 13th century icon of Our Lady which is now found in the Blessed Sacrament Chapel of this church. The crucifix in this chapel is also of note as it is said to have spoken to St Bridget in 1370.
✝St Paul is buried in the confessio in the main body of this church. Above his tomb are the chains that had been used to imprison him prior to his martyrdom. These chains were placed in this prominent location in 2008.

August

August 1st
Memorial of Alphonsus Liguori, bishop and doctor

St Alphonsus Liguori (d. 1787, Pagani, Italy) (Relics: Pagani, Italy)

Santuario della Madonna del Perpetuo Soccorso
(Sanctuary of Our Lady of Perpetual Help)
Via Merulana 26
✝This church is just south of the *Basilica of St Mary Major*. It is dedicated to St Alphonsus Liguori.
✝A miraculous image of the Blessed Virgin Mary entitled *Our Lady of Perpetual Help* is above the main altar.

Santa Maria ai Monti
(Our Lady at the Hills)
Via della Madonna dei Monti 41
✝This church is near the Cavour metro stop.
✝St Alphonsus Liguori said Mass here from April to June of 1762.
✝This church was built due to a miraculous discovery of an image of the Blessed Virgin Mary in a nearby Poor Clare convent. To celebrate this great find Pope Gregory XIII (d. 1585) commissioned the building of this church. This miraculous image is now placed above the main altar.

August 2nd
Optional memorial of Euseblus of Vercelli, bishop

St Eusebius of Vercelli (d. 371, Vercelli, Italy) (Relics: Vercelli, Italy)

Sant'Eusebio (Saint Eusebius)
Piazza Vittorio Emanuele 12a
✝This church is southeast of the *Basilica of St Mary Major*. It is dedicated to St Eusebius but probably not to St Eusebius the Bishop. Instead by tradition the remains of three early martyrs rest here: Eusebius, Orosius and Paulinus.

August 2nd
Optional memorial of Peter Julian Eymard, priest

St Peter Julian Eymard (d. 1868, La Mure, France) (Relics: Rome, Italy; Paris, France)

Chiesa San Claudio
(Church of Saint Claudius)
Via del Pozzetto 160
✝This church is near the Spanish Steps.
✝A relic of St Peter Julian Eymard is placed within a statue of his likeness that rests within an urn on the right side of the nave.
✝This church is managed by priests from the *Congregation of the Blessed Sacrament* which St Peter Julian Eymard founded in 1856.

August 4th
Memorial of John Vianney, priest

St John Vianney (d. 1859, Ars-sur-Formans, France) (Relics: Ars-sur-Formans, France)

August 5th
Optional memorial of The Dedication of the Basilica of Saint Mary Major

Basilica of St Mary Major
Piazza di Santa Maria Maggiore 42
✝A tradition claims that on a hot August 5th morning in 352 AD the ground where this basilica now stands was found cov-

ered in snow. Through a vision that same night a wealthy childless couple were asked to build a church in this spot dedicated to Mary. Thus was born the tradition of Our Lady of the Snows. This tradition is also partially supported by the fact that the *Liber Pontificalis* credits Pope Liberius, who lived during the time of this miracle, with the building of a church at this location. However, this document makes no mention of the miracle of the snow. In fact even Pope Sixtus III, who a century later rebuilt this first church into what is today the *Basilica of St Mary Major*, makes no mention of this miracle during his dedication. Therefore, historians remain incredulous. In fact, the first textual evidence of this story occurs only in the 9th century. Nevertheless, every year on August 5th this basilica keeps this tradition alive by releasing thousands of white petals into the air to imitate that first miraculous snowfall.

August 6th
Feast of The Transfiguration

St Peter's Basilica
Altar of the Transfiguration
✝This altar is located on the left side of the nave near the sacristy.
✝A mosaic above this altar depicts the Transfiguration of Christ. The original was completed by Raphael and now rests within the Vatican Museums.
✝The body of Blessed Innocent XI (d. 1689) rests below this mosaic.

Santa Maria della Concezione
(Our Lady of the Immaculate Conception)
Via Veneto 27
✝This church is just north of the Barberini metro stop.
✝The second chapel on the right side of

the nave is dedicated to the Transfiguration. The altarpiece was completed by Mario Balassi in 1667.

August 7th
Optional memorial of Sixtus II, pope and martyr, and Companions, martyrs

St Sixtus II (d. 258, Rome, Italy) (Relics: Rome, Italy)

San Sisto Vecchio
(Old Saint Sixtus)
Piazzale Numa Pompilio 8
✝This church is south of the Colosseum.
✝The relics of St Sixtus II were moved from the *Catacombs of San Callisto* to this church. A small stone located within the wall on the left side of the nave marks their location.
✝Pope Honorius III gave this church to the Dominican order with the issue of a Papal Bull dated December 3, 1218. This was the first Dominican monastery in Rome.
✝The Miracle of the Bread attributed to St Dominic occurred within the refectory of this monastery. Upon request this room can be visited.

Catacombs of San Callisto
Via Appia Antica 110/126
✝These catacombs are located south of the Aurelian Walls.
✝It was at this location in the year 258 that Roman soldiers burst into a chapel and arrested St Sixtus II and four other deacons while they were celebrating the liturgy. St Lawrence (d. 258) was not present for this arrest; however, a legend holds that St Lawrence was able to speak to St Sixtus just before the pope was martyred. In this conversation St Sixtus prophetically stated, "You shall follow me in three days." St Lawrence then in three days went on to suffer his own mar-

tyrdom by being burnt alive on a gridiron.

✝St Sixtus II, St Pontian (d. 235), St Fabian (d. 250), St Cornelius (d. 253) and a number of other early popes were originally buried here. The remains of St Sixtus II were later moved to *San Sisto Vecchio*, the remains of St Fabian to *San Sebastiano Fuori Le Mura, and* the remains of St Cornelius to *Santa Maria in Trastevere.*

Santi Domenico e Sisto
(Saints Dominic and Sixtus)
Largo Angelicum 1
✝This church is connected to the *Angelicum University*. It is dedicated to St Dominic (d. 1221) and to St Sixtus II.

August 7th
Optional memorial of Cajetan, priest

St Cajetan [Gaetano in Italian] (d. 1547, Naples, Italy) (Relics: Naples, Italy)

San Nicola dei Prefetti
(Saint Nicholas of the Prefects)
Via dei Prefetti 34
✝This church is north of the Pantheon.
✝In 1524 St Cajetan established his new religious order of Theatines in this church. However, they were forced out during the sacking of Rome in 1527.

Sant'Andrea della Valle
(Saint Andrew of the Valley)
Piazza Sant'Andrea della Valle / Piazza Vidoni 6
✝This church is located along the Corso Vittorio Emanuele. It was built by the Theatines in the 17th century.
✝The chapel with the Blessed Sacrament on the left side of the nave is dedicated to St Cajetan.

August 8th
Memorial of Dominic, priest

St Dominic (d. 1221, Bologna, Italy) (Relics: Bologna, Italy)

Santa Sabina (Saint Sabina)
Piazza Pietro d'Illiria 1
✝This church is located on the Aventine Hill just south of Circo Massimo.
✝In 1219 St Dominic and his friars received permission to move into this church. Three years later, on June 5, 1222, the church was given in perpetuity to the Dominican Order by Pope Honorius III. Today it serves as the Order's General Curia. The room in which St Dominic lived has been converted into a chapel and can be visited with permission. Also in the garden, visible from the narthex, is an orange tree that is said to have been planted by St Dominic himself.
✝The first chapel on the left side of the nave is dedicated to St Dominic. Within this chapel is a polished black stone that the Devil is said to have thrown at St Dominic.

San Sisto Vecchio
(Old Saint Sixtus)
Piazzale Numa Pompilio 8
✝This church is south of the Colosseum.
✝Pope Honorius III gave this church to the Dominican order with the issue of a Papal Bull dated December 3, 1218. This was the first Dominican monastery in Rome.
✝The Miracle of the Bread attributed to St Dominic occurred within the refectory of this monastery. Upon request this room can be visited.
✝The relics of St Sixtus II (d. 258) were moved from the *Catacombs of San Callisto* to this church. A small stone located

within the wall on the left side of the nave marks their location.

Santi Domenico e Sisto
(Saint Dominic and Sixtus)
Largo Angelicum 1
✝This church is connected to the *Angelicum University*. It is dedicated to St Dominic and to St Sixtus II (d. 258).

Santa Maria sopra Minerva
(Our Lady Above Minerva)
Piazza della Minerva 42
✝This church is near the Pantheon.
✝Within the second chapel on the right side of the nave are several frescoes by Gaspare Celio depicting episodes from the life of St Dominic. Also the Blessed Sacrament Chapel within the left transept is dedicated to St Dominic.
✝The body of St Catherine of Siena (d. 1380) rests under the main altar.

Basilica di San Clemente
(Basilica of Saint Clement)
Via Labicana 95 / Piazza San Clemente
✝This church is east of the Colosseum.
✝The chapel located in the back right corner of the nave is dedicated to St Dominic. Three paintings within this chapel depict scenes from his life.
✝The remains of St Clement I (d. 97) and of St Ignatius of Antioch (d. 107) rest beneath the main altar.
✝Also a chapel on the right side of the nave is dedicated to Saints Cyril (d. 869) and Methodius (d. 885). The extant remains of St Cyril rest within the altar of this chapel.

Santa Maria del Rosario in Prati
(Our Lady of the Rosary in Prati)
Via Germanico 94
✝This church is near the Ottaviano metro stop. It is dedicated to Our Lady of the Rosary.

✝A statue of St Dominic is placed within the fourth chapel on the right side of the nave.

August 9th
Optional memorial of Teresa Benedicta of the Cross, virgin and martyr

St Teresa Benedicta of the Cross (d. 1942, Auschwitz, Poland)

August 10th
Feast of Lawrence, deacon and martyr

St Lawrence (d. 258, Rome, Italy)
(Relics: Rome, Italy)

San Lorenzo fuori le Mura
(Saint Lawrence Outside the Walls)
Piazzale del Verano 3
✝This church is east of the Aurelian Walls.
✝The remains of St Lawrence, St Stephen, and St Justin lie in the confessio below the main altar. (Note: The relics are labeled as St Justin the Presbyter. Therefore, it is likely that this is not St Justin the Martyr.)
✝A marble stone slab beneath the choir floor is said to be the stone on which St Lawrence was placed after his execution. Also enshrined in this lower area is the body of Blessed Pius IX (d. 1878).

San Lorenzo in Panisperna
(Saint Lawrence in Panisperna)
Via Panisperna 90
✝This church is west of the *Basilica of St Mary Major*. It is often closed during the week. However, it is always open for the faithful during Sunday liturgies.
✝This church rests over the spot of St Lawrence's martyrdom. A chapel built under the porch marks where it occurred. Within this chapel is the oven that was used to roast St Lawrence alive.

✝Within the church the second chapel on the left side of the nave is dedicated to St Bridget (d. 1373). Her body was originally buried in this chapel before being moved to Sweden. She used to beg for alms for the poor outside of this church and prayed before the crucifix by the main altar.

San Lorenzo in Lucina
(Saint Lawrence in Lucina)
Via in Lucina 16/a
✝This church is north of the Pantheon.
✝The grill used to burn St Lawrence is preserved under the altar in the first chapel on the right side of the nave. This chapel also contains a number of paintings that depict scenes from the life of St Lawrence.

San Lorenzo in Fonte
(Saint Lawrence at the Spring)
Via Urbana 50
✝This church is near the Cavour metro stop.
✝Tradition holds that this was the location of St Lawrence's imprisonment.

San Lorenzo in Miranda
(Saint Lawrence in Miranda)
Via in Miranda 10
✝This church is in the Roman Forum. It is not open often.
✝A tradition suggests that this was the location where St Lawrence was condemned.

San Lorenzo in Damaso
(Saint Lawrence in Damaso)
Piazza della Cancelleria 1
✝This church is at the *Palazzo della Cancelleria* near Campo de' Fiori. It is dedicated to St Lawrence.

San Lorenzo in Palatio ad Sancta Sanctorum
(Saint Lawrence in the Palace at the Holy of Holies)
Piazza San Giovanni in Laterano
✝This is a private chapel at the top of the Scala Santa. It is dedicated to St Lawrence.

Basilica of St Paul Outside the Walls
Via Ostiense 186
✝This basilica is south of the Aurelian Walls.
✝In the right transept is a small chapel dedicated to St Lawrence.
✝St Paul is buried in the confessio. Above his tomb are the chains that had been used to imprison him prior to his martyrdom. These chains were placed in this prominent location in 2008.
✝Also a crucifix that is said to have spoken to St Bridget in 1370 is in the Blessed Sacrament Chapel.

August 11th
Memorial of Clare, virgin

St Clare (d. 1253, Assisi, Italy) (Relics: Assisi, Italy)

Santa Chiara (Saint Clare)
Piazza S. Chiara 42
✝This church is near the Pantheon. It is dedicated to St Clare.
✝Presently this church serves as the chapel for the seminarians at the French College.

San Lorenzo in Panisperna
(Saint Lawrence in Panisperna)
Via Panisperna 90
✝This church is west of the *Basilica of St Mary Major*. It is often closed during the week. However, it is always open for the faithful during Sunday liturgies.

✝The first chapel on the right side of the nave is dedicated to St Clare.

✝This church also rests over the spot of St Lawrence's martyrdom. A chapel built under the porch marks where it occurred. Within this chapel is the oven that was used to roast St Lawrence alive.

Sant'Antonio da Padova
(Saint Anthony of Padua)
Via Merulana 124

✝This church is near the *Basilica of St John Lateran.*

✝The second chapel on the left side of the nave is dedicated to St Clare.

August 12th
Optional memorial of Jane Frances de Chantal, religious

St Jane Frances de Chantal (d. 1641, Moulins, France) (Relics: Annecy, France)

August 13th
Optional memorial of Pontian, pope and martyr; Hippolytus, priest and martyr

St Pontian (d. 235, Sardinia, Italy)
St Hippolytus (d. 235, Sardinia, Italy)

In 235 both St Pontian and St Hippolytus were banished to the salt mines of Sardinia. At some point after their deaths their remains were returned to Rome. St Pontian was buried in the *Catacombs of San Callisto* as noted below and St Hippolytus was buried on the Via Tiburtina.

Catacombs of San Callisto
Via Appia Antica 110/126

✝These catacombs are located south of the Aurelian Walls.

✝St Pontian, St Fabian (d. 250), St Cornelius (d. 253), St Sixtus II (d. 258), and a number of other early popes were originally buried here. The remains of St Fabian were later moved to *San Sebastiano Fuori Le Mura*, the remains of St Cornelius to *Santa Maria in Trastevere*, and the remains of St Sixtus II to *San Sisto Vecchio*.

✝It was also at this location in the year 258 that Roman soldiers burst into a chapel and arrested St Sixtus II and four other deacons while they were celebrating the liturgy. St Lawrence (d. 258) was not present for this arrest; however, a legend holds that St Lawrence was able to speak to St Sixtus just before the pope was martyred. In this conversation St Sixtus prophetically stated, "You shall follow me in three days." St Lawrence then in three days went on to suffer his own martyrdom by being burnt alive on a gridiron.

August 14th
Optional memorial of Maximilian Mary Kolbe, priest and martyr

St Maximilian Mary Kolbe (d. 1941, Auschwitz, Poland)

Sant'Andrea delle Fratte
(Saint Andrew of the Bushes)
Via Sant'Andrea delle Fratte 1

✝This church is near the Spanish Steps.

✝The third altar on the left side of the nave is where the Blessed Virgin Mary appeared to Ratisbonne, an agnostic Jew, in 1842. Ratisbonne converted on the spot. In 1918 St Maximilian Mary Kolbe offered his first Mass in this very same chapel.

Santi Apostoli (Holy Apostles)
Piazza dei Santi Apostoli 51

†This church is just east of Piazza Venezia.

†The third chapel on the right side of the nave is dedicated to St Anthony of Padua. On the altar is a picture of St Maximilian Kolbe.

†Also upon a column within the second chapel on the left side of the nave is a monument honoring the 50th anniversary of St Maximilian Kolbe's martyrdom.

†Relics of St Philip and St James the Less also rest within the confessio.

Parrocchia Santa Dorotea
(Parish of Saint Dorothy)
Via San Dorotea 23
†This church is in Trastevere.
†A small statue of St Maximilian Mary Kolbe is in the left transept.

August 15th
Solemnity of The Assumption of The Blessed Virgin Mary

Santa Maria in Trastevere
(Our Lady in Trastevere)
Via della Paglia 14 / Piazza Santa Maria in Trastevere
†This church is located in Trastevere. It is dedicated to the Assumption of The Blessed Virgin Mary. A painting of the Assumption by Domenico Zampieri can be seen in the middle of the coffered wooden ceiling.

†Relics of the two popes, St Callistus I (d. 222) and St Cornelius (d. 253), rest under the main altar of this church. These relics are joined by others in particular those of the priest and martyr St Calepodius (d. 232).

Basilica of St Paul Outside the Walls
Via Ostiense 186
†This basilica is south of the Aurelian Walls.

†The chapel in the right transept is dedicated to the Assumption of our Lady.

†St Paul is buried in the confessio. Above his tomb are the chains that had been used to imprison him prior to his martyrdom. These chains were placed in this prominent location in 2008.

†Also a crucifix that is said to have spoken to St Bridget in 1370 is in the Blessed Sacrament Chapel.

Basilica of St John Lateran
Piazza San Giovanni in Laterano 4
†Within the second chapel on the left side of the nave is a painting of the Assumption by Giovanni Odazzi.

Santo Spirito in Sassia
(Holy Spirit in Sassia)
Via dei Penitenzieri 12
†This church is near the Vatican.
†The second chapel on the right side of the nave is dedicated to the Assumption.

Santissima Trinità dei Monti
(Most Holy Trinity of the Mounts)
Piazza della Trinità dei Monti
†This church is at the top of the Spanish Steps.
†Within the third chapel on the right side of the nave is a painting of the Blessed Virgin Mary entitled *The Assumption of the Virgin*. This masterpiece was completed by Daniele da Volterra.

La Maddalena (The Magdalene)
Piazza della Maddalena 53
†This church is just north of the Pantheon.
†The first chapel on the left side of the nave is dedicated to Our Lady of the Assumption.
†In the chapel in the right transept is a miraculous crucifix that is said to have

spoken to St Camillus de Lellis.

†In the third chapel on the right side of the nave are the remains of St Camillus de Lellis. He lived in the adjacent monastery and died here in 1614. His rooms can be visited by asking the sacristan. One of these rooms has been transformed into a chapel and contains the relic of his heart.

Santa Maria della Scala
(Our Lady at the Steps)
Piazza della Scala 23

†This church is located in Trastevere.

†The second chapel on the left side of the nave is dedicated to the Assumption of The Blessed Virgin Mary.

†The right foot of St Teresa of Avila (d. 1582) rests within a beautiful chapel to the left of the main sanctuary. It was gifted to this church in 1617. (This chapel is not visible from the nave of the church and it is rarely open to the public. However, if one kindly asks the sacristan access may be granted. If the sacristan is not present he or she can be called at the neighboring convent door.)

FOR ADDITIONAL MARIAN CHURCHES TO VISIT PLEASE SEE THE LIST AT THE END OF THIS BOOK.

August 16th
Optional memorial of Stephen of Hungary

St Stephen of Hungary (d. 1038, Hungary) (Relics: Budapest, Hungary)

Santo Stefano Rotondo al Celio
(Saint Stephen's Rotundo at the Celio)
Via di Santo Stefano Rotondo 7 / Via di Santo Stefano 7

†This church is southeast of the Colosseum. It is not open often.

†This is the Hungarian national church and it is dedicated to St Stephen of Hungary.

August 19th
Optional memorial of John Eudes, priest

St John Eudes (d. 1680, Caen, France)

August 20th
Memorial of Bernard, abbot and doctor

St Bernard (d. 1153, Clairvaux, France)
(Relics: Troyes, France)

Tre Fontane
(The Three Fountains)
Via Acque Salvie 1

†Located south of the Aurelian Walls.

†There are three churches located at this shrine, one of which is the church of *Santa Maria Scala Coeli*. This is the first church on the right as one enters. A crypt below the main sanctuary is believed to be the location where St Paul was imprisoned prior to his martyrdom. Also in this crypt St Bernard had a vision of souls entering heaven by a ladder, hence the name of the church which in English means *Our Lady Stairway to Heaven*.

†A second church on this property, *San Paolo alle Tre Fontane*, is believed to mark the spot of St Paul's martyrdom. This is the church located on the backside of the property. Legend says that after St Paul was decapitated his head bounced three times and with each bounce a fountain of water sprang up. Three grated areas along the eastern wall of this church cover up the locations of these three fountains. Also within this church is the column to which St Paul was bound and the table upon which he died.

San Bernardo alle Terme
(Saint Bernard at the Baths)
Via Torino 94
✝This church is north of Piazza della Repubblica. It is dedicated to St Bernard.
✝A very moving painting depicting a mystical vision of St Bernard being embraced by the crucified Christ is on the right side. It was completed by Giovanni Odazzi in the early 18th century.

Santissimo Nome di Maria al Foro Traiano
(The Most Holy Name of Mary at Trajan's Forum)
Piazza Foro Traiano 89
✝This church is near Trajan's column just east of Piazza Venezia.
✝The second chapel on the left side of the nave is dedicated to St Bernard.

August 21st
Memorial of Pius X, pope

St Pius X (d. 1914, Rome, Italy) (Relics: Rome, Italy)

St Peter's Basilica
Presentation Chapel
✝Located on the left side of the nave between the Baptistry and the Wedding Chapel.
✝The body of St Pius X rests under the altar in this chapel. He is known in particular for lowering the age of First Communion to the Age of Reason.

San Giuseppe al Trionfale
(Saint Joseph at the Trionfale)
Via Bernardino Telesio 4/B
✝This church is located in the Trionfale district just north of the Vatican.
✝The chapel to the left of the main sanctuary is dedicated to St Pius X.

Sant'Onofrio (Saint Onuphrius)
Piazza di Sant'Onofrio 2
✝This church is on the Janiculum Hill.
✝The second chapel on the left side of the nave is dedicated to St Pius X.

August 22nd
Memorial of The Queenship of The Blessed Virgin Mary

Santi Giovanni e Paolo
(Saints John and Paul)
Piazza dei Santi Giovanni e Paolo 13
✝This church is south of the Colosseum.
✝A chapel in the left transept is dedicated to the Coronation of The Blessed Virgin Mary.
✝Located beneath this church is a complex of well preserved ancient Roman houses. Among these is an ancient house church. These ruins can be visited.
✝St Paul of the Cross (d. 1775) is buried under the altar in the large side chapel on the right side of the nave. Upon request one can visit the room in which he died in the monastery adjacent to the church.

San Lorenzo in Damaso
(Saint Lawrence in Damaso)
Piazza della Cancelleria 1
✝This church is at the *Palazzo della Cancelleria* near Campo de' Fiori.
✝The altarpiece in the main sanctuary, completed by Federico Zuccari in the 16th century, depicts the Coronation of The Blessed Virgin Mary.

Gesu e Maria (Jesus and Mary)
Via del Corso 45
✝This church is near Piazza del Popolo. It is dedicated to the Holy Names of Jesus and Mary.
✝The large painting in the main sanctuary depicts the Coronation of The

Blessed Virgin Mary. It was completed by Giacinto Brandi in the 17th century.

Chiesa Nuova
(The New Church)
Via del Governo Vecchio 134
†This church is along the Corso Vittorio Emanuele.
†The chapel within the right transept is dedicated to the Coronation of The Blessed Virgin Mary.
†The body of St Philip Neri (d. 1595) is enshrined in the left transept. His private rooms can be visited on certain days of the week. They are located in the right wall of the left transept.

Santo Spirito in Sassia
(Holy Spirit in Sassia)
Via dei Penitenzieri 12
†This church is near the Vatican.
†The second chapel on the left side of the nave is dedicated to the Coronation of The Blessed Virgin Mary.

FOR ADDITIONAL MARIAN CHURCHES TO VISIT PLEASE SEE THE LIST AT THE END OF THIS BOOK.

August 23rd
Optional memorial of Rose of Lima, virgin

St Rose of Lima (d. 1617, Lima, Peru)
(Relics: Lima, Peru)

Santa Maria sopra Minerva
(Our Lady Above Minerva)
Piazza della Minerva 42
†This church is near the Pantheon.
†Within the third chapel on the right side of the nave are a number of works by Lazzaro Baldi depicting events from the life of St Rose of Lima.
†Also the body of St Catherine of Siena (d. 1380) rests under the main altar.

August 24th
Feast of Bartholomew, apostle

St Bartholomew (Relics: Rome, Italy; Benevento, Italy; Lipari, Sicily; Frankfurt, Germany)

According to the *Roman Martyrology* St Bartholomew suffered martyrdom in the Roman province of Armenia. It is recorded that he was first skinned alive and then put to death by decapitation. Five centuries later and half-way across the Mediterranean his relics were found in Lipari, Sicily. Most likely they arrived here through normal means; however, a pious tradition contends that this transfer occurred miraculously. This tradition claims that the sarcophagus of St Bartholomew was thrown into the sea by infidels. It then floated upon the water until it finally and miraculously came to the shores of the tiny island of Lipari. Regardless, how the relics arrived they remained on this island until the middle of the 9th century. At this time they were transferred to Benevento, Italy and then in the latter part of the 10th century they were brought to Rome by the Holy Roman Emperor, Otto III, where they were interred in the church of *San Bartolomeo all'Isola* on Tiber Island. This final transfer, however, is contested by the city of Benevento which continues to claim possession of the true relics of St Bartholomew.

San Bartolomeo all'Isola
(Saint Bartholomew on the Island)
Piazza San Bartolomeo, Tiber Island
†Relics of St Bartholomew rest within the red porphyry basin that supports the main altar.
†Enshrined in each of the side altars are relics of recent martyrs from around the world.
†An arm of St Adalbert (d. 997) is curr-

ently enshrined in the chapel to the left of the main sanctuary. It rests within a little metal box placed under the altar of this chapel.

✝This church also housed the relics of St Paulinus of Nola (d. 431) for about 1000 years until they were transferred to the Italian city of Nola in 1909.

San Bartolomeo e Alessandro dei Bergamaschi
(Saints Bartholomew and Alexander of the People of Bergamo)
Via di Pietra 70, Piazza Colonna
✝This church is off the Via del Corso near the Piazza Colonna. It is not open often. It is dedicated to St Bartholomew and St Alexander.

August 25th
Optional memorial of Louis

St Louis (d. 1270, Tunis, Tunisia) (Relics: Monreale, Sicily; Saint-Denis, France)

San Luigi dei Francesi
(Saint Louis of the French)
Piazza San Luigi dei Francesi 5
✝This church is near Piazza Navona and it is dedicated to St Louis.
✝The third chapel on the left side of the nave is dedicated to St Louis. A number of paintings placed within this chapel depict scenes from his life. Of particular interest is the painting on the right side-wall completed by Ludovico Gimignani which depicts St Louis receiving the Crown of Thorns in Paris. This unique relic, which is still preserved in this city, was first received by St Louis in 1239. It is now located within the treasury of *Notre Dame Cathedral* in Paris. On First Fridays throughout the year and on every

Friday during lent this relic is brought out for public veneration.

August 25th
Optional memorial of Joseph Calasanz, priest

St Joseph Calasanz (d. 1648, Rome, Italy) (Relics: Rome, Italy)

San Pantaleo (Saint Pantaleon)
Piazza San Pantaleo /
Piazza dei Massimi 4
✝This church is located along the Corso Vittorio Emanuele.
✝The relics of St Joseph Calasanz rest under the main altar of this church. His rooms can be visited in the adjacent convent.

Santa Maria ai Monti
(Our Lady at the Hills)
Via della Madonna dei Monti 41
✝This church is near the Cavour metro stop. St Joseph Calasanz would often visit the miraculous image of the Blessed Virgin Mary in this church. A plaque on the wall honors his devotion. This miraculous image is now placed above the main altar of this church.

August 27th
Memorial of Monica

St Monica (d. 387, Ostia, Italy) (Relics: Rome, Italy)

Sant'Agostino (Saint Augustine)
Piazza Sant'Agostino
✝This church is near Piazza Navona.
✝Relics of St Monica, the mother of St Augustine, rest within the Blessed Sacrament Chapel just to the left of the main sanctuary.

Sant'Aurea a Ostia Antica

(Saint Aurea at Old Ostia)
Piazza della Rocca 13
00119 Rome, Italy
✝This church is located just south of Rome at Ostia Antica.
✝On the right side of the nave is a chapel dedicated to St Monica. For many centuries her remains rested in this chapel. In 1425 they were relocated to the church of *Sant'Agostino* where they rest today.
✝Within this chapel is a work by Pietro da Cortona entitled the *Ecstasy of St Monica*.

Santa Monica dei Agostini

(Saint Monica of the Augustines)
Piazza del Sant'Uffizio
✝This church is near the Vatican and it is dedicated to St Monica. It is not open often.

August 28th
Memorial of Augustine, bishop and doctor

St Augustine (d. 430, Annaba, Algeria)
(Relics: Pavia, Italy; Annaba, Algeria)

Sant'Agostino (Saint Augustine)

Piazza Sant'Agostino
✝This church is near Piazza Navona.
✝The chapel in the right transept is dedicated to St Augustine.
✝Also the relics of St Augustine's mother, St Monica (d. 387), rest in the chapel to the left of the main altar.

Gesu e Maria (Jesus and Mary)

Via del Corso 45
✝This church is near Piazza del Popolo. It is dedicated to the Holy Names of Jesus and Mary.
✝The painting in the third chapel on the left side of the nave depicts St Augustine and St Monica venerating an image of Our Lady of Divine Help (*Madonna del Divino Aiuto*).

August 29th
Memorial of The Beheading of John the Baptist, martyr

St John the Baptist (Relics: Rome, Italy; Florence, Italy; Siena, Italy; Amiens, France; Munich, Germany; Damascus, Syria)

San Silvestro in Capite

(Saint Sylvester in Capite)
Piazza San Silvestro
✝This church is near the Spanish Steps.
✝A relic of the skull of St John the Baptist rests within the chapel to the left of the main entrance. The authenticity is uncertain since this same relic is said to be located at a number of other places throughout the world including the *Cathedral of Amiens* in France, the *Residenz Museum* in Munich, Germany, and the *Umayyad Mosque* in Damascus, Syria.
✝The remains of St Sylvester I (d. 335) rest in the confessio below the main altar. Also a work from 1688 depicting the legend of St Sylvester I baptizing Constantine can be seen in the apse vault.

Santa Maria degli Angeli

(Our Lady of the Angels)
Piazza della Repubblica
✝This church is at Piazza della Repubblica. It is a very spacious church built over the Baths of Diocletian.
✝A unique marble sculpture of St John the Baptist's head rests on the left side of the nave.

Santa Maria della Scala

(Our Lady at the Steps)

Piazza della Scala 23

†This church is located in Trastevere.

†The first chapel on the right side of the nave is dedicated to the Beheading of St John the Baptist.

†The right foot of St Teresa of Avila (d. 1582) rests within a beautiful chapel to the left of the main sanctuary. It was gifted to this church in 1617. (This chapel is not visible from the nave of the church and it is rarely open to the public. However, if one kindly asks the sacristan access may be granted. If the sacristan is not present he or she can be called at the neighboring convent door.)

San Giovanni Decollato

(Saint John Beheaded)

Via di San Giovanni Decollato 22

†This church is east of Tiber Island. It is dedicated to the Beheading of St John the Baptist. It is not open often.

SEE 'THE BIRTH OF JOHN THE BAPTIST' ON JUNE 24TH FOR ADDITIONAL CHURCHES IN HIS HONOR.

September

September 3rd
Memorial of Gregory the Great, pope and doctor

St Gregory the Great (d. 604, Rome, Italy) (Relics: Rome, Italy)

A major part of the relics of St Gregory the Great and the body of St Sebastian are said to have been taken to Soissons, France in 826 AD. Alban Butler in *The Lives of the Fathers, Martyrs, and Other Principal Saints* claims that in 1564 these relics were stolen and thrown into a ditch by Calvinists. This tradition then maintains that some of these desecrated relics were recovered and subsequently placed into surrounding churches in that area. Despite this tradition the veneration of their relics in Rome has been maintained for centuries.

St Peter's Basilica
Altar of St Gregory the Great
✝Located within the left transept near the entrance to the sacristy.
✝Relics of St Gregory the Great rest below this altar. The mosaic above this altar recounts a Eucharistic miracle attributed to him.

San Gregorio Magno al Celio
(Saint Gregory the Great at the Celio)
Piazza di San Gregorio 1
✝This church is south of the Colosseum. It is not open often.
✝The land upon which this church now rests was once owned by the family of St Gregory the Great. In the 6th century he built a monastery upon this property. It was from this monastery that St Augustine of Canterbury and his fellow missionaries were sent out to proclaim the Gospel in England. A plaque within this church recalls the importance of this event.

Santa Maria della Pietà
(Our Lady of Mercy)
Via del Portico d'Ottavia / Piazza di Monte Savello 9
✝This church is near the Jewish quarter and is alongside the Via Lungotevere De Cenci. It is known also as *San Gregorio a Ponte Quattro Capi*. It is not open often.
✝Tradition holds that this church is built over the location of St Gregory's birth home.

San Gregorio dei Muratori
(Saint Gregory of the Bricklayers)
Via Leccosa 75
✝This tiny church is near the Cavour Bridge along the Tiber River. It is difficult to find as it is at the end of a cul-de-sac and blends into the surrounding buildings. It is dedicated to St Gregory the Great. It is not open often.

September 8th
Feast of The Birth of The Blessed Virgin Mary

Santa Maria del Popolo
(Our Lady of the People)
Piazza del Popolo 12
✝This church is at Piazza del Popolo.
✝A painting within the second chapel on the left side of the nave depicts the birth of the Blessed Virgin Mary. It was started by Sebastiano del Piombo and completed by Francesco de' Rossi.

San Girolamo dei Croati
(Saint Jerome of the Croatians)
Via Tomacelli 132
✝This church is near the Tiber River just west of the Spanish Steps.

✝A painting in the second chapel on the right side of the nave depicts the birth of the Blessed Virgin Mary.

FOR ADDITIONAL MARIAN CHURCHES TO VISIT PLEASE SEE THE LIST AT THE END OF THIS BOOK.

September 9th
Memorial of Peter Claver, priest*

St Peter Claver (d. 1654, Cartagena, Colombia) (Relics: Cartagena, Colombia)

September 12th
Optional Memorial of The Most Holy Name of Mary

Santissimo Nome di Maria al Foro Traiano
(The Most Holy Name of Mary at Trajan's Forum)
Piazza Foro Traiano 89
✝This church is near Trajan's column just east of Piazza Venezia. It is dedicated to the Most Holy Name of Mary.

Gesu e Maria (Jesus and Mary)
Via del Corso 45
✝This church is near Piazza del Popolo. It is dedicated to the Holy Names of Jesus and Mary.

FOR ADDITIONAL MARIAN CHURCHES TO VISIT PLEASE SEE THE LIST AT THE END OF THIS BOOK.

September 13th
Memorial of John Chrysostom, bishop and doctor

St John Chrysostom (d. 407, NE Turkey) (Relics: Rome, Italy; Florence, Italy;

Istanbul, Turkey; Moscow, Russia; Mount Athos, Greece)

St Peter's Basilica
Chapel of the Immaculate Conception
✝Also known as the Wedding Chapel or the Chapel of the Choir.
✝This is the third chapel on the left side of the nave.
✝Some relics of St John Chrysostom rest below the altar within this chapel. In 2004 a major part of these relics were returned to the Ecumenical Patriarch of Constantinople.

September 14th
Feast of The Triumph of the Cross

Santa Croce in Gerusalemme
(Holy Cross In Jerusalem)
Piazza di Santa Croce in Gerusalemme 12
✝This church is east of the *Basilica of St John Lateran*.
✝Found here are relics of the True Cross brought to Rome by St Helena in 325.
✝These relics include: the Titulus Crucis (This is the sign that hung over the head of Christ and that declared him to be the King of the Jews), a Crucifixion nail, a fragment of the True Cross, two thorns from the Crown of Thorns, the greater part of the sponge used to give Christ vinegar, a piece of the cross from the good thief (St Dismas), and a finger of St Thomas the Apostle.
✝This chapel can be accessed by the staircase on the left side of the sanctuary.

San Marcello al Corso
(Saint Marcellus on the Corso)
Piazza di San Marcello 5
✝This church is north of Piazza Venezia.
✝A fire on the night of May 22, 1519 destroyed most of this church. Only the outer walls and a 15th century wooden crucifix survived. This miraculous cruc-

ifix can now be found in the fourth chapel on the right side of the nave. A relic of the true cross is also preserved within this chapel in a reliquary.

Scala Santa (Holy Steps)
Across from the *Basilica of St John Lateran*
†This building was the Papal Palace from the time of Constantine until the move to Avignon in 1313.
†It contains 28 marble steps that tradition holds were originally located at Pilate's house in Jerusalem. St Helena is credited for bringing these steps to Rome. These are believed to be the same steps that Christ walked upon during his Passion.

Santa Prassede (Saint Praxedes)
Via di Santa Prassede 9 / Via San Martino ai Monti
†This church is just south of the *Basilica of St Mary Major*.
†In a chapel on the right side of the nave is said to be the Pillar of Christ's scourging. Its authenticity, however, is doubtful primarily because it is made out of marble that seems to be too valuable for the punishment of criminals. A more realistic one is venerated in the *Church of the Holy Sepulchre* in Jerusalem.

Santa Sabina (Saint Sabina)
Piazza Pietro d'Illiria 1
†This church is located on the Aventine Hill just south of Circo Massimo.
†One of the oldest depictions of the crucifixion in Christian art is located on the uppermost left panel of the left entrance door. This wooden door dates back to the year 430 AD. (Note: This is not the entrance off of the street but the entrance from the narthex.)

St Peter's Basilica
†The Roman Station Mass occurs twice a year at this basilica. On both of these days relics of Christ's passion are presented to the public for veneration. The first occurs on the Saturday of the First Week of Lent. On this day the Lance of St Longinus and a relic of the True Cross are presented for veneration. The second occurs a few weeks later on the Sunday of the Fifth Week of Lent. On this day shortly after Vespers the Canons of the basilica present to the faithful the Veil of St Veronica from the balcony above the St Veronica statue.

Oratorio del Santissimo Crocifisso
(Oratory of the Most Holy Cross)
Piazza dell'Oratorio 69
†This small church is located near the Trevi Fountain.
†The crucifix above the main altar is a copy of the miraculous crucifix that survived the fire at *San Marcello al Corso* in 1519.
†Also many frescoes within this church depict events connected to the Cross. The first two on the right side of the nave were completed by Giovanni de' Vecchi.

September 15th
Memorial of Our Lady of Sorrows

St Peter's Basilica
Chapel of the Pietà
†This is the first chapel on the right side of the nave.
†Within this chapel is Michelangelo's Pietà completed in 1499.

Santa Maria in Via
(Our Lady of the Way)
Via del Mortaro 24
†This church is near the Spanish Steps.

✝Along the walls of this church are the Seven Sorrows of Our Lady. They are positioned like the Stations of the Cross. Also a statue of Mary pierced by seven swords is in the main sanctuary.

✝On September 26, 1256 a miraculous icon of the Blessed Virgin Mary appeared at this location. It was found painted on a stone and floating upon the water of an overflowing well. The first chapel on the right side of the nave preserves this miraculous well and icon. Cups are normally provided so that pilgrims can drink some of the water from this well.

Sant'Andrea della Valle
(Saint Andrew of the Valley)
Piazza Sant'Andrea della Valle / Piazza Vidoni 6

✝This church is located along the Corso Vittorio Emanuele.

✝The second chapel on the right side of the nave is dedicated to Our Lady of Sorrows. A reproduction of Michelangelo's Pietà is located within this chapel.

Santa Maria dell'Anima
(Our Lady of the Soul)
Via Santa Maria dell'Anima 64

✝This church is near Piazza Navona. It is the German national church.

✝A slightly altered reproduction of Michelangelo's Pietà is located in this church within the fourth chapel on the right side of the nave.

Santa Maria in Trastevere
(Our Lady in Trastevere)
Via della Paglia 14 / Piazza Santa Maria in Trastevere

✝This church is located in Trastevere.

✝The third chapel on the right side of the nave is entitled L'Addolorata. This chapel powerfully unites the sufferings of Jesus and Mary by placing the crucified Christ over the bust of a grieving Blessed Virgin Mary.

✝Relics of the two popes, St Callistus I (d. 222) and St Cornelius (d. 253), rest under the main altar of this church. These relics are joined by others in particular those of the priest and martyr St Calepodius (d. 232).

Santissima Trinità dei Monti
(Most Holy Trinity of the Mounts)
Piazza della Trinità dei Monti

✝This church is at the top of the Spanish Steps.

✝Within the first chapel on the left side of the nave is a copy of the Pietà by Theodor Wilhelm Achtermann. This unique and powerful work depicts Mary and three other individuals removing the body of Christ from the Cross.

San Marcello al Corso
(Saint Marcellus on the Corso)
Piazza di San Marcello 5

✝This church is located north of Piazza Venezia.

✝A chapel on the left side of the nave is dedicated to the Seven Sorrows of Mary.

Santa Croce in Gerusalemme
(Holy Cross In Jerusalem)
Piazza di Santa Croce in Gerusalemme 12

✝This church is east of the *Basilica of St John Lateran*.

✝Within the chapel located below the main sanctuary is a marble relief of the Pietà.

✝Also a chapel accessible by the staircase on the left side of the sanctuary preserves a number of relics from Christ's Passion.

FOR ADDITIONAL MARIAN CHURCHES TO VISIT PLEASE SEE THE LIST AT THE END OF THIS BOOK.

September 16th
Memorial of Cornelius, pope and martyr; Cyprian, bishop and martyr

St Cornelius (d. 253, Civitavecchia, Italy) (Relics: Rome, Italy; Aachen, Germany)

St Cyprian (d. 258, Carthage, Tunisia)

St Cornelius died in the Italian city of Civitavecchia in 253 AD. His remains were then transferred south to Rome and placed in the *Catacombs of San Callisto* on the Appian Way. Five centuries later his relics were transferred to the Roman church of *Santa Maria in Trastevere* by Pope Adrian I (772-795). Pope Gregory IV (827-844) then had his remains placed under the main altar of this same church during his pontificate. From here a tradition claims that the remains of both St Cornelius and the bishop, St Cyprian, were transferred to Compiègne, France. Some of the sources conflict, however, with regard to this tradition. For instance, the *Martyrology of Ado* mentions the transfer of St Cyprian but not the transfer of St Cornelius. As a result two separate traditions have arisen with regard to St Cornelius' relics. The Roman tradition holds that some of his relics still remain under the main altar in *Santa Maria in Trastevere*. In the 18th century some of these relics were transferred to the Roman church of *Santi Celso e Giuliano*. A sarcophagus with these relics can still be found in this church. On the other hand the highly venerated relic of St Cornelius' head in the *Kornelimünster Abbey* near Aachen, Germany demonstrates that the purported transfer of his relics to Compiègne in the 9th century may also have credence.

Santa Maria in Trastevere
(Our Lady in Trastevere)
Via della Paglia 14 / Piazza Santa Maria in Trastevere
✝This church is located in Trastevere.
✝Relics of the two popes, St Cornelius and St Callistus I (d. 222), rest under the main altar of this church. These relics are joined by others in particular those of the priest and martyr St Calepodius (d. 232).
✝Also the mosaic above the main altar depicts St Cornelius as the third individual to the right of Jesus Christ.

Santi Celso e Giuliano
(Saints Celsus and Julian)
Vicolo del Curato 12 / Via del Banco Santo Spirito
✝This church is located across the Tiber River from *Castel Sant'Angelo*. The main entrance to the church is on Via del Banco Santo Spirito.
✝Some relics of St Cornelius were transferred to this church in the 18th century. A sarcophagus containing these relics is located just to the right of the main entrance.

Catacombs of San Callisto
Via Appia Antica 110/126
✝These catacombs are located south of the Aurelian Walls.
✝St Cornelius, St Pontian (d. 235), St Fabian (d. 250), St Sixtus II (d. 258), and a number of other early popes were originally buried here. The remains of St Cornelius were later moved to *Santa Maria in Trastevere*, the remains of St Fabian to *San Sebastiano Fuori Le Mura*, and the remains of St Sixtus II to *San Sisto Vecchio*.
✝St Cecilia was also buried in these catacombs. In 821 her remains were removed and taken to *Santa Cecilia in Trastevere*.

✝Finally, it was at this location in the year 258 that Roman soldiers burst into a chapel and arrested St Sixtus II and four other deacons while they were celebrating the liturgy. St Lawrence (d. 258) was not present for this arrest; however, a legend holds that St Lawrence was able to speak to St Sixtus just before the pope was martyred. In this conversation St Sixtus prophetically stated, "You shall follow me in three days." St Lawrence then in three days went on to suffer his own martyrdom by being burnt alive on a gridiron.

September 17th
Optional memorial of Robert Bellarmine, bishop and doctor

St Robert Bellarmine (d. 1621, Rome, Italy) (Relics: Rome, Italy)

Sant'Ignazio (Saint Ignatius)
Via del Caravita 8/a
✝This church is east of the Pantheon.
✝The body of St Robert Bellarmine rests under the altar in the third chapel on the right side of the nave.
✝The remains of St Aloysius Gonzaga (d. 1591) rest under the altar in the right transept. His rooms are next to the church and can be visited by appointment.
✝The remains of St John Berchmans (d. 1621), the patron saint of altar servers, rest under the altar in the left transept.

San Roberto Bellarmino
(Saint Robert Bellarmine)
Via Panama 13
✝This church is north of Villa Borghese. It is dedicated to St Robert Bellarmine.

September 19th
Optional memorial of Januarius, bishop and martyr

St Januarius [Gennaro in Italian] (d. 305) (Relics: Naples, Italy)

September 20th
Optional memorial of Andrew Kim Taegon, priest and martyr; Paul Chong Hasang and Companions, martyrs (Korean martyrs)

Honored on this day are 103 martyrs who died in Korea from the years 1839-1867. (Relics: Mirinaeseongji-ro, South Korea; Seoul, South Korea)

September 21st
Feast of Matthew, apostle and evangelist

St Matthew (Relics: Salerno, Italy)

Santissima Trinità dei Pellegrini
(The Most Holy Trinity of the Pilgrims)
Via dei Pettinari 36/A
✝This church is located near Piazza Farnese.
✝Above the altar in the right transept is a statue of St Matthew.

San Luigi dei Francesi
(Saint Louis of the French)
Piazza San Luigi dei Francesi 5
✝This church is near Piazza Navona.
✝This church is known for its paintings. The most famous being *The Calling of St Matthew* by Caravaggio located in the *Contarelli Chapel*. This is the last chapel on the left side of the nave. The other two paintings in this chapel are also attributed to Caravaggio and are entitled *The Martyrdom of St Matthew* and *The Inspiration of St Matthew*.

Santa Maria in Aracoeli
(Our Lady in Aracoeli)
Piazza del Campidoglio 4
✝This church is on top of the Capitoline Hill.
✝The fifth chapel on the right side of the nave is dedicated to St Matthew.
✝Also relics of St Helena, the mother of Constantine, rest in the left transept.

September 23rd
Memorial of Pio of Pietrelcina, priest

St Pio of Pietrelcina (d. 1968, San Giovanni Rotondo, Italy) (Relics: San Giovanni Rotondo, Italy)

San Salvatore in Lauro
(Holy Savior in Lauro)
Piazza San Salvatore in Lauro 15
✝This church is west of Piazza Navona.
✝Some relics of St Padre Pio are kept within a side chapel in this church. This includes both a vial of blood from his stigmata and a stole.

September 26th
Optional memorial of Cosmas and Damian, martyrs

Saints Cosmas and Damian (d. 287, Syria) (Relics: Rome, Italy; Munich Germany)

Santi Cosma e Damiano
(Saints Cosmas and Damian)
Via dei Fori Imperiali 1
✝This church is located next to the Roman Forum.
✝Relics of Saints Cosmas and Damian rest under the altar in the lower church. Each year for the feast of Saints Cosmas and Damian these relics are brought out for public veneration.

San Giovanni Battista dei Fiorentini
(Saint John the Baptist of the Florentines)
Via Acciaioli 2
✝This church is just east of the Vatican. It is next to the Tiber River and the Corso Vittorio Emanuele.
✝The chapel in the right transept is dedicated to Saints Cosmas and Damian.
✝A relic of St Mary Magdalene's foot rests in a shrine to the left of the main sanctuary.

San Salvatore in Onda
(The Holy Savior in the Deluge)
Via dei Pettinari 51
✝This church is near Tiber Island.
✝A painting of Saints Cosmas and Damian is placed above an altar to the right of the main sanctuary.
✝The remains of St Vincent Pallotti (d. 1850) rest below the main altar.

September 27th
Memorial of Vincent de Paul, priest

St Vincent de Paul (d. 1660, Paris, France) (Relics: Paris, France)

San Silvestro al Quirinale
(Saint Sylvester at the Quirinale)
Via Ventiquattro (XXIV) Maggio 10
✝This church is east of Piazza Venezia. It is served by the Missionaries of St Vincent de Paul. A painting of their patron saint is in the main sanctuary. It is not open often.

September 28th
Optional memorial of Wenceslaus, martyr

St Wenceslaus (d. 935, Stará Boleslav, Czech Republic) (Relics: Prague, Czech Republic)

September 28th
Optional memorial of Lawrence Ruiz and Companions, martyrs

Honored on this day are 16 martyrs who died in Nagasaki, Japan from the years 1633-1637.

September 29th
Feast of Michael, Gabriel and Raphael, Archangels

Santa Maria degli Angeli
(Our Lady of the Angels)
Piazza della Repubblica
✝This church is at Piazza della Repubblica. It is a very spacious church built over the Baths of Diocletian.
✝Many angels are depicted within this church. Located near the entrance are two angels gracefully supporting shell-shaped holy water fonts. In the main sanctuary is a 16th century painting that depicts seven angels surrounding the Blessed Virgin Mary. An additional pair of sculpted angels then surround this painting.

Santi Michele e Magno
(Saints Michael and Magnus)
Borgo Santo Spirito 21/41
✝This church is located near the Vatican. It is not open often. To enter one must go up a flight of stairs on the south side of the Borgo Santo Spirito. It is dedicated to St Michael the Archangel.

Santissima Trinità dei Monti
(Most Holy Trinity of the Mounts)
Piazza della Trinità dei Monti
✝This church is at the top of the Spanish Steps.
✝Within the fourth chapel on the left side of the nave is a painting of St Michael the Archangel completed by Domenico Corvi in 1758.

Santa Maria della Concezione
(Our Lady of the Immaculate Conception)
Via Veneto 27
✝This church is just north of the Barberini metro stop.
✝The first chapel on the right side of the nave is dedicated to St Michael the Archangel. The altarpiece within this chapel is a painting by Guido Reni which masterfully portrays the archangel. Also of note is a famous painting by Gerard van Honthorst depicting the *Mocking of Jesus* upon the left side-wall of this same chapel.

Sant'Eustachio (Saint Eustace)
Piazza Sant'Eustachio 19
✝This church is just west of the Pantheon.
✝The second chapel on the left side of the nave is dedicated to St Michael the Archangel.

Santa Maria in Campitelli
(Our Lady in Campitelli)
Piazza di Campitelli 9
✝This church is near the Jewish quarter.
✝The first chapel on the right side of the nave is dedicated to St Michael the Archangel.
✝The body of St John Leonardi (d. 1609) is enshrined in the second chapel on the left side of the nave.

Santa Maria in Aracoeli
(Our Lady in Aracoeli)
Piazza del Campidoglio 4
✝This church is on top of the Capitoline Hill.
✝The seventh chapel on the left side of the nave is dedicated to St Michael the Archangel.

San Francesco d'Assisi a Ripa
(Saint Francis of Assisi in Ripa)
Piazza San Francesco d'Assisi 88
†This church is in the southern part of Trastevere.
†The third chapel on the left side of the nave is dedicated to St Michael the Archangel.
†St Francis of Assisi (d. 1226) stayed within a room in this church during a visit to Rome. Within this room is a stone that is said to have been used by him as a pillow.

Castel Sant'Angelo
(Castle of the Holy Angel)
†This mammoth circular building was built in the 2nd century to house the tomb of Emperor Hadrian. It is located along the Tiber River just east of the Vatican.
†Placed on top of this building is a statue of St Michael the Archangel. A tradition holds that as St Gregory the Great (d. 604) led a procession through the streets of Rome in an effort to bring an end to a plague he witnessed St Michael the Archangel upon this building. Hence the placement of the statue.

September 30th
Memorial of Jerome, priest and doctor

St Jerome (d. 420, Bethlehem, Judea)
(Relics: Rome, Italy)

Basilica of St Mary Major
Piazza di Santa Maria Maggiore 42
†The remains of St Jerome were brought to this basilica in the 12th century and placed next to the five highly venerated pieces of wood from the manger of the Lord. Up to the last century these relics from Christ's Nativity were located in the confessio within the chapel in the right transept. However, during the pon-

tificate of Pius IX they were removed and placed in their present location below the Papal Altar. There is some doubt if the relics of St Jerome were also moved at this time. The relics of St Jerome, therefore, either rest under the Papal Altar within the main body of the church or within the confessio of the chapel in the right transept.

San Girolamo della Carità
(Saint Jerome of Charity)
Via di Monserrato 62/a
†This church was built on the site of the house of St Paula. Tradition claims that St Jerome lived in this house when he was secretary to Pope St Damasus I (d. 384).

San Girolamo dei Croati
(Saint Jerome of the Croatians)
Via Tomacelli 132
†This church is near the Tiber River just west of the Spanish Steps.
†Several large paintings within the main sanctuary of this church depict scenes from the life of St Jerome. Both the church and the third chapel on the left side of the nave are dedicated to him.

St Peter's Basilica
Altar of St Jerome
†This altar is near the entrance to the confessional area.
†The mosaic above the altar depicts St Jerome receiving his last Communion.
†The body of St John XXIII rests under this altar.

Sant'Onofrio (Saint Onuphrius)
Piazza di Sant'Onofrio 2
†This church is on the Janiculum Hill.
†The hillside that this church rests upon was largely uninhabited prior to the 15th century. The present church was com-

missioned to provide a place of prayer
for a small community of hermits. As the
church took shape much of its art took on
themes that echo its eremitical origins.

✝St Jerome, like the church's patron
saint, Saint Onuphrius, was greatly
renowned as an ascetic. Three frescoes
found within the loggia located near the
entrance depict various ascetical scenes
from St Jerome's life. These were
completed by Domenichino in the 17th
century. St Jerome is also depicted
within the church in the first chapel on
the left side of the nave.

Santa Maria in Trastevere
(Our Lady in Trastevere)
Via della Paglia 14 / Piazza Santa Maria
in Trastevere

✝This church is located in Trastevere.

✝The fifth chapel on the left side of the
nave is dedicated to St Jerome.

✝Relics of the two popes, St Callistus I
(d. 222) and St Cornelius (d. 253), rest
under the main altar of this church.
These relics are joined by others in
particular those of the priest and martyr
St Calepodius (d. 232).

San Giovanni Battista dei Fiorentini
(Saint John the Baptist of the
Florentines)
Via Acciaioli 2

✝This church is just east of the Vatican.
It is next to the Tiber River and the Corso
Vittorio Emanuele.

✝The fourth chapel on the right side of
the nave is dedicated to St Jerome.

✝A relic of St Mary Magdalene's foot
also rests in a shrine to the left of the
main sanctuary.

October

October 1st
Memorial of Therese of the Child Jesus, virgin and doctor

St Therese of the Child Jesus (d. 1897, Lisieux, France) (Relics: Lisieux, France)

Santissima Trinità dei Monti
(Most Holy Trinity of the Mounts)
Piazza della Trinità dei Monti
✝This church is at the top of the Spanish Steps.
✝A painting of Our Lady called *Mater Admirabilis* is preserved within the convent chapel. St Therese of the Child Jesus (d. 1897) knelt in front of this painting during her visit to Rome and beseeched God for the grace to enter the convent at the age of 15. To visit this chapel enter the door at the *Instituto Del Sacro Cuore*. This door is not reached by the staircase to the church but by a second staircase on the left side.

Santa Cecilia in Trastevere
(Saint Cecilia in Trastevere)
Piazza di Santa Cecilia 22
✝This church is located in the southern part of Trastevere.
✝St Therese of the Child Jesus visited this church during her trip to Rome as a child. The chapel in the right transept honors her memory with a beautiful statue of her.
✝This church is built over the ruins of the house that St Cecilia had lived in prior to her martyrdom.
✝In 821 the body of St Cecilia was exhumed from the *Catacombs of San Callisto* by Pope St Paschal I (d. 824) and returned to this church. Today her remains rest within the crypt under the main altar.

Santa Maria della Vittoria
(Our Lady of the Victory)
Via XX Settembre 17
✝This church is north of Piazza della Repubblica.
✝The first chapel on the right side of the nave is dedicated to St Therese of the Child Jesus.
✝Also located in this church is Gian Lorenzo Bernini's famous sculpture entitled *The Ecstasy of St Teresa*.

October 2nd
Memorial of The Holy Guardian Angels

Santa Maria degli Angeli
(Our Lady of the Angels)
Piazza della Repubblica
✝This church is at Piazza della Repubblica. It is a very spacious church built over the Baths of Diocletian.
✝Many angels are depicted within this church. Located near the entrance are two angels gracefully supporting shell-shaped holy water fonts. In the main sanctuary is a 16th century painting that depicts seven angels surrounding the Blessed Virgin Mary. An additional pair of sculpted angels then surround this painting.

Oratorio dell'Angelo Custode
(Oratory of the Guardian Angel)
Piazza Poli 11
✝This small church is located near the Trevi Fountain. Its name is in the singular; therefore, its dedication is intended for each person's individual Guardian Angel.

Sant'Andrea delle Fratte
(Saint Andrew of the Bushes)
Via Sant'Andrea delle Fratte 1

†This church is near the Spanish Steps.
†The two masterfully sculpted angels on either side of the main sanctuary were created by Gian Lorenzo Bernini. They were originally designed for *Ponte Sant'Angelo*; however, they were deemed too beautiful to be placed outside.

San Carlo al Corso
(Saint Charles on the Corso)
Via del Corso 437
†This church is near the Spanish Steps.
†The large painting within the left transept depicts God the Father being worshiped by angels. It was completed by Tommaso Donini in 1632.
†The heart of St Charles Borromeo (d. 1584) rests within a reliquary in an altar located behind the main sanctuary.

Santa Maria in Aquiro
(Our Lady in Aquiro)
Via della Guglia 69/B
†This church is near the Pantheon.
†The first chapel on the left side of the nave is dedicated to the Guardian Angels.

October 4ᵗʰ
Memorial of Francis of Assisi

St Francis (d. 1226, Assisi, Italy)
(Relics: Assisi, Italy)

Basilica of St John Lateran
Piazza San Giovanni in Laterano 4
†The fourth chapel on the left side of the nave is dedicated to St Francis of Assisi. A painting within this chapel depicts St Francis receiving the stigmata.
†Within a small park just outside of this basilica is a large statue of St Francis. He is depicted facing the façade of the basilica with his arms outstretched. If one stands behind this statue at a certain distance it looks as if St Francis is hold-ing up the church. This recalls the dream of Pope Innocent III in 1209 when he saw the church being supported by St Francis.

Santissime Stimmate di San Francesco
(The Most Holy Stigmata of Saint Francis)
Largo delle Stimmate
†This church is near the Largo di Torre Argentina. It is dedicated to the holy stigmata of St Francis of Assisi. It is not open often.

San Francesco d'Assisi a Ripa
(Saint Francis of Assisi in Ripa)
Piazza San Francesco d'Assisi 88
†This church is in the southern part of Trastevere.
†St Francis of Assisi stayed within a room in this church during a visit to Rome. Within this room is a stone that is said to have been used by him as a pillow.

San Francesco d'Assisi a Monte Mario
(Saint Francis of Assisi on Monte Mario)
Piazzetta di Monte Gaudio 8
†This church is north of the Vatican.
†It is said that as St Francis journeyed from Assisi to Rome he caught his first glimpse of Rome from the hill upon which this church now rests. Upon seeing the city St Francis immediately fell to his knees in prayer.

Santa Maria della Concezione
(Our Lady of the Immaculate Conception)
Via Veneto 27
†This church is just north of the Barberini metro stop.
†The third chapel on the right side of nave is dedicated to St Francis of Assisi. The fresco on the left wall and the painting above the main altar were completed by Domenichino.

✝Also within the third chapel on the left side of the nave is a painting by Girolamo Muziano that depicts St Francis receiving the stigmata.

San Bernardo alle Terme
(Saint Bernard at the Baths)
Via Torino 94
✝This church is north of Piazza della Repubblica.
✝Within the chapel to the right of the main sanctuary is a very moving statue of St Francis of Assisi.

Santi Apostoli (Holy Apostles)
Piazza dei Santi Apostoli 51
✝This church is just east of Piazza Venezia.
✝The third chapel on the left side of the nave is dedicated to St Francis of Assisi.
✝Relics of St Philip and St James the Less rest within the confessio.

San Pietro in Montorio
(Saint Peter in Montorio)
Piazza San Pietro in Montorio 2
✝This church is located on the Janiculum hill.
✝Within the first chapel on the left side of the nave is a fresco completed by Giovanni de' Vecchi that depicts St Francis with his stigmata.
✝Also within the next chapel on the left side of the nave, which was designed by Gian Lorenzo Bernini, is a marble relief portraying The Ecstasy of St Francis.

Santa Maria in Trastevere
(Our Lady in Trastevere)
Via della Paglia 14 / Piazza Santa Maria in Trastevere
✝This church is located in Trastevere.
✝The third chapel on the left side of the nave is dedicated to St Francis of Assisi.

✝Relics of the two popes, St Callistus I (d. 222) and St Cornelius (d. 253), rest under the main altar of this church. These relics are joined by others in particular those of the priest and martyr St Calepodius (d. 232).

Santa Maria in Aracoeli
(Our Lady in Aracoeli)
Piazza del Campidoglio 4
✝This church is on top of the Capitoline Hill.
✝The chapel in the right transept is dedicated to St Francis. Several paintings within this chapel depict scenes from his life.
✝Also relics of St Helena, the mother of Constantine, rest in the left transept.

October 5th
Optional Memorial of Blessed Francis Xavier Seelos, priest*

Blessed Francis Xavier Seelos (d. 1867, New Orleans, Louisiana, USA) (Relics: New Orleans, Louisiana, USA)

October 6th
Optional memorial of Bruno, priest

St Bruno (d. 1101, Serra San Bruno, Italy) (Relics: Serra San Bruno, Italy)

Santa Maria degli Angeli
(Our Lady of the Angels)
Piazza della Repubblica
✝This church is at Piazza della Repubblica. It is a very spacious church built over the Baths of Diocletian.
✝A large statue of St Bruno is placed on the right side just as one enters the church. Shortly beyond this and also on the right side is a small chapel dedicated to St Bruno.

✝The spacious chapel located in the left transept is also dedicated to St Bruno. The large painting in this chapel by Giovanni Odazzi is entitled *The Apparition of the Virgin Mary to St Bruno.*

October 6th
Optional memorial of Blessed Marie Rose Durocher, virgin*

Blessed Marie Rose Durocher (d. 1849, Longueuil, Quebec, Canada) (Relics: Longueuil, Quebec, Canada)

October 7th
Memorial of Our Lady of the Rosary

Santa Maria in Aracoeli
(Our Lady in Aracoeli)
Piazza del Campidoglio 4
✝This church is on top of the Capitoline Hill.
✝The gilded ceiling within this church honors the Christian victory obtained at the Battle of Lepanto. This victory was largely accredited to the praying of the Rosary, hence the creation of the *Memorial of Our Lady of the Rosary.*
✝Also relics of St Helena, the mother of Constantine, rest in the left transept.

Santa Maria sopra Minerva
(Our Lady Above Minerva)
Piazza della Minerva 42
✝This church is near the Pantheon.
✝The *Capranica Chapel* located to the right of the main sanctuary is often called the *Chapel of the Rosary.* The frescoes covering the vault of this chapel, completed by Marcello Venusti in the 16th century, depict the traditional mysteries of the Rosary. Also the altarpiece by Michelangelo Cerruti portrays St Dominic receiving the Rosary from the Blessed Virgin Mary as St Catherine of Siena looks on.

✝The remains of St Catherine of Siena (d. 1380), which now rest beneath the altar in the main sanctuary, were originally placed within this chapel.

Santa Maria del Rosario in Prati
(Our Lady of the Rosary in Prati)
Via Germanico 94
✝This church is near the Ottaviano metro stop. It is dedicated to Our Lady of the Rosary. The stained glass windows above the main altar depict three mysteries of the Rosary. Also within the second chapel on the left side of the nave is a beautiful statue of Our Lady of the Rosary.

Basilica di San Clemente
(Basilica of Saint Clement)
Via Labicana 95 / Piazza San Clemente
✝This church is east of the Colosseum.
✝The chapel located to the left of the main sanctuary is dedicated to Our Lady of the Rosary. The painting above this altar depicts the Blessed Virgin Mary with both St Dominic and St Catherine of Siena.
✝The remains of St Clement I (d. 97) and of St Ignatius of Antioch (d. 107) rest beneath the main altar.
✝Also a chapel on the right side of the nave is dedicated to Saints Cyril (d. 869) and Methodius (d. 885). The extant remains of St Cyril rest within the altar of this chapel.

San Nicola dei Prefetti
(Saint Nicholas of the Prefects)
Via dei Prefetti 34
✝This church is north of the Pantheon.
✝An altar on the left side of the nave is dedicated to Our Lady of the Rosary.

Santa Maria dei Miracoli
(Our Lady of the Miracles)
Via del Corso 528
✝This church is at Piazza del Popolo.

†The second chapel on the left side of the nave is dedicated to the Rosary.

FOR ADDITIONAL MARIAN CHURCHES TO VISIT PLEASE SEE THE LIST AT THE END OF THIS BOOK.

October 9th
Optional memorial of Denis, bishop and martyr, and Companions, martyrs

St Denis (d. 3rd century, Paris, France)
(Relics: Saint-Denis, France)

San Luigi dei Francesi
(Saint Louis of the French)
Piazza San Luigi dei Francesi 5
†This church is near Piazza Navona.
†The first chapel on the right side of the nave is dedicated to St Denis. The altarpiece in this chapel depicts St Denis restoring sight to a blind man.

Basilica of St Paul Outside the Walls
Via Ostiense 186
†This basilica is south of the Aurelian Walls.
†In the right transept is a small chapel dedicated to St Lawrence. Above the altar in this chapel is a marble triptych depicting St Anthony, St Denis, and St Justina.
†St Paul is also buried within the confessio in this basilica. Above his tomb are the chains that had been used to imprison him prior to his martyrdom. These chains were placed in this prominent location in 2008.

October 9th
Optional memorial of John Leonardi, priest

St John Leonardi (d. 1609, Rome, Italy)
(Relics: Rome, Italy)

Santa Maria in Campitelli
(Our Lady in Campitelli)
Piazza di Campitelli 9
†This church is near the Jewish quarter.
†The body of St John Leonardi is enshrined in the second chapel on the left side of the nave.

October 11th
Optional memorial of John XXIII, pope

St John XXIII (d. 1963, Rome, Italy)
(Relics: Rome, Italy)

St Peter's Basilica
Altar of St Jerome
†Located on the right side of the nave at the base of the first column.
†The body of St John XXIII rests under this altar. He is known in particular for announcing the opening of the Second Vatican Council.

San Bartolomeo e Alessandro dei Bergamaschi
(Saints Bartholomew and Alexander of the People of Bergamo)
Via di Pietra 70, Piazza Colonna
†This church is off the Via del Corso near the Piazza Colonna. It is not open often.
†The first chapel on the right side of the nave is dedicated to St John XXIII. A relic of his zucchetto rests above the altar.

October 14th
Optional memorial of Callistus I, pope and martyr

St Callistus I (d. 222, Rome, Italy)
(Relics: Rome, Italy)

St Callistus I was originally buried in the *Cemetery of Calepodius* on the Aurelian Way. In the 8th century his remains were transferred to *Santa Maria in Trastevere* by Pope Adrian I (772-795). A few decades later during the pontificate of Pope Gregory IV (827-844) his body was relocated within this same church and placed directly under the main altar.

Santa Maria in Trastevere
(Our Lady in Trastevere)
Via della Paglia 14 / Piazza Santa Maria in Trastevere
✝This church is located in Trastevere.
✝Relics of the two popes, St Callistus I and St Cornelius (d. 253), rest under the main altar of this church. These relics are joined by others in particular those of the priest and martyr St Calepodius (d. 232).
✝Within a small grated niche at the end of the right aisle are several stones and a chain. The large marble stone is said to have been used as a weight to drown St Callistus I in a nearby well.
✝Also in the mosaics above the main altar St Callistus I is depicted as the individual next to the Blessed Virgin Mary.

San Callisto (St Callistus)
Piazza di San Callisto
✝This church is next to *Santa Maria in Trastevere*. It is not open often.
✝Tradition claims that it was in the location where this church now stands that St Callistus I suffered martyrdom by being thrown down a well.

October 15th
Memorial of Teresa of Jesus, virgin and doctor

St Teresa (d. 1582, Alba de Tormes, Spain) (Relics: Rome, Italy; Avila, Spain; Alba de Tormes, Spain)

Santa Maria della Scala
(Our Lady at the Steps)
Piazza della Scala 23
✝This church is located in Trastevere.
✝The right foot of St Teresa of Avila rests within this church in a beautiful chapel to the left of the main sanctuary. It was gifted to this church in 1617. (This chapel is not visible from the nave of the church and it is rarely open to the public. However, if one kindly asks the sacristan access may be granted. If the sacristan is not present he or she can be called at the neighboring convent door.)
✝Also the chapel in the right transept is dedicated to St Teresa of Avila.

Santa Maria della Vittoria
(Our Lady of the Victory)
Via XX Settembre 17
✝This church is north of Piazza della Repubblica.
✝Located here is Gian Lorenzo Bernini's famous sculpture entitled *The Ecstasy of St Teresa*.

Santa Teresa d'Avila
(St Teresa of Avila)
Corso d'Italia 37
✝This church is north of Piazza della Repubblica. It is dedicated to St Teresa of Avila.

Santuario della Madonna del Perpetuo Soccorso
(Sanctuary of Our Lady of Perpetual Help)

Via Merulana 26
†This church is just south of the *Basilica of St Mary Major*.
†The first chapel on the right side of the nave is dedicated to St Teresa of Avila.
†A miraculous image of the Blessed Virgin Mary entitled *Our Lady of Perpetual Help* is above the main altar.

Santa Maria in Traspontina
(Our Lady in Traspontina)
Via della Conciliazione 14
†This church is near the Vatican.
†The fourth chapel on the left side of the nave is dedicated to St Teresa of Avila.
†Also the third chapel on the right side of the nave contains a beautiful statue of Our Lady of Mt Carmel. A memorial at this chapel recalls that this church provided a new scapular for St John Paul II after the assassination attempt upon his life in 1981.

San Giovanni della Pigna
(Saint John of the Pigna)
Vicolo della Minerva 51
†This church is south of the Pantheon.
†The second chapel on the left side of the nave is dedicated to St Teresa of Avila.

October 16th
Optional memorial of Hedwig, religious

St Hedwig (d. 1243, Silesia, Poland) (Relics: Andechs, Germany; Berlin, Germany)

October 16th
Optional memorial of Margaret Mary Alacoque, virgin

St Margaret Mary Alacoque (d. 1690, Paray-le-Monial, France) (Relics: Paray-le-Monial, France)

St Peter's Basilica
Altar of the Sacred Heart
†Located at the base of the far left column.
†A mosaic above this altar depicts Christ revealing his Sacred Heart to St Margaret Mary Alacoque.

Casa Santa Maria (House of Our Lady)
Via dell'Umiltà 30
†Located south of the Trevi fountain.
†A community of Visitation Nuns occupied this residence during the early part of the 19th century. Therefore, the beatification of St Margaret Mary Alacoque was officially announced in a chapel located here.

Nostra Signora del Sacro Cuore
(Our Lady of the Sacred Heart)
Corso del Rinascimento 27
†This church is at Piazza Navona.
†The fourth chapel on the right side of the nave is dedicated to St Margaret Mary Alacoque.

October 17th
Memorial of Ignatius of Antioch, bishop and martyr

St Ignatius of Antioch (d. 107, Rome, Italy) (Relics: Rome, Italy)

Basilica di San Clemente
(Basilica of Saint Clement)
Via Labicana 95 / Piazza San Clemente
†This church is east of the Colosseum.
†The remains of St Ignatius of Antioch and of St Clement I (d. 97) rest below the main altar.
†Also a chapel on the right side of the nave is dedicated to Saints Cyril (d. 869) and Methodius (d. 885). The extant remains of St Cyril rest within the altar of this chapel.

✝Tradition claims that St Cyril discovered some bones and an anchor while in Crimea. These were believed to be the relics of St Clement I. St Cyril then carried these relics to Rome where they were placed in the *Basilica of San Clemente*.

October 18th
Feast of Luke, evangelist

St Luke (Relics: Rome, Italy; Padua, Italy; Prague, Czech Republic; Thebes, Greece)

St Peter's Basilica
Treasury Museum
✝A silver reliquary bust within this museum is said to contain the head of St Luke. This reliquary dates back to the 14th century and the relic is said to have come from Constantinople. However, this same relic is also said to be located in the *Cathedral of St Vitus* in Prague, Czech Republic. A recent study on the relics of St Luke was conducted at the request of Archbishop Antonio Mattiazzo of Padua in 1998. This study seems to suggest that the authentic relic of St Luke's head is the one within the *Cathedral of St Vitus*.

Santi Luca e Martina
(Saints Luke and Martina)
Via della Curia 2
✝This church is located in the Roman Forum and it is dedicated to St Luke and St Martina. The painting above the main altar is of St Luke painting the Blessed Virgin Mary. The church is not open often.

October 19th
Memorial of John de Brebeuf and Isaac Jogues, priests and martyrs, and Companions, martyrs*

Honored on this day are eight Jesuit martyrs who died in North America from the years 1642-1649. (Relics: Midland, Ontario, Canada)

Nostra Signora del Santissimo Sacramento e Santi Martiri Canadesi
(Our Lady of the Most Holy Sacrament and of the Holy Canadian Martyrs)
Via Giovanni Battista de Rossi 46
✝This is the national church of Canada and it is located in the Nomentano district northwest of the Bologna metro station. It was built in 1955 and it honors in a special way the North American Martyrs.

October 20th
Optional memorial of Paul of the Cross, priest*

St Paul of the Cross (d. 1775, Rome, Italy) (Relics: Rome, Italy)

Santi Giovanni e Paolo
(Saints John and Paul)
Piazza dei Santi Giovanni e Paolo 13
✝This church is south of the Colosseum.
✝St Paul of the Cross is buried under the altar in the large side chapel on the right side of the nave. Upon request one can visit the room in which he died in the monastery adjacent to the church.
✝Located beneath this church is a complex of well preserved ancient Roman houses. Among these is an ancient house church. These ruins can be visited.

Santa Maria ai Monti
(Our Lady at the Hills)
Via della Madonna dei Monti 41
†This church is near the Cavour metro stop.
†St Paul of the Cross said Mass here from 1745-1767.
†This church was built due to a miraculous discovery of an image of the Blessed Virgin Mary in a nearby Poor Clare convent that had fallen into ruins. To celebrate this great find Pope Gregory XIII (d. 1585) commissioned the building of this church. This miraculous image is now placed above the main altar.

October 22nd
Memorial of John Paul II, pope

St John Paul II (d. 2005, Rome, Italy)
(Relics: Rome, Italy)

St Peter's Basilica
Chapel of St Sebastian
†Located on the right side of the nave just after Michelangelo's statue of the Pietà.
†In 2011 the remains of St John Paul II were removed from the crypt of this basilica and placed within the altar of this chapel. Since this basilica is visited by thousands of people every day the tomb is roped off to provide a small area of prayer. Access to this area is granted if one asks to pray at the tomb.

Santa Maria in Traspontina
(Our Lady in Traspontina)
Via della Conciliazione 14
†This church is near the Vatican.
†The third chapel on the right side of the nave contains a beautiful statue of Our Lady of Mt Carmel. A memorial at this chapel recalls that this church provided a

new scapular for St John Paul II after the assassination attempt upon his life in 1981.

Santo Spirito in Sassia
(Holy Spirit in Sassia)
Via dei Penitenzieri 12
†This church is near the Vatican.
†Within the fourth chapel on the left side of the nave is a painting of St John Paul II. Also preserved here is a small relic of him.

October 23rd
Optional memorial of John of Capistrano, priest

St John of Capistrano (d. 1456, Ilok, Croatia) (Relics: Ilok, Croatia)

San Francesco d'Assisi a Ripa
(Saint Francis of Assisi in Ripa)
Piazza San Francesco d'Assisi 88
†This church is in the southern part of Trastevere.
†The second chapel on the right side of the nave is dedicated to St John of Capistrano. The paintings and frescoes within this chapel depict various scenes from his life. They were all completed by Domenico Muratori.
†St Francis of Assisi (d. 1226) stayed within a room in this church during a visit to Rome. Within this room is a stone that is said to have been used by him as a pillow.

Santa Maria in Aracoeli
(Our Lady in Aracoeli)
Piazza del Campidoglio 4
†This church is on top of the Capitoline Hill.
†A small altar located just to the left of the front row of pews is dedicated to St John of Capistrano. The painting above

this altar depicts him holding a red flag while meditating upon a wooden cruci-fix.

October 24th
Optional memorial of Anthony Mary Claret, bishop

St Anthony Mary Claret (d. 1870, Fontfroide, France) (Relics: Vic, Spain)

October 28th
Feast of Simon and Jude, apostles

St Simon (Relics: Rome, Italy)

St Jude (Relics: Rome, Italy; Chicago, Illinois, USA)

St Peter's Basilica
St Joseph's Altar
†Located in the left transept where the Blessed Sacrament is reserved.
†Relics of the two apostles, St Simon and St Jude, rest under this altar.

San Salvatore in Lauro
(Holy Savior in Lauro)
Piazza San Salvatore in Lauro 15
†This church is west of Piazza Navona.
†A small bone fragment from an arm of St Jude rests within a side chapel in this church.

November

November 1ˢᵗ
Solemnity of All Saints

Santa Maria sopra Minerva
(Our Lady Above Minerva)
Piazza della Minerva 42
†This church is near the Pantheon.
†The *Altieri Chapel* located to the right of the main sanctuary has the unique status of being dedicated to all the saints.
†Also the body of St Catherine of Siena (d. 1380) rests under the main altar.

November 2ⁿᵈ
Optional memorial of All Souls

November 3ʳᵈ
Optional memorial of Martin de Porres, religious

St Martin de Porres (d. 1639, Lima, Peru) (Relics: Lima, Peru)

Santissima Trinità dei Spagnoli
(The Most Holy Trinity of the Spanish)
Via dei Condotti 41
†This church is near the Spanish Steps.
†A small statue of St Martin de Porres is in the first chapel on the right side of the nave.

November 4ᵗʰ
Memorial of Charles Borromeo, bishop

St Charles Borromeo (d. 1584, Milan, Italy) (Relics: Rome, Italy; Milan, Italy)

San Carlo al Corso
(Saint Charles on the Corso)
Via del Corso 437
†This church is near the Spanish Steps.
†The dedication of this church is to the great 16ᵗʰ century Archbishop of Milan, St Charles Borromeo. A relic of his heart rests within a reliquary in an altar located behind the main sanctuary.

San Carlo ai Catinari
(Saint Charles at the Catinari)
Piazza Benedetto Cairoli 117
†This church is near the Largo di Torre Argentina. It is dedicated to St Charles Borromeo.
†The painting above the main altar depicts St Charles Borromeo leading a procession of the faithful.

San Carlo alle Quattro Fontane
(Saint Charles at the Four Fountains)
Via del Quirinale 23
†This church is south of the Barberini metro stop. It is a small Baroque church created by Francesco Borromini. It is dedicated to St Charles Borromeo.

Chiesa Nuova
(The New Church)
Via del Governo Vecchio 134
†This church is along the Corso Vittorio Emanuele.
†The chapel to the right of the main sanctuary is dedicated to St Charles Borromeo.
†The body of St Philip Neri (d. 1595) is enshrined in the left transept. His private rooms can be visited on certain days of the week. They are located in the right wall of the left transept.

November 9ᵗʰ
Feast of The Dedication of the Basilica of Saint John Lateran

Basilica of St John Lateran
Piazza San Giovanni in Laterano 4
†Positioned above the Papal Altar of this church are two busts of St Peter and St Paul. According to tradition the skulls or parts of the skulls of St Peter and St Paul

are within these busts. Also located within the Papal Altar is a wooden table that St Peter and many of the earliest popes are said to have celebrated the Eucharist upon.

†Located to the left of the Papal Altar is another very ancient table. This table rests above the altar where the Blessed Sacrament is reserved. It is placed directly behind a bronze relief of the Last Supper. Tradition claims that it was upon this table that Jesus and the apostles celebrated the Last Supper.

November 10th
Memorial of Leo the Great, pope and doctor

St Leo the Great (d. 461, Rome, Italy) (Relics: Rome, Italy)

St Peter's Basilica
Altar of St Leo the Great
†Located in the far left corner of the left transept.
†The remains of St Leo the Great rest under this altar.
†St Leo was known both for his exemplar defense of orthodox theology and for his efforts in halting the advance of the Barbarian tribes. A marble relief of his important meeting with Attila the Hun is placed above this altar.

November 11th
Memorial of Martin of Tours, bishop

St Martin of Tours (d. 397, Candes-Saint-Martin, France) (Relics: Tours, France)

San Martino ai Monti
(Saint Martin at the Hills)
Viale Monte Oppio 28
†This church is south of the *Basilica of St Mary Major*.

†The third chapel on the right side of the nave is dedicated to St Martin of Tours. A painting above this altar depicts him giving his cloak to a beggar.
†The greater part of the remains of St Martin I (d. 655) were transferred from Crimea to this church in Rome. They now rest in the confessio below the main altar. This confessio also houses the relics of many other saints taken from the *Catacombs of Priscilla*.

San Rocco (Saint Roch)
Largo San Rocco 1
†This church is near the Tiber River just west of the Spanish Steps.
†The chapel in the left transept is dedicated to St Martin of Tours. The painting in this chapel depicts him dividing his cloak with a beggar.

November 12th
Memorial of Josaphat, bishop and martyr

St Josaphat (d. 1623, Vitebsk, Russia) (Relics: Rome, Italy)

St Peter's Basilica
Altar of St Basil
†Located within the confessional area on the back side of the first column.
†The remains of St Josaphat rest below this altar. During the early part of the 17th century he valiantly tried to bring Christians within the Polish-Lithuanian Kingdom of Eastern Europe into full communion with Church of Rome. As a result of his efforts he suffered martyrdom in 1623.

November 13th
Memorial of Frances Xavier Cabrini, virgin*

St Frances Xavier Cabrini (d. 1917, Chicago, Illinois, USA) (Relics: New York City, New York, USA; Chicago, Illinois, USA; Rome, Italy; Codogno, Italy; Sant'Angelo Lodigiano, Italy)

Chiesa del Santissimo Redentore e Santa Francesca Cabrini
(Church of the Most Holy Redeemer and Saint Frances Cabrini)
Via Sicilia 215
✝This church is north of Piazza della Repubblica.
✝The skull of St Frances Xavier Cabrini rests within this church. It is placed within a statue of her likeness that reposes within an urn on the right side of the nave.

November 15th
Optional memorial of Albert the Great, bishop and doctor

St Albert the Great (d. 1280, Cologne, Germany) (Relics: Cologne, Germany)

November 16th
Optional memorial of Gertrude, virgin

St Gertrude the Great (d. 1301, Helfta, Germany)

November 16th
Optional memorial of Margaret of Scotland

St Margaret of Scotland (d. 1093, Scotland) (Relics: Dunfermline, Scotland)

November 17th
Memorial of Elizabeth of Hungary, religious

St Elizabeth of Hungary (d. 1231,

Marburg, Germany) (Relics: Vienna, Austria)

Sant'Antonio da Padova
(Saint Anthony of Padua)
Via Merulana 124
✝This church is near the *Basilica of St John Lateran.*
✝The third chapel on the left side of the nave is dedicated to St Elizabeth of Hungary.

November 18th
Optional memorial of The Dedication of the Basilicas of Saints Peter and Paul, apostles

St Peter's Basilica
✝Tradition holds that St Peter was crucified upside down in the middle of Nero's Circus. The *Altar of The Crucifixion*, located in the left transept of *St Peter's Basilica*, is very close to the actual site where this crucifixion took place.
✝The bones of St Peter are in the confessio below the Papal Altar and his jawbone can be seen on the Scavi tour.
✝Tradition also holds that within the large bronze chair located above the *Altar of the Chair* in the apse of the church is a second smaller chair made out of wood. This second chair is said to consist of fragments from the original Episcopal chair that St Peter once sat in.

Basilica of St Paul Outside the Walls
Via Ostiense 186
✝St Paul is buried in the confessio of this church. Above his tomb are the chains that had been used to imprison him prior to his martyrdom. These chains were placed in this prominent location in 2008.

✝Also a crucifix that is said to have spoken to St Bridget in 1370 is in the Blessed Sacrament Chapel.

✝Lining the nave are 266 medallions depicting every pope from the last 2000 years.

November 18th
Optional memorial of Rose Philippine Duchesne, virgin*

St Rose Philippine Duchesne (d. 1852, St Charles, Missouri, USA) (Relics: St Charles, Missouri, USA)

November 21st
Memorial of The Presentation of The Blessed Virgin Mary

St Peter's Basilica
Presentation Chapel
✝This is the second chapel on the left side of the nave. The large mosaic in this chapel depicts the Presentation of The Blessed Virgin Mary. The original painting that this mosaic replaced hangs within the Roman church *Santa Maria degli Angeli*.
✝The body of St Pius X (d. 1914) also rests under this altar.

Santa Maria in Monticelli
(Our Lady in Monticelli)
28 Via di Santa Maria in Monticelli
✝This church is near the Largo di Torre Argentina.
✝The painting in the main sanctuary depicts the Presentation of The Blessed Virgin Mary

Chiesa Nuova
(The New Church)
Via del Governo Vecchio 134
✝This church is along the Corso Vittorio Emanuele.

✝The transept chapel on the left side of the nave is dedicated to the Presentation of The Blessed Virgin Mary.
✝The body of St Philip Neri (d. 1595) is also enshrined in the left transept. His private rooms can be visited on certain days of the week. They are located in the right wall of the left transept.

FOR ADDITIONAL MARIAN CHURCHES TO VISIT PLEASE SEE THE LIST AT THE END OF THIS BOOK.

November 22nd
Memorial of Cecilia, virgin and martyr

St Cecilia (d. Sicily) (Relics: Rome, Italy)

Santa Cecilia in Trastevere
(Saint Cecilia in Trastevere)
Piazza di Santa Cecilia 22
✝This church is located in the southern part of Trastevere. It is built over the ruins of the house that St Cecilia had lived in prior to her martyrdom.
✝In 821 the body of St Cecilia was exhumed from the *Catacombs of San Callisto* by Pope St Paschal I (d. 824) and returned to this church. Today her remains rest within the crypt under the main altar.
✝The recumbent statue of St Cecilia below the main altar was completed by Stefano Maderno in the late 16th century. A gash on her neck recalls the miraculous events surrounding her martyrdom. Tradition claims that St Cecilia was condemned to execution first by drowning and then by decapitation. Both attempts failed. The second method, however, left her greatly wounded. The executioner struck her neck three times with a sword but being

unable to sever her head fled in fear. She survived for three days, offered all she had to the poor, and then expired.

Catacombs of San Callisto

Via Appia Antica 110/126

†These catacombs are located south of the Aurelian Walls.

†St Cecilia was originally buried in these catacombs. In 821 her remains were removed and taken to *Santa Cecilia in Trastevere*.

†It was at this location in the year 258 that Roman soldiers burst into a chapel and arrested St Sixtus II and four other deacons while they were celebrating the liturgy. St Lawrence (d. 258) was not present for this arrest; however, a legend holds that St Lawrence was able to speak to St Sixtus just before the pope was martyred. In this conversation St Sixtus prophetically stated, "You shall follow me in three days." St Lawrence then in three days went on to suffer his own martyrdom by being burnt alive on a gridiron.

†St Sixtus II (d. 258), St Pontian (d. 235), St Fabian (d. 250), St Cornelius (d. 253), and a number of other early popes were originally buried here. The remains of St Sixtus II were later moved to *San Sisto Vecchio*, the remains of St Fabian to *San Sebastiano Fuori Le Mura*, and the remains of St Cornelius to *Santa Maria in Trastevere*.

San Luigi dei Francesi

(Saint Louis of the French)

Piazza San Luigi dei Francesi 5

†This church is near Piazza Navona.

†The second chapel on the right side of the nave is dedicated to St Cecilia. The altarpiece within this chapel is entitled *The Ecstasy of St Cecilia*. It was completed by Guido Reni and is a copy

of a work done by Raphael. Frescoes completed by Domenichino line the sidewalls and the vault. They depict various scenes from the life of St Cecilia.

San Carlo ai Catinari

(Saint Charles at the Catinari)

Piazza Benedetto Cairoli 117

†This church is near the Largo di Torre Argentina. The third chapel on the right side of the nave, located in the transept arm, is dedicated to St Cecilia.

Sant'Agnese in Agone

(Saint Agnes in Agone) Piazza Navona

†A marble relief to the left of the main sanctuary depicts the death of St Cecilia. It was completed by Antonio Raggi in the 17th century.

†Also a relic of St Agnes' skull is present in a chapel on the left side of the nave. According to tradition she was martyred here in 304 AD.

November 23rd
Optional memorial of Clement I, pope and martyr

St Clement I (d. 97) (Relics: Rome, Italy)

Legend holds that St Clement I was exiled to the Crimean region of Ukraine. After converting many people in the region it is believed that he was thrown into the sea with an iron anchor attached to his body. Many years later St Cyril is said to have found some bones and an anchor in Crimea. These were believed to be the relics of St Clement I. He then carried these relics to Rome where they were placed in the *Basilica of San Clemente*.

Basilica di San Clemente

(Basilica of Saint Clement)

Via Labicana 95 / Piazza San Clemente
† This church is east of the Colosseum.
† The remains of St Clement I and of St Ignatius of Antioch (d. 107) rest beneath the main altar. On the feast of St Clement I a reliquary bust containing his skull is festively carried in procession through the streets of Rome.
† Also a chapel on the right side of the nave is dedicated to Saints Cyril (d. 869) and Methodius (d. 885). The extant remains of St Cyril rest within the altar of this chapel.

San Girolamo dei Croati
(Saint Jerome of the Croatians)
Via Tomacelli 132
† This church is near the Tiber River just west of the Spanish Steps.
† The first chapel on the left side of the nave contains a painting that depicts Saints Cyril and Methodius giving the relics of St Clement I to Pope Adrian II.

November 23rd
Optional memorial of Columban, abbot

St Columban (d. 615, Bobbio, Italy) (Relics: Bobbio, Italy)

November 23rd
*Optional memorial of Blessed Miguel Agustin Pro, priest and martyr**

Blessed Miguel Agustin Pro (d. 1927, Mexico City, Mexico) (Relics: Mexico City, Mexico)

November 24th
Optional memorial of Andrew Dung-Lac, priest and martyr, and Comp-anions, martyrs (Vietnamese martyrs)

More than 100,000 Vietnamese Catholics died for their faith during the seventeenth, eighteenth, and nineteenth centuries. One hundred seventeen of

these martyrs were canonized in 1988 and are honored on this day. A further martyr, Blessed Andrew Phú Yên, was beatified in the year 2000. (Relics: Paris, France; Penang, Malaysia)

November 25th
Optional memorial of Catherine of Alexandria, virgin and martyr

St Catherine of Alexandria (d. 305, Alexandria, Egypt) (Relics: Mount Catherine, Egypt)

Basilica di San Clemente
(Basilica of Saint Clement)
Via Labicana 95 / Piazza San Clemente
† This church is east of the Colosseum.
† The chapel located in the back left corner of the nave is dedicated to St Catherine of Alexandria.
† The remains of St Clement I (d. 97) and of St Ignatius of Antioch (d. 107) rest beneath the main altar.
† Also a chapel on the right side of the nave is dedicated to Saints Cyril (d. 869) and Methodius (d. 885). The extant remains of St Cyril rest within the altar of this chapel.

Sant'Agostino (Saint Augustine)
Piazza Sant'Agostino
† This church is near Piazza Navona.
† The first chapel on the right side of the nave is dedicated to St Catherine of Alexandria.
† Relics of St Monica (d. 387) rest in the chapel to the left of the main altar.

Sant'Antonio dei Portoghesi
(Saint Anthony of the Portuguese)
Via dei Portoghesi 2
† This church is northeast of Piazza Navona.
† The first chapel on the right side of the nave is dedicated to St Catherine of Alexandria.

Santissima Trinità dei Spagnoli
(The Most Holy Trinity of the Spanish)
Via dei Condotti 41
†This church is near the Spanish Steps.
†Three paintings within the second chapel on the right side of the nave depict scenes from the life of St Catherine of Alexandria.

Santa Caterina dei Funari
(Saint Catherine of the Funari)
Via dei Funari
†This church is near the Jewish quarter and it is dedicated to St Catherine of Alexandria. It is not open often.
†A painting of the martyrdom of St Catherine of Alexandria is placed above the main altar.

Santa Caterina della Rota
(Saint Catherine of the Rota)
Via di San Girolamo della Carità 80
†This church is near Piazza Farnese and it is dedicated to St Catherine of Alexandria. It is not open often.

November 30ᵗʰ
Feast of Andrew, apostle

St Andrew (Relics: Amalfi, Italy; Florence, Italy; Patras, Greece; Edinburgh, Scotland; Cologne, Germany; Kiev, Ukraine)

Tradition claims that St Andrew was martyred and buried in Patras, Greece. Later most of his relics were transferred to the city of Constantinople and a small portion to Scotland. The relics in Constantinople were taken by the crusaders after their violent sacking of the city in 1204 and transferred to the *Duomo di Sant'Andrea* in Amalfi, Italy. It is from this source that many cities within Europe have received their relics of St Andrew.

Sant'Andrea della Valle
(Saint Andrew of the Valley)
Piazza Sant'Andrea della Valle / Piazza Vidoni 6
†This church is located along the Corso Vittorio Emanuele.
†The large paintings in the sanctuary depict the martyrdom of St Andrew.

Sant'Andrea delle Fratte
(Saint Andrew of the Bushes)
Via Sant'Andrea delle Fratte 1
†This church is near the Spanish Steps. It is dedicated to St Andrew. Within the sanctuary are five large paintings depicting his martyrdom.
†The third altar on the left side of the nave is where the Blessed Virgin Mary appeared to Ratisbonne, an agnostic Jew, in 1842. Ratisbonne converted on the spot. In 1918 St Maximilian Mary Kolbe (d. 1941) offered his first Mass in this very same chapel.

Sant'Andrea al Quirinale
(Saint Andrew at the Quirinale)
Via del Quirinale 29
†This church is south of the Barberini metro stop. It was designed by Gian Lorenzo Bernini and it is dedicated to St Andrew.
†The remains of St Stanislaus Kostka (d. 1568), a young Jesuit novice who died in Rome at the age of seventeen, rest here. The room in which he died has been converted into a chapel and can be visited by asking the sacristan.

Sant'Andrea a Ponte Milvio
(Saint Andrew at the Milvian Bridge)
Via Flaminia 441
✝This church is near the Milvian Bridge.
✝The advancement of the Ottoman Turks into the Byzantine Empire threatened the safety of many Christian relics. Therefore, in 1462 the relic of St Andrew's skull was brought to Rome for safe keeping. The small church of *Sant'Andrea a Ponte Milvio* marks the spot where this relic was first received in Rome. This relic remained in Rome at *St Peter's Basilica* until its return to Patras, Greece in 1964.

Il Gesu (The Jesus)
Via degli Astalli 16
✝This church is located along the Corso Vittorio Emanuele.
✝The first chapel on the right side of the nave is dedicated to St Andrew.
✝St Ignatius of Loyola (d. 1556) is buried under the altar in the left transept.
✝An arm of St Francis Xavier (d. 1552) also rests within a reliquary above the altar in the right transept.

December

St Francis Xavier (d. 1552, Shangchuan Island, China) (Relics: Rome, Italy; Goa, India; Antwerp, Belgium)

Il Gesu (The Jesus)
Via degli Astalli 16
✝This church is located along the Corso Vittorio Emanuele. It honors a number of Jesuit saints.
✝An arm of St Francis Xavier rests within a reliquary above the altar in the right transept. With this arm he is said to have baptized thousands of individuals in India and the Far East.
✝St Ignatius of Loyola (d. 1556), the founder of the Jesuits, is buried under the altar in the left transept. His rooms are located in the Generalate next to the church and may be visited.
✝The remains of St Peter Faber (d. 1546), an early companion of St Ignatius, are also located here. They are said to rest below the main entrance to this church having been placed here when the church was built in the 16th century. During the placement of these relics it was impossible to separate the bones of St Peter Faber from the bones of other individuals; therefore, his bones are buried together with theirs.

San Francesco Saverio del Caravita
(Saint Francis Xavier of Caravita)
Via del Caravita 7
✝This oratory is east of the Pantheon and it is dedicated to St Francis Xavier. It is not open often.

St John Damascene (d. 750, Jerusalem) (Relics: Mar Saba Monastery)

St Nicholas (d. 350, Myra, Turkey) (Relics: Bari, Italy; Venice, Italy)

In 1993 a small grave was found on Gemiler Island east of Rhodes. Historians believe that the body of St Nicholas was originally buried in this grave and then subsequently transferred to Myra. From Myra the bones of St Nicholas were stolen by Italian merchants in 1087 and taken to the two Italian cities of Bari and Venice. The merchants from Bari raided the tomb first and in their haste they took only the large bone fragments. The Venetian merchants came later and took the remaining smaller bone fragments. A scientific study in 1992 confirmed that both collections are from the same skeleton.

San Nicola dei Prefetti
(Saint Nicholas of the Prefects)
Via dei Prefetti 34
✝This church is north of the Pantheon. Both the church and an altar on the right side of the nave are dedicated to St Nicholas.

San Nicola in Carcere
(Saint Nicholas at the Prisons)
Via del Teatro di Marcello 46 / Via del Foro Olitorio
✝This church is near Tiber Island. It is dedicated to St Nicholas.

La Maddalena (The Magdalene)
Piazza della Maddalena 53
✝This church is just north of the Pantheon.
✝The third chapel on the left side of the nave is dedicated to St Nicholas.
✝In the third chapel on the right side of the nave are the remains of St Camillus de Lellis. He lived in the adjacent monastery and died here in 1614. His rooms can be visited by asking the sacristan.

Santa Maria in Campitelli
(Our Lady in Campitelli)
Piazza di Campitelli 9
✝This church is near the Jewish quarter.
✝The third chapel on the right side of the nave is dedicated to St Nicholas.
✝The body of St John Leonardi (d. 1609) is enshrined in the second chapel on the left side of the nave.

December 7th
Memorial of Ambrose, bishop and doctor

St Ambrose (d. 397, Milan, Italy)
(Relics: Milan, Italy)

Sant'Ambrogio della Massima
(Saint Ambrose)
Via S Ambrogio 3
✝This church is located west of Piazza Venezia near the Fontana delle Tartarughe. It is set behind some buildings and is not easy to notice from the street. It is not open often.
✝Tradition holds that this church rests on land that was formerly the location of a house owned by St Ambrose's father and occupied by his older sister.
✝Relics of St Polycarp (d. 155) are set in a marble memorial stone under the main altar.

San Carlo al Corso
(Saint Charles on the Corso)
Via del Corso 437
✝This church is near the Spanish Steps. It was formerly called *Santi Ambrogio e Carlo al Corso*; therefore, it is dedicated to both St Ambrose and St Charles Borromeo.
✝The heart of St Charles Borromeo (d. 1584) rests within a reliquary in an altar located behind the main sanctuary.

December 8th
Solemnity of The Immaculate Conception of The Blessed Virgin Mary

St Peter's Basilica
Chapel of the Immaculate Conception / Chapel of the Choir
✝This is the third chapel on the left side of the nave. It is dedicated to the Immaculate Conception. The mosaic of the Blessed Virgin Mary within this chapel was made in 1750. Blessed Pius IX (d. 1878) crowned this image on December 8, 1854 when he declared the Dogma of the Immaculate Conception. Fifty years later the twelve stars were added to the crown by St Pius X (d. 1914).

Santa Maria del Popolo
(Our Lady of the People)
Piazza del Popolo 12
✝This church is at Piazza del Popolo.
✝A painting of the Immaculate Conception, completed by Carlo Maratta in 1686, is placed within the second chapel on the right side of the nave.

Santissima Trinità dei Monti
(Most Holy Trinity of the Mounts)
Piazza della Trinità dei Monti
✝This church is at the top of the Spanish Steps.

✝The third chapel on the left side of the nave is dedicated to the Immaculate Conception. Philipp Veit, a 19th century German painter, completed the Marian altarpiece. The frescoes upon the side walls depicting the Annunciation and the Visitation were completed by Joseph Ernst Tunner.

San Carlo al Corso
(Saint Charles on the Corso)
Via del Corso 437
✝This church is near the Spanish Steps.
✝The chapel in the right transept is dedicated to the Immaculate Conception.
✝The heart of St Charles Borromeo (d. 1584) rests within a reliquary in an altar located behind the main sanctuary.

Santi Apostoli (Holy Apostles)
Piazza dei Santi Apostoli 51
✝This church is just east of Piazza Venezia.
✝The second chapel on the right side of the nave is dedicated to the Immaculate Conception.
✝Relics of St Philip and St James the Less also rest within the confessio.

Sant'Antonio dei Portoghesi
(Saint Anthony of the Portuguese)
Via dei Portoghesi 2
✝This church is northeast of Piazza Navona.
✝The chapel in the left transept is dedicated to the Immaculate Conception.

FOR ADDITIONAL MARIAN CHURCHES TO VISIT PLEASE SEE THE LIST AT THE END OF THIS BOOK.

December 9th
Optional memorial of Juan Diego*

St Juan Diego (d. 1548, Tlayacac, Cuautitlan, Mexico)

December 11th
Optional memorial of Damasus I, pope

St Damasus I (d. 384, Rome, Italy)
(Relics: Rome, Italy)

San Lorenzo in Damaso
(Saint Lawrence in Damaso)
Piazza della Cancelleria 1
✝This church is at the *Palazzo della Cancelleria* near Campo de' Fiori. It is believed to have been founded in the very home of St Damasus I whose remains now rest under the main altar.

December 12th
Feast of Our Lady of Guadalupe*

Nostra Signora di Guadalupe e San Filippo Martire
(Our Lady of Guadalupe and Saint Philip the Martyr)
Via Aurelia 675
✝This church is outside of the Aurelian Walls and is west of the Vatican. It is the Mexican national church.
✝An image of Our Lady of Guadalupe is in the main sanctuary.

San Nicola in Carcere
(St Nicholas at the Prisons)
Via del Teatro di Marcello 46 / Via del Foro Olitorio
✝This church is near Tiber Island.
✝About halfway down the left aisle is a chapel with an image of Our Lady of Guadalupe.

San Giovanni della Malva in Trastevere
(Saint John of Malva in Trastevere)
Piazza del San Giovanni della Malva
†This church is located in Trastevere.
†A large image of Our Lady of Guadalupe is above the altar on the left side of the nave.

Chiesa Latino Americana
(Latin American Church)
Santa Maria della Luce 70
†This church is located in Trastevere.

FOR ADDITIONAL MARIAN CHURCHES TO VISIT PLEASE SEE THE LIST AT THE END OF THIS BOOK.

December 13th
Memorial of Lucy, virgin and martyr

St Lucy (d. 304, Syracuse, Sicily) (Relics: Syracuse, Sicily; Venice, Italy)

Santa Lucia del Gonfalone
(Saint Lucy of the Gonfalone)
Via dei Banchi Vecchi 12
†This church is located between Via Giulia and the Corso Vittorio Emanuele. It is dedicated to St Lucy.
†A large statue of St Lucy is within a chapel on the right side of the nave.

Santa Lucia in Selci
(Saint Lucy in Selci)
Via in Selci 82
†This church is near the Cavour metro stop. It is dedicated to St Lucy. It is not open often.

December 14th
Memorial of John of the Cross, priest and doctor

St John of the Cross (d. 1591, Ubeda, Spain) (Relics: Segovia, Spain; Ubeda, Spain)

Santa Maria della Vittoria
(Our Lady of the Victory)
Via XX Settembre 17
†This church is north of Piazza della Repubblica.
†The second chapel on the left side of the nave is dedicated to St John of the Cross.
†Also located in this church is Gian Lorenzo Bernini's famous sculpture entitled *The Ecstasy of St Teresa*.

December 21st
Optional memorial of Peter Canisius, priest and doctor

St Peter Canisius (d. 1597, Fribourg, Switzerland) (Relics: Fribourg, Switzerland)

December 23rd
Optional memorial of John of Kanty, priest

St John of Kanty (d. 1473, Kraków, Poland) (Relics: Kraków, Poland)

December 25th
Solemnity of Christmas

During the Christmas season many churches set up Nativity Scenes. Some of the best are located in the following churches.

St Peter's Basilica
Piazza San Pietro

Santi Cosma e Damiano
(Saints Cosmas and Damian)
Via dei Fori Imperiali 1
†Located next to the Roman Forum.

Santa Maria in Via
(Our Lady of the Way)
Via del Mortaro 24
†Located near the Spanish Steps.

San Marcello al Corso
(Saint Marcellus on the Corso)
Piazza di San Marcello 5
†Located north of Piazza Venezia.

Sant'Eustachio (Saint Eustace)
Piazza Sant'Eustachio 19
†Located just west of the Pantheon.

Santa Maria in Traspontina
(Our Lady in Traspontina)
Via della Conciliazione 14
†Located near the Vatican.

Sant'Ignazio (Saint Ignatius)
Via del Caravita 8/a
†Located east of the Pantheon.

San Giacomo in Augusta /
San Giacomo degli Incurabili
(Saint James in Augusta / Saint James of
the Incurables)
Via del Corso 499
†Located near Piazza del Popolo.

Santa Maria in Aracoeli
(Our Lady in Aracoeli)
Piazza del Campidoglio 4
†This church is on top of the Capitoline
Hill.
†During Midnight Mass a wooden statue
of the baby Jesus is taken from a little
chapel to the left of the main sanctuary
and ceremonially placed within the
Chapel of the Crib. The original statue
that had been used in this ceremony was
stolen in 1994. This original statue had
been carved in the 15th century from
olive wood taken from the Garden of
Gethsemane. Today a replica is used.

Basilica of St Mary Major
Piazza di Santa Maria Maggiore 42
†A reliquary within the confessio below
the Papal Altar holds five pieces of wood
believed to be from the crib of Jesus
Christ. These relics were brought to
Rome in the 7th century.
†Preserved within the museum of this
church is one of the oldest nativity sets
in the world. The pieces were sculpted
by Arnolfo di Cambio in the late 13th
century. This museum is accessed on the
right side of the nave through the
baptistry chapel.

December 26th
Feast of Stephen, first martyr

St Stephen (Relics: Rome, Italy)

Tradition claims that the tomb of St
Stephen was miraculously discovered in
Jerusalem in 415 AD through a special
revelation given to a priest named
Lucian. Since this discovery the relics of
St Stephen have been distributed to a
variety of cities. Among these is Rome
where a long-standing tradition holds
that a large portion of his remains rest in
San Lorenzo fuori le Mura.

San Lorenzo fuori le Mura
(Saint Lawrence Outside the Walls)
Piazzale del Verano 3
†This church is east of the Aurelian
Walls.

✝The remains of St Lawrence (d. 258), St Stephen, and St Justin lie in the confessio below the main altar. (Note: The relics are labeled as St Justin the Presbyter. Therefore, it is likely that this is not St Justin the Martyr.)

✝A marble stone slab beneath the choir floor is said to be the stone on which St Lawrence was placed after his execution. Also enshrined in this lower area is the body of Blessed Pius IX (d. 1878).

Basilica of St Paul Outside the Walls
Via Ostiense 186

✝This basilica is south of the Aurelian Walls.

✝In the left transept is a small chapel dedicated to St Stephen.

✝St Paul is buried in the confessio. Above his tomb are the chains that had been used to imprison him prior to his martyrdom. These chains were placed in this prominent location in 2008.

✝Also a crucifix that is said to have spoken to St Bridget in 1370 is in the Blessed Sacrament Chapel.

San Martino ai Monti
(Saint Martin at the Hills)
Viale Monte Oppio 28

✝This church is south of the *Basilica of St Mary Major*.

✝The fourth chapel on the right side of the nave is dedicated to St Stephen.

✝The greater part of the remains of St Martin I (d. 655) were transferred from Crimea to this church in Rome. They now rest in the confessio below the main altar. This confessio also houses the relics of many other saints taken from the *Catacombs of Priscilla*.

Santo Stefano Protomartire
(Saint Stephen the First Martyr)
Via San Stefano del Cacco 26

✝This church is south of the Pantheon and it is dedicated to St Stephen. It is not open often.

December 27th
Feast of John, apostle and evangelist

Tradition holds that St John was originally buried in Ephesus. Later in the 6th century a large basilica was built over his tomb. However, due to a number of earthquakes and the encroachment of the Turks the church was abandoned and his relics lost. Today the location of his relics is unknown. However, his original tomb, now empty, is marked and venerated in Ephesus, Turkey.

Basilica of St John Lateran
Piazza San Giovanni in Laterano 4

✝This basilica is dedicated to both St John the Evangelist and St John the Baptist.

✝Within the *Colonna Chapel* to the left of the main sanctuary is a painting completed by Giuseppe Cesari of St John the Evangelist and St John the Baptist pointing to Christ. Another painting of these two saints is on the left wall of the *Lancellotti Chapel*. Also within the fourth chapel on the right side of the nave is a painting that depicts St John the Evangelist at Patmos. Finally, within the baptistry next to the basilica is a chapel dedicated to St John the Evangelist.

San Giovanni in Oleo
(St John in Oil)
Via di San Giovanni a Porta Latina

✝This is a small octagonal devotional shrine located southeast of the Colosseum. It is not open often.

✝A legend holds that Emperor Domitian attempted to execute St John here by placing him into a pot of boiling oil. St

John survived this attempt upon his life and as a result was exiled to the island of Patmos.

San Giovanni a Porta Latina
(Saint John at the Latin Gate)
Via di San Giovanni a Porta Latina 17
✝This church is southeast of the Colosseum and it is dedicated to St John the Evangelist.

San Giovanni della Malva in Trastevere
(Saint John of Malva in Trastevere)
Piazza del San Giovanni della Malva
✝This church is located in Trastevere. It is dedicated to St John the Evangelist.

December 28th
Feast of Holy Innocents, martyrs

Santissima Trinità dei Monti
(Most Holy Trinity of the Mounts)
Piazza della Trinità dei Monti
✝This church is at the top of the Spanish Steps.
✝A painting within the third chapel on the right side of the nave depicts the massacre of the Holy Innocents. This work was completed by Michele Alberti in the 16th century.

December 29th
Optional memorial of Thomas Becket, bishop and martyr

St Thomas Becket (d. 1170, Canterbury, United Kingdom) (Relics: Canterbury, United Kingdom)

December 31st
Optional memorial of Sylvester I, pope

St Sylvester I (d. 335) (Relics: Rome, Italy)

San Silvestro in Capite
(Saint Sylvester in Capite)
Piazza San Silvestro
✝This church is near the Spanish Steps.
✝The remains of St Sylvester I rest in the confessio below the main altar. They were transferred to this church in the 8th century from the *Catacombs of Priscilla*. On his feast day a relic of his skull is brought out for veneration.
✝Depicted within the apse vault above the main altar is the popular legend of St Sylvester I baptizing Constantine.
✝Within the chapel to the left of the main entrance is a relic of the skull of St John the Baptist. The authenticity is uncertain since this same relic is said to be located at a number of other places throughout the world including the *Cathedral of Amiens* in France, the *Residenz Museum* in Munich, Germany, and the *Umayyad Mosque* in Damascus, Syria.

San Silvestro al Quirinale
(Saint Sylvester at the Quirinale)
Via Ventiquattro (XXIV) Maggio 10
✝This church is east of Piazza Venezia. It is not open often.
✝The first chapel on the right side of the nave is dedicated to St Sylvester I. Three paintings within this chapel depict alleged events from his life.

San Martino ai Monti
(Saint Martin at the Hills)
Viale Monte Oppio 28
✝This church is south of the *Basilica of St Mary Major*.
✝A tradition claims that the pope, St Sylvester I, and many other bishops met here to prepare for the Council of Nicaea. They then reconvened at this same church after the Council to announce the newly formulated Nicene Creed. Constantine was in attendance for

this. The large painting on the left side of the nave created in 1640 recalls one of these meetings. This tradition, however, is often tied to the 'Symmachian Forgeries' thus throwing some doubt on its credibility. Nevertheless, it does seem probable that some agreement was achieved between Constantine and St Sylvester I that allowed for the success of the Council of Nicaea.

✝The greater part of the remains of St Martin I (d. 655) were transferred from Crimea to this church in Rome. They now rest in the confessio below the main altar. This confessio also houses the relics of many other saints taken from the *Catacombs of Priscilla.*

Santa Croce in Gerusalemme
(Holy Cross In Jerusalem)
Piazza di Santa Croce in Gerusalemme 12

✝This church is east of the *Basilica of St John Lateran.*

✝A painting above the third altar on the left side of the nave depicts St Sylvester I revealing to Constantine an image of Saints Peter and Paul.

✝Also a chapel accessible by the staircase on the left side of the sanctuary preserves a number of relics from Christ's Passion.

Moveable Feasts

Feast of The Holy Family
(First Sunday After Christmas)

Santa Maria dell'Anima
(Our Lady of the Soul)
Via Santa Maria dell'Anima 64
✝This church is near Piazza Navona. It is the German national church.
✝The altarpiece within the main sanctuary, completed by Giulio Romano, depicts the Holy Family.

Santuario della Madonna del Perpetuo Soccorso
(Sanctuary of Our Lady of Perpetual Help)
Via Merulana 26
✝This church is just south of the *Basilica of St Mary Major.*
✝The third chapel on the right side of the nave is dedicated to the Holy Family.
✝A miraculous image of the Blessed Virgin Mary entitled *Our Lady of Perpetual Help* is above the main altar.

Oratorio dell'Angelo Custode
(Oratory of the Guardian Angel)
Piazza Poli 11
✝This small church is located near the Trevi Fountain.
✝Over the main altar is a large painting of the Holy Family.

Gesu e Maria (Jesus and Mary)
Via del Corso 45
✝This church is near Piazza del Popolo. It is dedicated to the Holy Names of Jesus and Mary.
✝The painting in the second chapel on the left side of the nave depicts the Holy Family. It was completed by Giacinto Brandi in 1660.

San Carlo al Corso
(Saint Charles on the Corso)
Via del Corso 437
✝This church is near the Spanish Steps.
✝The third chapel on the right side of the nave is dedicated to the Holy Family.
✝The heart of St Charles Borromeo (d. 1584) rests within a reliquary in an altar located behind the main sanctuary.

Il Gesu (The Jesus)
Via degli Astalli 16
✝This church is located along the Corso Vittorio Emanuele.
✝The second chapel on the left side of the nave is dedicated to the Holy Family.
✝St Ignatius of Loyola (d. 1556) is buried under the altar in the left transept.
✝An arm of St Francis Xavier (d. 1552) also rests within a reliquary above the altar in the right transept.

Solemnity of Epiphany of the Lord

(Traditionally, this Solemnity was celebrated on January 6th. However, in the United States it is celebrated on the Sunday that falls between January 2nd and January 8th.)

Chiesa Nuova
(The New Church)
Via del Governo Vecchio 134
✝This church is along the Corso Vittorio Emanuele.
✝The second chapel on the left side of the nave is dedicated to the Epiphany. The painting within this chapel depicts the Magi adoring the Christ child.
✝The body of St Philip Neri (d. 1595) is also enshrined in the left transept. His private rooms can be visited on certain days of the week. They are located in the right wall of the left transept.

San Girolamo dei Croati
(Saint Jerome of the Croatians)

Via Tomacelli 132

✝This church is near the Tiber River just west of the Spanish Steps.

✝The large painting in the right transept depicts the Three Kings giving gifts to the Christ Child.

Santissima Trinità dei Monti

(Most Holy Trinity of the Mounts)
Piazza della Trinità dei Monti
✝This church is at the top of the Spanish Steps.
✝The fifth chapel on the right side of the nave contains three paintings from the 16th century that depict the Adoration of the Magi, the Nativity, and the Circumcision.

Feast of The Baptism of the Lord

(Traditionally this Feast was celebrated on January 13th the octave of the Epiphany. However, now in the United States it is celebrated on the first Sunday after January 6th except in the years when Epiphany is moved to either Sunday January 7th or Sunday January 8th. On these years the Feast of the Baptism of the Lord is celebrated on the Monday that follows the celebration of Epiphany.)

San Giovanni Battista dei Fiorentini

(Saint John the Baptist of the Florentines)
Via Acciaioli 2
✝This church is just east of the Vatican. It is next to the Tiber River and the Corso Vittorio Emanuele.
✝In the sanctuary is a large sculpture of the Baptism of Christ.
✝A relic of St Mary Magdalene's foot rests in a shrine to the left of the main sanctuary.

St Peter's Basilica

✝The first chapel on the left side of the

nave contains a large mosaic of the Baptism of the Lord. The original painting that this mosaic replaced hangs within the Roman church *Santa Maria degli Angeli*.

San Pietro in Montorio

(Saint Peter in Montorio)
Piazza San Pietro in Montorio 2
✝This church is located on the Janiculum hill.
✝Within the left transept is a large painting of the Baptism of the Lord.

San Giacomo in Augusta /
San Giacomo degli Incurabili

(Saint James in Augusta / Saint James of the Incurables)
Via del Corso 499
✝This church is near Piazza del Popolo.
✝The third chapel on the right side of the nave is dedicated to the Baptism of the Lord.

Holy Thursday

San Lorenzo in Damaso

(Saint Lawrence in Damaso)
Piazza della Cancelleria 1
✝This church is at the *Palazzo della Cancelleria* near Campo de' Fiori.
✝A large painting of the Last Supper is placed within the first chapel on the left side of the nave.

Good Friday

Santissima Trinità dei Monti

(Most Holy Trinity of the Mounts)
Piazza della Trinità dei Monti
✝This church is at the top of the Spanish Steps.
✝Within the fourth chapel on the right side of the nave is a very moving work entitled *The Flagellation of Jesus*. This painting was completed by Louis Vincent Leon Pallière in 1817.

Santa Maria dell'Anima

(Our Lady of the Soul)

Via Santa Maria dell'Anima 64

✝This church is near Piazza Navona. It is the German national church.

✝Within the fourth chapel on the left side of the nave is a powerful image of *The Deposition of Christ* by Francesco Salviati.

Basilica of St John Lateran

Piazza San Giovanni in Laterano 4

✝Within the second chapel on the right side of the nave is marble sculpture of *The Deposition of Christ* by Pietro Tenerani.

Santissima Trinità dei Monti

(Most Holy Trinity of the Mounts)

Piazza della Trinità dei Monti

✝This church is at the top of the Spanish Steps.

✝Within the second chapel on the left side of the nave is a painting of *The Deposition of Christ* by Daniele da Volterra.

San Giovanni Battista dei Fiorentini

(Saint John the Baptist of the Florentines)

Via Acciaioli 2

✝This church is just east of the Vatican. It is next to the Tiber River and the Corso Vittorio Emanuele.

✝The chapel to the left of the main sanctuary is dedicated to the Passion of Christ.

✝A relic of St Mary Magdalene's foot also rests in a shrine to the left of the main sanctuary.

San Pietro in Montorio

(Saint Peter in Montorio)

Piazza San Pietro in Montorio 2

✝This church is located on the Janiculum hill. Within the first chapel on the right side of the nave is a painting depicting the scourging of Christ by Sebastiano del Piombo.

Il Gesu (The Jesus)

Via degli Astalli 16

✝This church is located along the Corso Vittorio Emanuele. The second chapel on the right side of the nave is dedicated to the Passion of Christ.

✝St Ignatius of Loyola (d. 1556) is buried under the altar in the left transept.

✝An arm of St Francis Xavier (d. 1552) also rests within a reliquary above the altar in the right transept.

Solemnity of Easter

Chiesa San Claudio

(Church of Saint Claudius)

Via del Pozzetto 160

✝This church is near the Spanish Steps.

✝Within the chapel on the left side of the nave is a painting of the Resurrection. It was completed by Jean François de Troy in 1740.

Santa Maria del Popolo

(Our Lady of the People)

Piazza del Popolo 12

✝This church is at Piazza del Popolo.

✝In the *Cerasi Chapel*, to the left of the main altar, are two exceptional works by Caravaggio entitled the *Crucifixion of St Peter* and the *Conversion of St Paul*. These two works are on the side walls of the chapel and face each other. In between these two works is Annibale Carracci's, *Assumption*. It is said that the positioning of these paintings show both Peter and Paul acknowledging the grace of the Resurrection as it is being realized through the Assumption of The Blessed Virgin Mary.

La Maddalena (The Magdalene)
Piazza della Maddalena 53
✝This church is just north of the Pantheon.
✝To the sides of the main altar are reliefs depicting two events following the Resurrection. The one is of the three Marys at the empty tomb. (Mk 16:1) The other is of Mary Magdalene mistaking Jesus for a gardener. (Jn 20:15)
✝In the chapel in the right transept is a miraculous crucifix that is said to have spoken to St Camillus de Lellis.
✝In the third chapel on the right side of the nave are the remains of St Camillus de Lellis. He lived in the adjacent monastery and died here in 1614. His rooms can be visited by asking the sacristan. One of these rooms has been transformed into a chapel and contains the relic of his heart.

Basilica of St John Lateran
Piazza San Giovanni in Laterano 4
✝On the right side of the nave, near the entrance and above the large statue of St Thaddaeus, is a relief of the Resurrection of Christ.

Nostra Signora del Sacro Cuore
(Our Lady of the Sacred Heart)
Corso del Rinascimento 27
✝This church is at Piazza Navona.
✝The first chapel on the right side of the nave was originally dedicated to the Resurrection. Remnants from this previous dedication still remain within the chapel. This includes a number of frescoes completed by Baldassare Croce and Cesare Nebbia which depict various post-resurrection events from the Gospels.

Solemnity of Divine Mercy

Santo Spirito in Sassia
(Holy Spirit in Sassia)

Via dei Penitenzieri 12
✝This church is near the Vatican.
✝The fourth chapel on the right side of the nave is dedicated to St Faustina and Divine Mercy.

Solemnity of The Ascension of the Lord

San Nicola in Carcere
(Saint Nicholas at the Prisons)
Via del Teatro di Marcello 46 / Via del Foro Olitorio
✝This church is near Tiber Island.
✝To the left of the main altar is a painting of the Ascension.

Santa Maria in Aracoeli
(Our Lady in Aracoeli)
Piazza del Campidoglio 4
✝This church is on top of the Capitoline Hill. A painting in the sixth chapel on the left side of the nave depicts the Ascension. It was completed by Girolamo Muziano in the 16th century.

Chiesa Nuova
(The New Church)
Via del Governo Vecchio 134
✝This church is along the Corso Vittorio Emanuele.
✝The third chapel on the right side of the nave is dedicated to the Ascension.
✝The body of St Philip Neri (d. 1595) is also enshrined in the left transept. His private rooms can be visited on certain days of the week. They are located in the right wall of the left transept.

Solemnity of Pentecost

Pantheon / Santa Maria dei Martiri
(Our Lady of the Martyrs)
Piazza della Rotonda
✝This ancient temple was converted into a Christian church in the year 609. It now honors the Blessed Virgin Mary and the Christian martyrs.

✝At the end of the Mass on Pentecost thousands of rose petals are dropped from the opening in the dome onto the people below.

Santo Spirito in Sassia
(Holy Spirit in Sassia)
Via dei Penitenzieri 12
✝This church is near the Vatican. It is dedicated to the Holy Spirit.
✝Both the large painting in the main sanctuary and a smaller painting in the first chapel on the right side of the nave depict the Pentecost.

Chiesa Nuova
(The New Church)
Via del Governo Vecchio 134
✝This church is located along the Corso Vittorio Emanuele.
✝The fourth chapel on the right side of the nave is dedicated to the Holy Spirit.
✝The body of St Philip Neri (d. 1595) is also enshrined in the left transept. His private rooms can be visited on certain days of the week. They are located in the right wall of the left transept.

San Silvestro in Capite
(Saint Sylvester in Capite)
Piazza San Silvestro
✝This church is near the Spanish Steps.
✝The third chapel on the right side of the nave is dedicated to the Holy Spirit.
✝A relic of the skull of St John the Baptist rests within the chapel to the left of the main entrance. The authenticity is uncertain since this same relic is said to be located at a number of other places throughout the world including the *Cathedral of Amiens* in France, the *Residenz Museum* in Munich, Germany, and the *Umayyad Mosque* in Damascus, Syria.

✝The remains of St Sylvester I (d. 335) rest in the confessio below the main altar. Also a work from 1688 depicting the legend of St Sylvester I baptizing Constantine can be seen in the apse vault.

Solemnity of The Most Holy Trinity
(First Sunday After Pentecost)

Santissima Trinità dei Pellegrini
(Most Holy Trinity of the Pilgrims)
Via dei Pettinari 36/A
✝This church is located near Piazza Farnese. It is dedicated to the Most Holy Trinity.

Santissima Trinità dei Monti
(Most Holy Trinity of the Mounts)
Piazza della Trinità dei Monti
✝This church is at the top of the Spanish Steps. It is dedicated to the Most Holy Trinity.
✝Within the various side chapels in this church are many distinguished pieces of religious art.

Santissima Trinità dei Spagnoli
(Most Holy Trinity of the Spanish)
Via dei Condotti 41
✝This church is near the Spanish Steps. It is dedicated to the Most Holy Trinity.

San Giacomo in Augusta /
San Giacomo degli Incurabili
(Saint James in Augusta / Saint James of the Incurables)
Via del Corso 499
✝This church is near Piazza del Popolo.
✝The large painting in the main sanctuary depicts the Holy Trinity. It was completed by Francesco Grandi in 1862.

Il Gesu (The Jesus)
Via degli Astalli 16
†This church is located along the Corso Vittorio Emanuele.
†The third chapel on the left side of the nave is dedicated to the Holy Trinity.
†St Ignatius of Loyola (d. 1556) is buried under the altar in the left transept.
†An arm of St Francis Xavier (d. 1552) also rests within a reliquary above the altar in the right transept.

Solemnity of The Most Holy Body and Blood of Christ – Corpus Christi
(Thursday After Holy Trinity Sunday) OR (In The United States The Sunday After Holy Trinity Sunday)

Sant'Anastasia
(Saint Anastasius)
Piazza di Sant'Anastasia
†This church is near Circo Massimo. It has Perpetual Adoration of the Blessed Sacrament twenty-four hours a day in a chapel to the left of the main sanctuary.

Chiesa San Claudio
(Church of Saint Claudius)
Via del Pozzetto 160
†This church is near the Spanish Steps.
†A relic of St Peter Julian Eymard (d. 1868) is placed within a statue of his likeness that rests within an urn on the right side of the nave.
†St Peter Julian Eymard is often called the Apostle of the Eucharist since he is the founder of the *Congregation of the Most Blessed Sacrament*. This church is run by this community; therefore, Eucharistic devotion is strongly promoted including frequent adoration of the Blessed Sacrament.

Basilica of St John Lateran
Piazza San Giovanni in Laterano 4
†A table located above the altar where the Blessed Sacrament is reserved on the left side of the nave is claimed to be the table upon which Jesus and the apostles celebrated the Last Supper. It is placed directly behind a bronze relief depicting the Last Supper.

Santa Maria sopra Minerva
(Our Lady Above Minerva)
Piazza della Minerva 42
†This church is near the Pantheon.
†Within the *Aldobrandini Chapel* is a painting of the Institution of the Eucharist. This is the sixth chapel on the right side of the nave. The First Blessed Sacrament Confraternity to be approved by the Holy See was established in this chapel.
†Also the body of St Catherine of Siena (d. 1380) rests under the main altar.

Solemnity of The Most Sacred Heart of Jesus
(Friday Following The Second Sunday After Pentecost)

St Peter's Basilica
Altar of the Sacred Heart
†Located at the base of the far left column.
†A mosaic above this altar depicts Christ revealing his Sacred Heart to St Margaret Mary Alacoque.

Il Gesu (The Jesus)
Via degli Astalli 16
†This church is located along the Corso Vittorio Emanuele.
†The beautiful chapel to the right of the main sanctuary is dedicated to the Sacred Heart of Jesus.
†St Ignatius of Loyola (d. 1556) is buried under the altar in the left transept.
†An arm of St Francis Xavier (d. 1552) also rests within a reliquary above the altar in the right transept.

Sacro Cuore di Gesu a Castro Pretorio
(Sacred Heart of Jesus at Castro Pretorio)
Via Marsala 42
✝This church is near the Termini Train Station. It is dedicated to the Sacred Heart of Jesus.
✝The church was built by St John Bosco and finished in 1887.

Nostra Signora del Sacro Cuore
(Our Lady of the Sacred Heart)
Corso del Rinascimento 27
✝This church is at Piazza Navona. It is dedicated to Our Lady of the Sacred Heart.

San Lorenzo in Damaso
(Saint Lawrence in Damaso)
Piazza della Cancelleria 1
✝This church is at the *Palazzo della Cancelleria* near Campo de' Fiori.
✝The third chapel on the right side of the nave is dedicated to the Sacred Heart of Jesus.

**San Giacomo in Augusta /
San Giacomo degli Incurabili**
(Saint James in Augusta / Saint James of the Incurables)
Via del Corso 499
✝This church is near Piazza del Popolo.
✝The first chapel on the left side of the nave is dedicated to the Sacred Heart of Jesus.

Santa Maria sopra Minerva
(Our Lady Above Minerva)
Piazza della Minerva 42
✝This church is near the Pantheon.
✝The first chapel on the left side of the nave is dedicated to the Sacred Heart of Jesus.
✝Also the body of St Catherine of Siena (d. 1380) rests under the main altar.

Santa Maria in Trastevere
(Our Lady in Trastevere)
Via della Paglia 14 / Piazza Santa Maria in Trastevere
✝This church is located in Trastevere.
✝The fourth chapel on the left side of the nave is dedicated to the Sacred Heart of Jesus.
✝Relics of the two popes, St Callistus I (d. 222) and St Cornelius (d. 253), rest under the main altar of this church. These relics are joined by others in particular those of the priest and martyr St Calepodius (d. 232).

Sacro Cuore del Suffragio
(Sacred Heart of Suffrage)
Lungotevere Prati 12
✝This church is next to the Tiber River north of *Castel Sant'Angelo*. It is dedicated to the Sacred Heart of Jesus.

Memorial of The Immaculate Heart of Mary
(Saturday Following The Second Sunday After Pentecost)

San Lorenzo in Lucina
(Saint Lawrence in Lucina)
Via in Lucina 16/a
✝This church is north of the Pantheon.
✝The chapel to the left of the main altar is dedicated to the Immaculate Heart of The Blessed Virgin Mary.
✝The grill used to burn St Lawrence (d. 258) is preserved under the altar in the first chapel on the right side of the nave.

Sant'Eustachio (Saint Eustace)
Piazza Sant'Eustachio 19
✝This church is just west of the Pantheon.
✝The third chapel on the left side of the nave is dedicated to the Immaculate Heart of The Blessed Virgin Mary.

Solemnity of Christ The King
(Last Sunday In Ordinary Time)

Santi Cosma e Damiano
(Saints Cosmas and Damian)
Via dei Fori Imperiali 1
✝This church is located next to the Roman Forum.
✝The mosaic within the apse depicts Christ at his Second Coming. When it was created in the 6th century it was intended to be viewed from a greater distance. In the 17th century, however, the church was restored and the floor raised about 25 feet to its present location. Thus the mosaic is now much closer than it was intended.

Parrocchia Sacro Cuore di Cristo Re
(Sacred Heart Parish of Christ the King)
Viale Giuseppe Mazzini 32
✝This church is north of the Vatican.
✝The large painting in the main sanctuary depicts Christ the King.

Marian Churches

Basilica of St Mary Major
Piazza di Santa Maria Maggiore 42

✝This basilica has two large transept chapels. Within the *Pauline Chapel* in the left transept is a miraculous image of the Blessed Virgin Mary entitled *Protectress of the Roman People*. Tradition credits St Luke for the creation of this image.

✝Within the porphyry base of the Papal Altar in the main body of this church are some relics of St Matthias. Also prominently placed within the confessio below this altar are five pieces of wood believed to be from the crib of Jesus Christ.

✝The remains of St Jerome (d. 420) were brought to this basilica in the 12th century. There is some doubt as to their exact location. They either rest under the Papal Altar within the main body of the church or within the confessio in the right transept.

Santuario della Madonna del Divino Amore
(Sanctuary of Our Lady of Divine Love)
Via Ardeatina 1221
00134 Rome, Italy

✝This sanctuary is located south of the city of Rome. It is a very popular and important Roman shrine to Our Lady.

Santa Maria sopra Minerva
(Our Lady Above Minerva)
Piazza della Minerva 42

✝This church is near the Pantheon.

✝A painting of the Annunciation completed in the late 15th century by Antoniazzo Romano is found in the fifth chapel on the right side of the nave. Also the chapel in the right transept is dedicated to the Annunciation.

Santa Maria in Trastevere
(Our Lady in Trastevere)
Via della Paglia 14 / Piazza Santa Maria in Trastevere

✝This church is located in Trastevere. It is dedicated to the Assumption of The Blessed Virgin Mary. A painting of the Assumption by Domenico Zampieri can be seen in the middle of the coffered wooden ceiling.

✝Relics of the two popes, St Callistus I (d. 222) and St Cornelius (d. 253), rest under the main altar of this church. These relics are joined by others in particular those of the priest and martyr St Calepodius (d. 232).

Santuario della Madonna del Perpetuo Soccorso
(Sanctuary of Our Lady of Perpetual Help)
Via Merulana 26

✝This church is just south of the *Basilica of St Mary Major*. It is dedicated to St Alphonsus Liguori.

✝A miraculous image of the Blessed Virgin Mary entitled *Our Lady of Perpetual Help* is above the main altar.

Santa Maria ai Monti
(Our Lady at the Hills)
Via della Madonna dei Monti 41

✝This church is near the Cavour metro stop.

✝This church was built due to a miraculous discovery of an image of the Blessed Virgin Mary in a nearby Poor Clare convent that had fallen into ruins. To celebrate this great find Pope Gregory XIII (d. 1585) commissioned the building of this church. This miraculous image is now placed above the main altar.

Santa Maria in Via
(Our Lady of the Way)
Via del Mortaro 24
† This church is near the Spanish Steps.
† On September 26, 1256 a miraculous icon of the Blessed Virgin Mary appeared at this location. It was found painted on a stone and floating upon the water of an overflowing well. The first chapel on the right side of the nave preserves this miraculous well and icon. Cups are normally provided so that pilgrims can drink some of the water from this well.

Santa Maria in Traspontina
(Our Lady in Traspontina)
Via della Conciliazione 14
† This church is near the Vatican.
† The third chapel on the right side of the nave contains a beautiful statue of Our Lady of Mt Carmel. A memorial at this chapel recalls that this church provided a new scapular for St John Paul II after the assassination attempt upon his life in 1981.

Santa Maria in Aracoeli
(Our Lady in Aracoeli)
Piazza del Campidoglio 4
† This church is on top of the Capitoline Hill.
† Twelve paintings in the upper nave depict events from the life of the Blessed Virgin Mary.
† Also relics of St Helena, the mother of Constantine, rest in the left transept.

Sant'Andrea delle Fratte
(Saint Andrew of the Bushes)
Via Sant'Andrea delle Fratte 1
† This church is near the Spanish Steps.
† The third altar on the left side of the nave is where the Blessed Virgin Mary appeared to Ratisbonne, an agnostic Jew, in 1842. Ratisbonne converted on the spot. In 1918 St Maximilian Mary Kolbe

(d. 1941) offered his first Mass in this very same chapel.

San Carlo ai Catinari
(Saint Charles at the Catinari)
Piazza Benedetto Cairoli 117
† This church is near the Largo di Torre Argentina.
† Within the first chapel on the right side of the nave is a beautiful painting of the Annunciation by Giovanni Lanfranco.
† Also a chapel in the right transept preserves a copy of the miraculous image of the Blessed Virgin Mary entitled *Mother of Divine Providence*. The original is located in a Barnabite church in Trastevere.

Chiesa Nuova
(The New Church)
Via del Governo Vecchio 134
† This church is located along the Corso Vittorio Emanuele.
† Nearly all of the side chapels are dedicated to different events in the life of the Blessed Virgin Mary.

Additional Marian Churches to See

Santa Maria del Popolo
(Our Lady of the People)
Piazza del Popolo 12
† This church is at Piazza del Popolo.

Santissimo Nome di Maria al Foro Traiano
(The Most Holy Name of Mary at Trajan's Forum)
Piazza Foro Traiano 89
† This church is near Trajan's column just east of Piazza Venezia.

Santa Maria di Loreto
(Our Lady of Loreto)

Piazza della Madonna di Loreto 26
†This church is near Trajan's column just east of Piazza Venezia. This is the smaller of the two churches that are located here.

Santa Maria in Via Lata
(Our Lady on Via Lata)
Via del Corso 306
†This church is north of Piazza Venezia.
†It is believed that this church is built over a location where St Paul resided while he was under house arrest in Rome.

Santa Maria degli Angeli
(Our Lady of the Angels)
Piazza della Repubblica
†This church is at Piazza della Repubblica. It is a very spacious church built over the Baths of Diocletian.
†In the main sanctuary is a painting that depicts seven angels surrounding the Blessed Virgin Mary. An additional pair of sculpted angels then surround this painting.

Santa Maria della Vittoria
(Our Lady of the Victory)
Via XX Settembre 17
†This church is located north of Piazza della Repubblica.
†Located here is Gian Lorenzo Bernini's famous sculpture entitled *The Ecstasy of St Teresa*.

Santa Maria in Aquiro
(Our Lady in Aquiro)
Via della Guglia 69/B
†This church is near the Pantheon.
†The third chapel on the left side of the nave is dedicated to Our Lady of Lourdes

Santa Maria dell'Umiltà
(Our Lady of Humility)

Via dell'Umiltà 30
†This church is south of the Trevi Fountain. It is the church at the *Casa Santa Maria*.

Santa Maria della Pace
(Our Lady of Peace)
Vicolo del Arco della Pace 5
†This church is near Piazza Navona.

Santa Maria dell'Anima
(Our Lady of the Soul)
Via Santa Maria dell'Anima 64
†This church is near Piazza Navona. It is the German national church.

Santa Maria in Campitelli
(Our Lady in Campitelli)
Piazza di Campitelli 9
†This church is near the Jewish quarter.
†The body of St John Leonardi (d. 1609) is enshrined in the second chapel on the left side of the nave.

Santa Maria in Domnica
(Our Lady in Domnica)
Via della Navicella 10
†This church is south of the Colosseum.
†The 9th century mosaic within the apse depicts Pope St Paschal I (d. 824) humbly kneeling at the foot of the Blessed Virgin Mary as angels to the right and to the left look on.

Santa Maria della Consolazione
(Our Lady of Consolation)
Piazza della Consolazione 94
†This church is east of Tiber Island.
†In 1506 a hospital was founded adjacent to this church. It was at this hospital that St Aloysius Gonzaga (d. 1591) contracted the plague while caring for the sick. He eventually died from this disease at the age of twenty-three.
†The image of the Blessed Virgin Mary

above the main altar was purchased in 1385 to console the nearby prisoners who were awaiting execution.

Santa Maria della Scala
(Our Lady at the Steps)
Piazza della Scala 23
✝This church is located in Trastevere.
✝A miraculous image of the Blessed Virgin Mary entitled *Madonna della Scala* is venerated in the left transept.

Santa Maria dei Miracoli
(Our Lady of the Miracles)
Via del Corso 528
✝This church is at Piazza del Popolo.
✝Within the second chapel on the right side of the nave is statue of Mary entitled Our Lady of Betharram.

Santa Maria di Montesanto
(Our Lady of Montesanto)
Via del Babuino 197
✝This church is at Piazza del Popolo

Santa Maria in Monticelli
(Our Lady in Monticelli)
28 Via di Santa Maria in Monticelli
✝This church is near the Largo di Torre Argentina.
✝The painting in the main sanctuary depicts the Presentation of The Blessed Virgin Mary.

Santa Maria in Trivio
(Our Lady in Trivio)
Piazza dei Crociferi 49
✝This church is near the Trevi Fountain.

Santa Maria in Monterone
(Our Lady in Monterone)
75 Via Monterone
✝This church is located south of the Pantheon.

Santa Maria Annunziata in Borgo
(Annunciation of Mary in the Borgo)
Borgo Santo Spirito
✝This small church is near the Vatican and the Corso Vittorio Emanuele Bridge.

Santa Maria delle Grazie alle Fornaci
(Our Lady of Graces at the Fornaci)
Piazza di Santa Maria alle Fornaci 30
✝This church is south of the Vatican.

Santa Maria Odigitria al Tritone
(Our Lady Odigitria at the Tritone)
Via del Tritone 82
✝This church is just west of the Barberini metro stop.

Sant'Andrea della Valle
(Saint Andrew of the Valley)
Piazza Sant'Andrea della Valle / Piazza Vidoni 6
✝This church is located along the Corso Vittorio Emanuele.
✝The chapel in the left transept is dedicated to the purity of the Blessed Virgin Mary.

Il Gesu (The Jesus)
Via degli Astalli 16
✝This church is located along the Corso Vittorio Emanuele.
✝The small chapel to the left of the main sanctuary is entitled *Our Lady of the Way Chapel*. It is named after the previous church that was located here and contains a number of very humble and prayerful images of our Lady including one from the 15th century that St Ignatius would have known from the previous church.
✝St Ignatius of Loyola (d. 1556) is buried under the altar in the left transept.
✝An arm of St Francis Xavier (d. 1552) also rests within a reliquary above the altar in the right transept.

References & Indexes

INDEX

Elizabeth of Portugal	*Coimbra, Portugal*	134
	Chapels and Churches in Rome	251
Ephrem	*Chapels and Churches in Rome*	246 (N/A)
Eusebius of Vercelli	*Vercelli, Italy*	101
	Chapels and Churches in Rome	261
Fabian	*Rome, Italy*	64
	Chapels and Churches in Rome	36, 215
Faustina	*Kraków, Poland*	178
Felicity	*Carthage, Tunisia*	192
	Chapels and Churches in Rome	227 (N/A)
Fidelis of Sigmaringen	*Feldkirch, Austria*	170
	Chur, Switzerland	170
	Chapels and Churches in Rome	236
Frances of Rome	*Rome, Italy*	66
	Chapels and Churches in Rome	7, 227
Frances Xavier Cabrini	*New York City, New York, USA*	200
	Chicago, Illinois, USA	200
	Rome, Italy	66
	Codogno, Italy	101
	Sant'Angelo Lodigiano, Italy	101
	Chapels and Churches in Rome	296
Francis de Sales	*Annecy, France*	147
	Treviso, Italy	92
	Chapels and Churches in Rome	218
Francis of Assisi	*Assisi, Italy*	113
	Chapels and Churches in Rome	11, 286

Rose Philippine Duchesne	**St Charles, Missouri, USA**	205
	Chapels and Churches in Rome	298 (N/A)
Scholastica	**Monte Cassino, Italy**	117
	Juvigny-sur-Loison, France	143
	Chapels and Churches in Rome	222
Sebastian	**Rome, Italy**	64
	Chapels and Churches in Rome	37, 216
Seven Holy Founders	*Florence, Italy*	116
	Chapels and Churches in Rome	223
Sharbel Makhluf	**Annaya, Jbeil District, Lebanon**	193
	Chapels and Churches in Rome	256 (N/A)
Simon	**Rome, Italy**	85
	Chapels and Churches in Rome	16, 294
Sixtus II	**Rome, Italy**	85
	Chapels and Churches in Rome	262
Stanislaus	**Kraków, Poland**	180
	Chapels and Churches in Rome	234
Stephen	**Rome, Italy**	76
	Jerusalem, Israel	193
	Chapels and Churches in Rome	38, 307
Stephen of Hungary	**Budapest, Hungary**	180
	Chapels and Churches in Rome	268
Sylvester I	**Rome, Italy**	73
	Chapels and Churches in Rome	28, 309
Teresa Benedicta of the Cross	*Chapels and Churches in Rome*	264 (N/A)

Teresa of Avila	Avila, Spain	139
	Alba de Tormes, Spain	139
	Rome, Italy	86
	Chapels and Churches in Rome	10, 290
Therese of the Child Jesus	Lisieux, France	154
	Chapels and Churches in Rome	285
Thomas	Ortona, Italy	132
	Mylapore, India	194
	Rome, Italy	86
	Chapels and Churches in Rome	18, 251
Thomas Aquinas	Toulouse, France	155
	Aquino, Italy	120
	Naples, Italy	126
	Chapels and Churches in Rome	219
Thomas Becket	Canterbury, United Kingdom	159
	Chapels and Churches in Rome	309 (N/A)
Thomas More	London, United Kingdom	160
	Canterbury, United Kingdom	160
	Chapels and Churches in Rome	248
Timothy	Termoli, Italy	132
	Chapels and Churches in Rome	219 (N/A)
Titus	Heraklion, Crete, Greece	195
	Chapels and Churches in Rome	219 (N/A)
Turibius of Mogrovejo	Lima, Peru	206
	Chapels and Churches in Rome	230

Vincent	***Castres, France***	155
	Lisbon, Portugal	135
	Chapels and Churches in Rome	217
Vincent de Paul	***Paris, France***	156
	Chapels and Churches in Rome	281
Vincent Ferrer	***Vannes, France***	156
	Chapels and Churches in Rome	234
Wenceslaus	***Prague, Czech Republic***	176
	Chapels and Churches in Rome	281 (N/A)

INDEX

Various Liturgical Feasts

Marian Feasts

Floor Plans

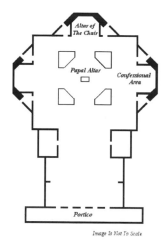

St Peter's Basilica

Basilica of St Mary Major

General Bibliography

Cruz, Joan Carroll. *Relics*. Huntington, Indiana: Our Sunday Visitor, 1984.

Korn, Frank J. *A Catholic's Guide To Rome*. Mahwah, New Jersey: Paulist Press, 2000.

Liturgy of the Hours. New York: Catholic Book Publishing Corporation, 1975.

Ofenbach, Elvira. *Sulle Orme Dei Santi A Roma*. Vatican City: Libreria Editrice Vaticana, 2003.

Pontifical North American College. *Procedamus In Pace: A Guide To The Station Churches Of Rome*.

Sicari, Giovanni. *Reliquie Insigni e "Corpi santi" a Roma*. Rome: Alma Roma, 1998. (Roman Monograph, 12)

Tylenda, Joseph S.J. *The Pilgrim's Guide to Rome's Principal Churches*. Collegeville, Minnesota: Michael Glazier Books by The Liturgical Press, 1993.

The websites of various individual churches.

Personal Visits.

The Liturgical Calendar

January 1st
Solemnity of The Blessed Virgin Mary,
Mother of God

January 2nd
Memorial of Basil the Great and Gregory
Nazianzen, bishops and doctors

January 3rd
Optional Memorial of The Most Holy
Name of Jesus

January 4th
Memorial of Elizabeth Ann Seton,
religious*

January 5th
Memorial of John Neumann, bishop*

January 6th
Optional Memorial of André Bessette,
religious*

January 7th
Optional memorial of Raymond of
Penyafort, priest

January 13th
Optional memorial of Hilary, bishop and
doctor

January 17th
Memorial of Anthony, abbot

January 20th
Optional memorial of Fabian, pope and
martyr

January 20th
Optional memorial of Sebastian, martyr

January 21st
Memorial of Agnes, virgin and martyr

January 23rd
Optional memorial of Vincent, deacon
and martyr*

January 23rd
Optional memorial of Marianne Cope,
virgin*

January 24th
Memorial of Francis de Sales, bishop and
doctor

January 25th
Feast of The Conversion of Paul, apostle

January 26th
Memorial of Timothy and Titus, bishops

January 27th
Optional memorial of Angela Merici,
virgin

January 28th
Memorial of Thomas Aquinas, priest and
doctor

January 31st
Memorial of John Bosco, priest

February 2nd
Feast of The Presentation of the Lord

February 3rd
Optional memorial of Blaise, bishop and
martyr

February 3rd
Optional memorial of Ansgar, bishop

February 5th
Memorial of Agatha, virgin and martyr

February 6th
Memorial of Paul Miki and Companions,
martyrs

February 8th
Optional memorial of Jerome Emiliani, priest

February 8th
Optional memorial of Josephine Bakhita, virgin

February 10th
Memorial of Scholastica, virgin

February 11th
Optional memorial of Our Lady of Lourdes

February 14th
Memorial of Cyril, monk; and Methodius, bishop

February 17th
Optional memorial of The Seven Holy Founders of the Servite Order

February 21st
Optional memorial of Peter Damian, bishop and doctor

February 22nd
Feast of the Chair of St Peter, apostle

February 23rd
Memorial of Polycarp, bishop and martyr

March 3rd
Optional memorial of Katharine Drexel, virgin*

March 4th
Optional memorial of Casimir

March 7th
Memorial of Perpetua and Felicity, martyrs

March 8th
Optional memorial of John of God, religious

March 9th
Optional memorial of Frances of Rome, religious

March 17th
Optional memorial of Patrick, bishop

March 18th
Optional memorial of Cyril of Jerusalem, bishop and doctor

March 19th
Solemnity of Joseph, husband of Mary

March 23rd
Optional memorial of Turibius of Mogrovejo, bishop

March 25th
Solemnity of The Annunciation

April 2nd
Optional memorial of Francis of Paola, hermit

April 4th
Optional memorial of Isidore, bishop and doctor

April 5th
Optional memorial of Vincent Ferrer, priest

April 7th
Memorial of John Baptist de la Salle, priest

April 11th
Memorial of Stanislaus, bishop and martyr

April 13th
Optional memorial of Martin I, pope and martyr

April 21st
Optional memorial of Anselm, bishop and doctor

April 23rd
Optional memorial of George, martyr

April 23rd
Optional Memorial of Adalbert, bishop and martyr

April 24th
Optional memorial of Fidelis of
Sigmaringen, priest and martyr

April 25th
Feast of Mark, evangelist

April 28th
Optional Memorial of Peter Chanel,
priest and martyr

April 28th
Optional Memorial of Louis Grignion de
Montfort, priest

April 29th
Memorial of Catherine of Siena, virgin
and doctor

April 30th
Optional memorial of Pius V, pope

May 1st
Optional Memorial of Saint Joseph the
Worker

May 2nd
Memorial of Athanasius, bishop and
doctor

May 3rd
Feast of Philip and James, apostles

May 10th
Optional memorial of Damien Joseph de
Veuster of Moloka'i, priest*

May 12th
Optional memorial of Nereus and
Achilleus, martyrs

May 12th
Optional memorial of Pancras, martyr

May 13th
Optional memorial of Our Lady of Fatima

May 14th
Feast of Matthias, apostle

May 15th
Optional memorial of Isidore*

May 18th
Optional memorial of John I, pope and
martyr

May 20th
Optional memorial of Bernardine of
Siena, priest

May 21st
Optional memorial of Christopher
Magallanes, priest and martyr, and
Companions, martyrs

May 22nd
Optional memorial of Rita of Cascia,
religious

May 25th
Optional memorial of Bede the Venerable,
priest and doctor

May 25th
Optional memorial of Gregory VII, pope

May 25th
Optional memorial of Mary Magdalene
de Pazzi, virgin

May 26th
Memorial of Philip Neri, priest

May 27th
Optional memorial of Augustine of
Canterbury, bishop

May 31st
Feast of The Visitation of The Blessed
Virgin Mary

June 1st
Memorial of Justin, martyr

June 2nd
Optional memorial of Marcellinus and
Peter, martyrs

June 3rd
Memorial of Charles Lwanga and
Companions, martyrs (Uganda martyrs)

June 5th
Memorial of Boniface, bishop and martyr

June 6th
Optional memorial of Norbert, bishop

June 9th
Optional memorial of Ephrem, deacon
and doctor

June 11th
Memorial of Barnabas, apostle

June 13th
Memorial of Anthony of Padua, priest and
doctor

June 19th
Optional memorial of Romuald, abbot

June 21st
Memorial of Aloysius Gonzaga, religious

June 22nd
Optional memorial of Paulinus of Nola,
bishop

June 22nd
Optional memorial of John Fisher, bishop
and martyr; Thomas More, martyr

June 24th
Solemnity of the Birth of John the Baptist

June 27th
Optional memorial of Cyril of Alexandria,
bishop and doctor

June 28th
Memorial of Irenaeus, bishop and martyr

June 29th
Solemnity of Peter and Paul, apostles

June 30th
Optional memorial of The First Martyrs
of the Church of Rome

July 1st
Optional memorial of Blessed Junipero
Serra, priest*

July 3rd
Feast of Thomas, apostle

July 5th
Optional memorial of Elizabeth of
Portugal*

July 5th
Optional memorial of Anthony Zaccaria,
priest

July 6th
Optional memorial of Maria Goretti,
virgin and martyr

July 9th
Optional Memorial of Augustine Zhao
Rong, priest and martyr, and
Companions, martyrs (Chinese martyrs)

July 11th
Memorial of Benedict, abbot

July 13th
Optional memorial of Henry

July 14th
Memorial of Kateri Tekakwitha, virgin*

July 15th
Memorial of Bonaventure, bishop and
doctor

July 16th
Optional memorial of Our Lady of Mt
Carmel

July 18th
Optional memorial of Camillus de Lellis,
priest*

July 20th
Optional Memorial of Apollinaris, bishop
and martyr

July 21st
Optional memorial of Lawrence of
Brindisi, priest and doctor

July 22nd
Memorial of Mary Magdalene

July 23rd
Optional memorial of Bridget, religious

July 24th
Optional Memorial of Sharbel Makhluf,
priest

July 25th
Feast of James, apostle

July 26th
Memorial of Joachim and Anne, parents
of The Blessed Virgin Mary

July 29th
Memorial of Martha

July 30th
Optional memorial of Peter Chrysologus,
bishop and doctor

July 31st
Memorial of Ignatius of Loyola, priest

August 1st
Memorial of Alphonsus Liguori, bishop
and doctor

August 2nd
Optional memorial of Eusebius of
Vercelli, bishop

August 2nd
Optional memorial of Peter Julian
Eymard, priest

August 4th
Memorial of John Vianney, priest

August 5th
Optional memorial of The Dedication of
the Basilica of Saint Mary Major

August 6th
Feast of The Transfiguration

August 7th
Optional memorial of Sixtus II, pope and
martyr, and Companions, martyrs

August 7th
Optional memorial of Cajetan, priest

August 8th
Memorial of Dominic, priest

August 9th
Optional memorial of Teresa Benedicta of
the Cross, virgin and martyr

August 10th
Feast of Lawrence, deacon and martyr

August 11th
Memorial of Clare, virgin

August 12th
Optional memorial of Jane Frances de
Chantal, religious

August 13th
Optional memorial of Pontian, pope and
martyr; Hippolytus, priest and martyr

August 14th
Optional memorial of Maximilian Mary
Kolbe, priest and martyr

August 15th
Solemnity of The Assumption of The
Blessed Virgin Mary

August 16th
Optional memorial of Stephen of Hungary

August 19th
Optional memorial of John Eudes, priest

August 20th
Memorial of Bernard, abbot and doctor

August 21st
Memorial of Pius X, pope

August 22nd
Memorial of The Queenship of The
Blessed Virgin Mary

August 23rd
Optional memorial of Rose of Lima,
virgin

August 24th
Feast of Bartholomew, apostle

August 25th
Optional memorial of Louis

August 25th
Optional memorial of Joseph Calasanz,
priest

August 27th
Memorial of Monica

August 28th
Memorial of Augustine, bishop and doctor

August 29th
Memorial of The Beheading of John the
Baptist, martyr

September 3rd
Memorial of Gregory the Great, pope and
doctor

September 8th
Feast of The Birth of The Blessed Virgin
Mary

September 9th
Memorial of Peter Claver, priest*

September 12th
Optional Memorial of The Most Holy
Name of Mary

September 13th
Memorial of John Chrysostom, bishop
and doctor

September 14th
Feast of The Triumph of the Cross

September 15th
Memorial of Our Lady of Sorrows

September 16th
Memorial of Cornelius, pope and martyr;
Cyprian, bishop and martyr

September 17th
Optional memorial of Robert Bellarmine,
bishop and doctor

September 19th
Optional memorial of Januarius, bishop
and martyr

September 20th
Optional memorial of Andrew Kim
Taegon, priest and martyr; Paul Chong
Hasang and Companions, martyrs

September 21st
Feast of Matthew, apostle and evangelist

September 23rd
Memorial of Pio of Pietrelcina, priest

September 26th
Optional memorial of Cosmas and
Damian, martyrs

September 27th
Memorial of Vincent de Paul, priest

September 28th
Optional memorial of Wenceslaus, martyr

September 28th
Optional memorial of Lawrence Ruiz and
Companions, martyrs

September 29th
Feast of Michael, Gabriel and Raphael,
Archangels

September 30th
Memorial of Jerome, priest and doctor

October 1st
Memorial of Therese of the Child Jesus,
virgin and doctor

October 2nd
Memorial of The Holy Guardian Angels

October 4th
Memorial of Francis of Assisi

October 5th
Optional Memorial of Blessed Francis Xavier Seelos, priest*

October 6th
Optional memorial of Bruno, priest

October 6th
Optional memorial of Blessed Marie Rose Durocher, virgin*

October 7th
Memorial of Our Lady of the Rosary

October 9th
Optional memorial of Denis, bishop and martyr, and Companions, martyrs

October 9th
Optional memorial of John Leonardi, priest

October 11th
Optional memorial of John XXIII, pope

October 14th
Optional memorial of Callistus I, pope and martyr

October 15th
Memorial of Teresa of Jesus, virgin and doctor

October 16th
Optional memorial of Hedwig, religious

October 16th
Optional memorial of Margaret Mary Alacoque, virgin

October 17th
Memorial of Ignatius of Antioch, bishop and martyr

October 18th
Feast of Luke, evangelist

October 19th
Memorial of John de Brebeuf and Isaac Jogues, priests and martyrs, and Companions, martyrs*

October 20th
Optional memorial of Paul of the Cross, priest*

October 22nd
Memorial of John Paul II, pope

October 23rd
Optional memorial of John of Capistrano, priest

October 24th
Optional memorial of Anthony Mary Claret, bishop

October 28th
Feast of Simon and Jude, apostles

November 1st
Solemnity of All Saints

November 2nd
Optional memorial of All Souls

November 3rd
Optional memorial of Martin de Porres, religious

November 4th
Memorial of Charles Borromeo, bishop

November 9th
Feast of The Dedication of the Basilica of Saint John Lateran

November 10th
Memorial of Leo the Great, pope and doctor

November 11th
Memorial of Martin of Tours, bishop

November 12th
Memorial of Josaphat, bishop and martyr

November 13th
Memorial of Frances Xavier Cabrini,
virgin*

November 15th
Optional memorial of Albert the Great,
bishop and doctor

November 16th
Optional memorial of Gertrude, virgin

November 16th
Optional memorial of Margaret of
Scotland

November 17th
Memorial of Elizabeth of Hungary,
religious

November 18th
Optional memorial of The Dedication of
the Basilicas of Saints Peter and Paul,
apostles

November 18th
Optional memorial of Rose Philippine
Duchesne, virgin*

November 21st
Memorial of The Presentation of The
Blessed Virgin Mary

November 22nd
Memorial of Cecilia, virgin and martyr

November 23rd
Optional memorial of Clement I, pope
and martyr

November 23rd
Optional memorial of Columban, abbot

November 23rd
Optional memorial of Blessed Miguel
Agustin Pro, priest and martyr*

November 24th
Optional memorial of Andrew Dung-Lac,
priest and martyr, and Companions,
martyrs (Vietnamese martyrs)

November 25th
Optional memorial of Catherine of
Alexandria, virgin and martyr

November 30th
Feast of Andrew, apostle

December 3rd
Memorial of Francis Xavier, priest

December 4th
Optional memorial of John Damascene,
priest and doctor

December 6th
Optional memorial of Nicholas, bishop

December 7th
Memorial of Ambrose, bishop and doctor

December 8th
Solemnity of The Immaculate Conception
of The Blessed Virgin Mary

December 9th
Optional memorial of Juan Diego*

December 11th
Optional memorial of Damasus I, pope

December 12th
Feast of Our Lady of Guadalupe*

December 13th
Memorial of Lucy, virgin and martyr

December 14th
Memorial of John of the Cross, priest and
doctor

December 21st
Optional memorial of Peter Canisius,
priest and doctor

December 23rd
Optional memorial of John of Kanty,
priest

December 25th
Solemnity of Christmas

December 26th
Feast of Stephen, first martyr

December 27th
Feast of John, apostle and evangelist

December 28th
Feast of Holy Innocents, martyrs

December 29th
Optional memorial of Thomas Becket,
bishop and martyr

December 31st
Optional memorial of Sylvester I, pope

Relics Organized By Location

Gianna Beretta Molla**
Jerome Emiliani, priest
John Bosco, priest
Pier Giorgio Frassati** (Blessed)

Near Bologna
Anne, mother of The Blessed Virgin
Mary
Apollinaris, bishop and martyr
Dominic, priest
Peter Chrysologus, bishop and doctor
Peter Damian, bishop and doctor

Central Italy

Near Florence
Andrew, apostle
Bernardine of Siena, priest
Catherine of Siena, virgin and doctor
Clare, virgin
Elizabeth Ann Seton, religious
Francis of Assisi
Gemma Galgani**
John Chrysostom, bishop and doctor
John the Baptist, martyr
Mary Magdalene de Pazzi, virgin
Philip, apostle
Rita of Cascia, religious
Romuald, abbot

Near Rome
Benedict, abbot
Bonaventure, bishop and doctor
Justin, martyr
Maria Goretti, virgin and martyr
Scholastica, virgin
Thomas Aquinas, priest and doctor

Southern Italy

Near Naples
Alphonsus Liguori, bishop and doctor
Andrew, apostle
Bartholomew, apostle
Cajetan, priest
Gregory VII, pope
Januarius, bishop and martyr
Matthew, apostle and evangelist
Paulinus of Nola, bishop
Philomena, martyr**
Thomas Aquinas, priest and doctor

Calabria & Sicily
Agatha, virgin and martyr
Bartholomew, apostle
Blaise, bishop and martyr
Bruno, priest
Francis of Paola, hermit
Louis
Lucy, virgin and martyr
Paulinus of Nola, bishop

Adriatic Coast of Italy
Nicholas, bishop
Pio of Pietrelcina, priest
Thomas, apostle
Timothy, bishop

Algeria
Augustine, bishop and doctor

Austria
Anne, mother of The Blessed Virgin
Mary
Elizabeth of Hungary, religious
Fidelis of Sigmaringen, priest and
martyr

Belgium
Basil the Great, bishop and doctor
Damien Joseph de Veuster, priest*
Francis Xavier, priest

Canada
André Bessette, religious*
Anne, mother of The Blessed Virgin
Mary
Marie Rose Durocher, virgin* (Blessed)
Kateri Tekakwitha*
John de Brebeuf, priest and martyr*

Colombia
Peter Claver, priest*

Croatia
Blaise, bishop and martyr
John of Capistrano, priest

Cyprus
Barnabas, apostle
Lazarus**

Relics Organized
By Saint

Adalbert, bishop and martyr
Rome, Italy
Prague, Czech Republic
Gniezno, Poland
Agatha, virgin and martyr
Catania, Sicily, Italy
Agnes, virgin and martyr
Rome, Italy
Albert the Great, bishop and doctor
Cologne, Germany
Aloysius Gonzaga, religious
Rome, Italy
Castiglione delle Stiviere, Italy
Alphonsus Liguori, bishop and doctor
Pagani, Italy
Ambrose, bishop and doctor
Milan, Italy
André Bessette, religious*
Montreal, Quebec, Canada
Andrew, apostle
Amalfi, Italy
Florence, Italy
Patras, Greece
Edinburgh, Scotland
Cologne, Germany
Kiev, Ukraine
Angela Merici, virgin
Brescia, Italy
Anne, mother of The Blessed Virgin Mary
Apt, France
Bologna, Italy
Sainte-Anne d'Auray, France
Sainte-Anne de Beaupré, Quebec, Canada
Vienna, Austria
Anselm, bishop and doctor
-
Ansgar, bishop
-
Anthony, abbot
Zaafarana, Egypt
Saint-Antoine l'Abbaye, France
Arles, France

Anthony Mary Claret, bishop
Vic, Spain
Anthony of Padua, priest and doctor
Padua, Italy
Anthony Zaccaria, priest
Milan, Italy
Apollinaris, bishop and martyr
Ravenna, Italy
Düsseldorf, Germany
Remagen, Germany
Athanasius, bishop and doctor
Venice, Italy
Cairo, Egypt
Augustine, bishop and doctor
Pavia, Italy
Annaba, Algeria
Augustine of Canterbury, bishop
-
Barnabas, apostle
Famagusta, Cyprus
Bartholomew, apostle
Rome, Italy
Benevento, Italy
Lipari, Sicily, Italy
Frankfurt, Germany
Basil the Great, bishop and doctor
Mount Athos, Greece
Bruges, Belgium
Bede the Venerable, priest and doctor
Durham, United Kingdom
Benedict, abbot
Monte Cassino, Italy
Saint-Benoît-sur-Loire, France
Brescia, Italy
Bernard, abbot and doctor
Troyes, France
Bernardine of Siena, priest
L'Aquila, Italy
Blaise, bishop and martyr
Rome, Italy
Maratea, Italy
Dubrovnik, Croatia

Thomas Aquinas, priest and doctor
Toulouse, France
Aquino, Italy
Naples, Italy
Thomas Becket, bishop and martyr
Canterbury, United Kingdom
Thomas More, martyr
London, United Kingdom
Canterbury, United Kingdom
Timothy, bishop
Termoli, Italy
Titus, bishop
Heraklion, Crete, Greece
Turibius of Mogrovejo, bishop
Lima, Peru
Vietnamese martyrs
Penang, Malaysia
Paris, France
Vincent de Paul, priest
Paris, France
Vincent Ferrer, priest
Vannes, France

Vincent, deacon and martyr*
Castres, France
Lisbon, Portugal
Wenceslaus, martyr
Prague, Czech Republic

*Note: The Saints listed with an (*) have Memorials or Feasts specific to the National Calendar of the United States of America as requested by the United States Conference of Catholic Bishops and approved by the Holy See. In certain cases the (*) indicates that in the United States of America the Feast Day of a particular saint has been transferred to accommodate a certain national memorial.

*Also those marked with (**) are Saints or Blesseds of importance but are not on the Universal Roman Catholic Liturgical Calendar.

Roman Churches Included In This Book